101

GREAT WAYS
TO IMPROVE
YOUR LIFE

Selected and Introduced by

DAVID RIKLAN

A PRODUCT OF

SELFGROWTH.COM

D1010199

101 Great Ways to Improve Your Life
By David Riklan

Published by
Self Improvement Online, Inc.
http://www.SelfGrowth.com
20 Arie Drive, Marlboro, NJ 07746

Copyright © 2006 by David Riklan
All rights reserved.
ISBN 0-9745672-6-4
Manufactured in the United States

Cover Design:
Peri Poloni
Knockout Design
http://www.knockoutbooks.com

This book is dedicated to my wife, Michelle, and our three wonderful children: Joshua, Jonathan, and Rachel.

ACKNOWLEDGEMENTS

This book was truly created through a team effort that took countless hours of writing, revisions, and updates. It could not have been created alone.

I'd like to acknowledge each and every author that contributed to this book—in fact, there would *be* no book without the inspiring wisdom and words of each of our contributing authors. Thank you all.

In addition to all of the contributors to the book, there were two people involved that deserve a very special thanks.

Stephanie Anastasio and Kristina Kanaley were the hearts and souls responsible for the creation of this book. Without their sincere dedication, hard work, motivation, blood, sweat, and tears (yes, there were tears), this book would never have been completed. Stephanie and Kristina worked hand-in-hand with each of our authors to create this powerful self-improvement book—and, in many ways, were more responsible for the completion of this book than I was.

I would also like to thank many other members of our self-improvement team. Todd Lesser and Jamie Albert provided many hours of valuable feedback and insights which were instrumental in the completion of the book. Joe De Palma provided staunch support for this project and helped me stay focused on this new endeavor. Adriene Hayes has assisted in countless aspects of our business. Gary Dong, Douglas Pak and Greg Aronne have all helped to expand our self-improvement message around the world. Jerry Kimbrough, the latest member of our team, helped us finish up this comprehensive project with his keen editing and writing skills.

Peggy McColl has continued to be a great source of inspiration for my business, my Web site, and my books.

Many special thanks are due to my friends and family, who have provided much-needed support and encouragement throughout the process.

Finally, a special thanks to my wife, Michelle, who is a continual source of motivation for everything that I do.

TABLE OF CONTENTS

Contents

Contents

Contents

Contents

Contents

Contents

Contents

Contents

Contents

Contents

INTRODUCTION – BY DAVID RIKLAN

I've come to believe that you can learn something from just about everybody.

And it doesn't matter if that person is a teacher, a religious leader, a family member, or a stranger you meet at the grocery store. I follow the credo that *everyone* has a pearl of knowledge to impart—about ways of leading a better life, of improving your self-image, or even something as seemingly mundane as finding the quickest way to save time at the Department of Motor Vehicles.

It's through this very sentiment that this book was born.

In *101 Great Ways to Improve Your Life,* I have compiled an amazing collection of 101 great chapters, all written by self-improvement experts from different walks of life—and all with their own unique perspectives and philosophies on the process of personal growth. Each author has a distinctive voice and a method of teaching that is all his or her own.

Many of these experts are already established authors, while others run their own successful businesses. But there's one common thread that ties all of these teachers together—they're all phenomenal educators who have learned how to help other people improve their lives.

And they want to help you improve yours. So do I.

WHAT YOU CAN LEARN FROM THIS BOOK

You *can* find or create great wealth and success.
You *can* improve your communication skills and learn about true love.
You *can* double your reading speed in a matter of minutes.
You *can* learn not to dwell on the negative aspects of your life.
You *can* escape from a job you hate and find a career you love.

In short, you *can* do a lot of things—you simply might not know where to start or what to do. This book will show you how. These 101 articles are written on a wide range of topics: anger management, business, integrity, spirituality, and dozens of others. From identifying your passion to controlling your stress to building self-confidence, this book covers it all. There's something in here for *everyone.*

1

I've organized this book by topic, to simplify the information-gathering process. If you're looking for tips on avoiding procrastination, all you have to do is find the word "procrastination" in the table of contents, locate the corresponding page number, and commence reading. If you're trying to bolster your creativity, locate the word "creativity," and flip to that page. It's as simple as that. I hope this makes it easy to find exactly what you're looking for.

These self-improvement experts all have phenomenal messages—they're just waiting for you to listen. By getting these experts together, I'm essentially enabling you to examine the concept of self-improvement from 101 different vantage points. Listen to each expert's message—I'm certain you'll find many that resonate well with your overall life philosophy. And if you find someone whose teachings and philosophies don't necessarily mesh with your own, that's okay. Not every chapter of this book will apply to each individual person—one reader might think a particular section is inspiring, while another might not.

You may find that you agree with the message of 10 experts, or 20 experts, or you may feel that they *all* have important things to say. That's natural. There's really no panacea, no cure-all remedy, that can magically solve all of your problems and fast-track you down the path to self-improvement. If I felt there *was* such a method, this book would be a heck of a lot shorter.

A PRODUCT OF SELFGROWTH.COM

Virtually everything under the sun connected in some way to self-improvement can be tracked down at SelfGrowth.com. The site offers literally thousands of unique self-improvement articles, written by hundreds of experts. And that is exactly how we came up with the idea for *101 Great Ways*.

There are so many good writers who submit content to our site—all with their own forte and writing style. We wanted to gather the best these authors had to offer. We wanted to put their ideas, their values, and their ways of thinking into one source so that you, the reader, can feed off their expertise. And I think in the end we succeeded.

We wanted you to come away with the motivation to try something new, to look at things in different ways, and to apply our experts' techniques to your own life. We've seen so many articles that have had this effect. They're in here. All you need to do is find the ideas that work for you.

I like to describe *101 Great Ways* as a compilation of high-quality information on ways to improve your life. SelfGrowth.com is dedicated to providing that same quality of information on the Web. So, on behalf of everyone here at Self Improvement Online, Inc., good luck, and enjoy our work. Whether in print or online, I'm sure you will find the expert—or hopefully *several* experts—to suit your individual goals in life.

1

Myths and Misconceptions That Keep Us Chained

Cindy Stone & Joe van Koeverden

In today's world of self-help gurus, celebrity help shows, and spiritual masters, we are inundated with all kinds of advice and preaching about how we should be in this world. We should be fearless. We should be authentic. We should be ethical. We should never be angry. We should always be peaceful. We should have purpose. We should have goals.

Instead of following a guru, celebrity, or master, I have chosen to take as my guide on this journey through life my once-abandoned, still slightly wild dog, Harry. He constantly reminds me of what is natural in this life, how vital real freedom is, and what authenticity truly is, but mostly, he taught me the gift of true acceptance. Not acquiescence, but acceptance. Acquiescence is when we comply with something or give in to something that is not necessarily what we want or in our best interests to elevate our lives. True acceptance is when we discover the deeper patterns and rhythms of nature, when we know deep inside who we truly are (without the overlaying of cultural, parental, or authoritarian beliefs or the suppression of our true natures as loving, connected beings).

I can't tell you how many people come into my practice feeling as though they have somehow failed the current spiritual tests of being fearless, never angry, and emotionally, even like a Zen monk. Others have successfully suppressed all excitement and energy in their lives to appear in total emotional evenness, yet they wonder why they feel little joy in their lives. How sad that we have unwittingly placed more ways for us humans to deny, control, or manipulate what is natural to ourselves and to this world and become ever more alienated from our true selves. Let's dispel just four of the common myths and misconceptions one by one. Doing so will make a world of difference to the richness of your life.

1. **Be fearless.** Fear is a natural response to dangerous situations. Without fear we cannot adequately protect ourselves from potential accidents, fraudulent or mean people, hungry, people-eating beasts, or other life-threatening experiences. Fear becomes a problem when instead of managing fear, it begins to manage us. When our fears reside in our imaginations, beliefs, or emotions, fear is managing us, and we can limit our life experience to comply with our perceived fears.

   Instead of denying fear, we could develop courage to face our fears. We would stay in contact with our natural defense mechanism, and we could take our courage by the hand to walk through our emotional fears. At first, it may feel like walking through a ring of fire, but knowing that our denied emotions are playing tricks on us, we can learn to develop our capacity for courage.

2. **No anger.** Anger seems to be one of the least understood of our emotions. Any social change of any importance in this world has come about because of anger: the American Civil Rights movement and the end of apartheid, the Berlin Wall, and British rule in India were all accomplished through the anger generated by social injustice. Anger does not necessarily mean violence, though when anger is experienced as hopelessness incapable of impelling change, violence often becomes fused within it. Anger separate from violence and bitter resentment is energizing. Anger is life-changing. Anger is a very powerful emotion that when understood can suffuse a depressed person with life-giving energy, vitality, positive purpose, and happiness.

   Like any other emotion, anger has its natural role in our world. Anger's duty is to inform us of social and personal injustice, inequality, and abuse. We need our anger to inform us when our world is not in harmony so that we can take action to ensure proper boundaries, safety, and equality. Anger also infuses our sense of obligation to protect those who are weaker, defenseless,

6

or whose voices are not being heard. We need to understand anger, to *listen* to those who are angry and find ways of empowering change in their lives or in the lives of those they care about and to tease apart the coupling of anger with violence. This alone could cause significant world change.

3. **Be happy, not sad.** When we exchange our feelings as if they have no more relevance than exchanging currencies on a stock market, we risk denying emotions that contain vital information about how the self is experiencing and perceiving the world. These emotions then go underground and become distorted, making healing more difficult. An emotion that may have begun as a simple expression on the surface of the self, once underground can become a deeply imbedded pattern of unconscious behavior, or worse, a somatic illness. Emotions do not deliver reality, but they do hold keys to how we are experiencing the world and what we can do to heal a fractured self to become whole, energized, and engaged again.

4. **Be authentic.** Most often, the demand for authenticity comes along with the demand for what I call the emotional flat line. How can we be authentic when we are busy denying, repressing, or changing our real feelings for those feelings we believe are more desirable ones? Being authentic is just being real. We need to get real, with real feelings and with a real understanding of the human condition.

5. **Commit to a guru or expert.** What we need is true freedom, that which requires us to be accountable for creating our own lives and living them fully in keeping with the values that serve to elevate all those with whom we share the planet. All too often, today's charismatic gurus and experts generate income off the vulnerable backs of people eager to submit to a "higher authority," promising that any dream can come true. I have nothing against making money from a service, talent, or product offered, but when the service, talent, or product manipulates others through grandiose promises that create dependency, it is a problem. We all need help and support, to learn new things, and we need to pay for this, but what we don't need are more experts and gurus claiming to deliver people to their full potential through accountability couched in a militaristic demand for conformity and compliance. Let's develop free thinkers: people and leaders who are in touch

with themselves, their humanity, and our world. It is the deeper pattern of nature to allow each of us to unfold naturally to our own rhythm of life.

Accepting "who we are with all of our insecurities and vulnerabilities, without limiting ourselves to who we think we are" (*The Incidental Guru*) frees us, allowing us to be real and to find our own true path.

ABOUT THE AUTHORS

Cindy Stone, MA, is a practicing psychotherapist, executive coach, speaker, and the author of *The Incidental Guru; Lessons in Healing from a Dog* (Fitzhenry & Whiteside, 2002) and the upcoming *Leader of the Pack; Enlightened Leadership and the Responsible Use of Power* (http:// www.incidentalguru.com). Joe van Koeverden, MBA, teaches at Ryerson University and is a professional speaker, workshop facilitator, and business consultant with experience as CEO of a large crown corporation. Cindy and Joe work with organizations, corporations, executives, entrepreneurs, and exceptional individuals to create meaningful conversations for authentic collaborative leadership, alignment of purpose, and sustainable economic ecological development. Cindy and Joe are principals of vanKoeverdenStone & Associates (http://www.ceomylife.ca).

2

The Power of Small

Rick Beneteau

Routinely, I rise out of bed before the birds and watch the sunlight flood my office every morning. See, I love this time of day, but what I don't love is being rudely rousted out of a deep sleep before my normal rise-and-shine time, and every day, for the past few months, I have been.

I sleep with the windows open, and at around 4 A.M. each and every morning, rain or shine, a very obnoxious bird has been screeching his mating call somewhere close-by at what seems like 130 decibels. Many times, I've wearily peered out the window in an attempt to glimpse firsthand what sounded like a pterodactyl-sized creature on some kind of steroids, but never would this clever little creature reveal himself.

I appreciate nature as much as the next person, but this large sound at this wee hour of the morning is not music to my ears. My fine-feathered foe once put me in such a highly agitated state that I thought about locating a "sportsman" in the neighborhood to take him out, but that was only wishful fantasizing. It's been a few months now, though, and I've gotten pretty used to my tree-dwelling alarm; looking on the positive side, I could even thank him for the extra hour of work I am able to put in every day.

In fact, one day last week, I was pounding away on my laptop on the front porch swing, when lo and behold—*that piercing sound again*! And it was *near*! Imagine my surprise when, after peeking out from under the canopy, I saw perched on the telephone line above this teeny-weeny finch, smaller than my prized canary, warbling away what was really a beautiful anthem, at least when heard at that normal hour of the day. Oh my, the power of small!

We can all learn a lesson from this tiny finch: how many times in your life have you thought that you were "too small" to make a difference? How many times has this thought actually stopped you from doing something you knew in your heart was worthwhile? Perhaps it was something like changing careers, starting a new business, creating your own product, or even buying that dream home. If you're at all like me, I'll bet you've thought this plenty of times.

Instead, think about this: every great achievement in this world has its roots in a single thought in the mind of a single human being. There are no exceptions—the greatest inventions, the biggest corporations, and the tallest skyscrapers were all borne of the single idea of one individual.

So, what separates us from the Henry Fords and Bill Gates of this world? They possessed total self-belief and a firm conviction in their ideas to just build it, no matter the size, no matter the scope, and no matter the naysayers around them, all the while knowing full well that the road to achieving their goals was going to be paved with major setbacks and failures.

> There are some people who live in a dream world, and there are some who face reality; and then there are those who turn one into the other.
>
> –Douglas Everett

You've heard many of the stories about icons like Ford and Gates and about people like Abraham Lincoln, Thomas Edison, and Gandhi. Their journeys were filled with great adversity, devastating setbacks, and heartbreaking failures, but still, because of the sheer level of their belief in themselves and in what they set out to achieve, they were able to leave a legacy that today affects every one of us, every hour of every day.

There are millions of everyday people who will never become household names but who have made magnificent differences in their lives and in the lives of those around them. Take, for instance, the single mother who is reluctantly forced onto the welfare rolls due to a deadbeat dad and pounds the pavement until she lands a job, determined to excel, and works her way up the ladder until she ends up with a wonderful career to the benefit of herself and her family. How about the foreign medical student whose family sacrifices everything in order to send him to a "free country" for his education and who, through sheer determination, graduates at the top of his class but decides not to chase the almighty big bucks that await him in the "land of promise" and instead returns to his native land so that he can help to alleviate the dire suffering of the people there. Consider the entrepreneur who takes a single idea and, no matter what obstacles he faces and the many sacrifices he has to make, creates a successful business with a product that impacts thousands, or even millions, of people.

I am privileged to know so many individuals who have accomplished great things only because of the great belief they had in themselves and in their ideas. As such, I firmly believe that every human being *can* accomplish great things. I can tell you with all the sincerity I possess that this great universe of ours awaits your simple and sincere decision so that it can begin to fill you with all the power you need to make your dream a reality. It's a matter of truly making that decision and then opening yourself up to receiving that invisible assistance.

> The Creator has not given you a longing to do that
> which you have no ability to do.
> —Orison Swett Marden

Now, back to my miniscule, winged friend. On cue, and still prior to daylight, he shakes me out of my peaceful slumber. He knows nothing else, no other way. He just cranks it up at an enormous volume at nature's call, oblivious to the fact he is impacting me on a major scale by doing the only thing he was designed to do—how we all should be, don't you agree?

The power of small!

ABOUT THE AUTHOR

Rick is cocreator of the breakthrough Make Every Day A Great Day program. Read the powerful, life-changing testimonials, and discover how this revolutionary product can dramatically change your life, too: http://www.MakeEveryDayAGreatDay.com/yes. Subscribe *free* to Rick's popular *ARISE!* e-zine and e-chieve: http://www.arise.themirrorezine.com.

3

ADDICTION AND RECOVERY

Knowing Addiction and Doing Recovery: "The Slugger's Path"

John Baldasare

Anyone who has lived with an addiction or has had a close-up experience with someone struggling to overcome addictive behaviors knows that all of the theories and research are of little consequence. The real-world, nitty-gritty fight to reclaim one's life is beyond the lab, the classroom, or the latest article in a science digest. It matters not if the addictive behavior involves drugs, food, sex, gambling, or any other behavior that can hijack the brain and cause dysfunction and debilitation. What is most important in a time of dire need is a clear solution. A simple solution, one easily understood by any person, is likely best. This article is intended to offer a recovery path for all people, applicable to every type of addictive behavior. This method, the "Slugger's Path," is based on the direct observation of thousands in the recovery process and what they did to recover their lives. You will find no fancy notions, no sophisticated research, and no academic posturing in this article; you will only find one addiction treatment professional's biases based on close encounters over a 30-year career.

The "Slugger's Path" is designed for the average person. It is a knowledge base and an action plan modeled on a baseball metaphor. Keeping it simple, an addict needs to know five things about addiction, and he needs to do five things to attain recovery; helpers, friends, and family should know these things, too.

Five Things the Addict Needs to Know

First, addiction is about being sick—it is neither a moral issue nor a criminal matter. Addictive illness has identifiable symptoms, a marked progression, and is fatal. Good medical research shows that addiction is a brain-based disease that no one chooses and has much to do with heredity and trauma. Anyone watching can easily see the overall and ongoing physical, mental, emotional, social, and spiritual deterioration in the active addict. It is devastating to individual addicts, those close to them, and to society as a whole. A person can be very sick, as in late-stage alcoholism, requiring hospitalization, or a little sick, as in feeling depressed after that second piece of chocolate cake.

Second, the addict is quite lonely. Lying about one's behavior is a symptom of addiction. Secrets, isolation, and a sense of separation and rejection are increasingly prevalent as the disease progresses. This is a painful place. Attempts at connection fail again and again. Addicts feel forsaken and forgotten. Relief is temporary with further acting out the addictive behavior.

Third, the addict is unable to resolve his situation, in spite of much effort and individual application of willpower. Many attempts are made to improve the addict's situation, but these always ultimately fail because an addict cannot cure his addiction on his own. This often is referred to as being powerless. The inherent result is great frustration—the disease has the power.

Fourth, the addict feels much guilt as he increasingly fails at performing responsibly in life due to the mental, emotional, and physical effects of his illness. Guilt comes from believing that he is doing wrong or that he is not up to doing things "correctly" or well.

Fifth, the addict feels shame as he is continuously judged and as he judges himself harshly in a destructive and pervasive manner. Ultimately, hopelessness sets in, and thoughts of self-destruction result. Shame is believing that he is a bad person and wholly undeserving.

In summary, an addict is sick, lonely, unable, guilt-ridden, and shame-filled. These characteristics can be remembered with the acronym s.l.u.g.s. This is clearly a lower state of consciousness and a definite downward spiral in life. In order to overcome this debilitating condition, recover the self, and move to a higher state of consciousness and overall health, the addict simply needs to follow the path provided below. This path is as clearly laid out as the base path, the five fingers on your hand, a five-pointed star, five steps up, or any other visual cue you choose to use.

Five Things the Addict Needs to Do

Going with the baseball metaphor, picture yourself up to bat in the biggest game of your life. You look down and see the letter "S" on home plate, representing both your starting point and your goal. That "S" stands for Sobriety, the beginning of the recovery process and your first commitment. The hallmark of this level of recovery is achieving a period of abstinence that is long enough to allow the entire process to start working. This is individualized in nature due to the degree and severity of individual addictions. The person may need intense medical supervision, medications, and a controlled environment in order to succeed in this phase. Once the person is detoxed safely and has some level of stability, he is ready for level two: Love.

Love is a very important part of the recovery process. The very best treatment centers have workers who can express caring and positive regard consistently. It is sometimes hard to love an addict, but no less crucial if you want to contribute to the person's recovery. So, in level two of the process the addict commits to accepting help from qualified helpers, commits to working at self-love and self-care, and begins making an effort to support others in need.

The third value/commitment in recovery is Unity. This is the "joining-up" phase, when the addict embraces Alcoholics Anonymous or another support group. This, again, is a crucial part of the whole recovery process. Studies have shown that group involvement over time is a big factor in positive outcomes.

The fourth of the five values of recovery is Growth. This, too, is an essential element for full recovery. Growth comes from being sober, loved and loving, and united. It is also nurtured and enhanced through activities and commitments around working the 12 Steps, getting psychotherapy, exercise programs, and many other self-improvement practices.

Back to home, the place of peace, Spirituality is the final commitment. Spirituality involves acceptance of a Higher Power, living in the now, prayer and meditation, and an attitude of gratitude.

So, be a Slugger, not a drugger. Win at life. Keep your whole focus on SLUGS, not drugs, and you will experience, in time, full recovery from any addiction and great peace of mind . That is the goal we all share, after all. And it really is the best high.

ABOUT THE AUTHOR

John Baldasare holds a Master's degree in Counseling and a Bachelor's degree in Sociology, both from Wright State University in Dayton, Ohio. He has worked as a therapist, educator, and director in addiction treatment programs continuously since 1973 and was the Executive Director of the renowned Sierra Tucson in Arizona in the early 1990s as well as the Director and CEO at facilities in Ohio and Virginia. John has spoken at national forums and continues to maintain the SluggersPath.com Web site, responding to e-mails and inquiries. John has three grown children and an almost-teenage granddaughter.

4

ADVERSITY

Using Self-Talk to Overcome Adversity

Michael J. Russ

While living on this planet, you can count on one thing: adversity. Sooner or later, something is going to upset your applecart. The good news is that no event can add up to the end of the world unless you say so: adversity is inevitable and presents itself to test your inner strength and provide an opportunity for personal growth. According to *Webster's New World Dictionary*, adversity is defined as "misfortune, a wretched or troubled state, a calamity or a disaster." This means that it could reveal itself to be anything from a minor event to what you would interpret as a full-scale, life-altering catastrophe. The extent to which adversity affects you will be determined by your perspective, past experience, and degree of personal involvement.

Life is easy to live when everything is going smoothly. The real challenge is continuing to feel good about yourself when adversity hits you between the eyes. This is where self-talk becomes so vitally important. Self-talk is what you think and say about yourself, both in your head and out loud to others. Self-talk used before adversity comes into your life is just as important for overcoming it as is the self-talk used after it happens.

The self-talk you use before adversity strikes bolsters self-confidence and strengthens your ability to deal with whatever comes your way. How you feel about yourself before experiencing adversity has everything to do with the way it affects you and how you decide to work through it. Negative self-talk makes it more difficult to shake off adversity and extends your recovery time indefinitely because this kind of self-talk inhibits you from accepting your circumstances so that you can move forward. However, when you use self-talk that promotes optimism and self-confidence in advance of adversity, it becomes easier to maintain a positive perspective. For instance, when you repeatedly use encouraging self-talk, you build self-confidence and a strong self-image that lessens the impact of peer pressure, loss, verbally abusive people, and other adverse circumstances.

After the adversity you can employ conscious self-talk that lessens its impact, enhances creativity, builds optimism, and supports a healthy self-image. This is when you want to repeat thoughts like "I am getting through this" or "This is just a minor interruption; I will deal with it and move on." The important thing is to consciously use more positive self-talk than negative. You do this is by monitoring your self-talk.

Make it a point to be aware of what you are thinking and saying about yourself so that you can determine whether its current trend is positive or negative, fearful or hopeful, and most important, whether it reinforces a positive image of who you are. In the face of adversity, be alert to whether your self-talk is stuck in the past with "shoulds" and "coulds."

Being conscious of the path of your self-talk gives you the mental agility to change its direction when it falls short of supporting you, your intentions, and your goals. For example, when you encounter misfortune, self-talk emphasizing your aptitude for finding yourself in sticky situations falls short of being fully supportive and fails to reinforce a positive self-image. Even when said in jest, these comments are just as destructive because humor only masks what you truly believe to be the truth about yourself. Furthermore, these comments act like a magnet, attracting even more of these experiences to your doorstep.

Being able to recognize when your self-talk is in a downward spiral is essential. If it is, you need to ask yourself if your self-talk is inhibiting your ability to get through adverse situations. Your answer will ignite a dialogue of self-talk that will help you find your way to the other side of what has happened. You can aid this process by transforming repetitive self-talk from that of a victim to someone who encourages and supports his recovery with thoughts like "I can get over this" or "I am a survivor." Transforming the path of your self-talk requires awareness, desire, and a conscious effort, and the results are worth your commitment.

Another way that you can use self-talk to overcome adversity is by designing positive statements upon which you can draw the moment adversity happens in order to reignite the energy, passion, and purpose you originally had for accomplishing your goals and intentions. These statements could be as basic as "I can do this" or "I can overcome any obstacle." Repeated over and over again, these statements are a very powerful influence and represent a conscious way of supporting yourself in the face of the most devastating adversity.

Self-talk provides you with a way of turning misery into something positive through the use of self-actualization. The process involves dropping iffy language that begins with "I can't," "I don't," and "I'll try" and replacing it with purposeful thoughts and statements about you and what you are doing. When adversity seeks to get the best of you, this linguistic transformation fosters trust, enhances self-confidence, fortifies your resolve, and limits damaging effects to your attitude and feelings.

Something else that factors into the management of adversity is your expectation of perfection. Of course, you want to use self-talk that promotes perfection, yet adversity is something you should expect and for which you should be ready. Factor the possibility of imperfection into everything you do so that you can keep a clear head and maintain your mental agility when things don't go as planned. To cultivate this mind-set, use self-talk that promotes open-mindedness and solution-based thinking.

Regardless of the adversity you face in life, it's just a bump in the road that you have to get beyond in order to learn or experience something that will benefit you later in life. Self-talk is something you use every day. Keep a steady eye on yours, and you will always be one step ahead.

ABOUT THE AUTHOR

Michael J. Russ, President and Founder of Powerful Living International, LLC, lives in Panama City Beach, Florida. He is passionate about travel, teaching, public speaking, writing, and conveying ideas that help people live life with more passion and purpose. Michael has authored several audio books, presents corporate workshops, and writes regularly for several online magazines. For more information about Michael and his books, please visit his Web site at http://www.powerfulliving.org.

5

11 Positive Attitudes of Aging: Keep Life from Losing Its Luster

Shirley W. Mitchell

What an awesome time to be Fabulous after 50! We are stepping over the threshold of the new millennium. The explosion of knowledge and communication will thrust us into new beginnings, adventures, and ways of thinking and living.

Age doesn't dull one's luster because the shine comes from within! How does one experience the fountain of youth?

I will stay young at heart! I will keep growing and going. I recently downsized from a large family home to a luxury townhouse on the golf course—the first ever house I picked out for myself and bought. It is positively fabulous and perfect for my needs. I have never lived in a two-story home. I chose to put my bedroom upstairs to force myself to climb the stairs several times a day and to capture the gorgeous view from a higher perch. The sunlight that fills my bedroom each morning fills my soul and gives me a shine from inside all day. My motto is "Keep moving. Exercise is the golden egg of aging."

On my journey beyond youth, I will stay young at heart by living the moment, laughing, and embracing a positive attitude. My goal is to be in the moments of my life, to experience, enjoy, and savor the magic as the minutes tick by. Each day is a precious jewel. If I have the courage to make each day a pearl, at the end of my life I will have a string of pearls.

Laughter has so many healthy benefits for our body, soul, and spirit, so why do we stay stressed so often? Laughter is a stress buster!

Returning home from a speaking engagement, I sat at the airport, reading the *Wall Street Journal*, sipping a cup of coffee, enjoying my time alone—my space—waiting for my flight. Usually a warm, outgoing, approachable person, today I was enjoying the peace and quiet. Hiding behind the newspaper, I did not make eye contact with anyone.

A white cane tapped my shoe. A fit, fabulous gentleman sat in the seat next to me. I kept reading, hoping he did not desire to talk; however, travel was an adventure for him, and he wanted to talk.

With perfect diction, he asked, "Where is your destination?"

"Birmingham, Alabama," I responded with a smile.

"Hey, that's where I'm planning to attend a reunion with my buddies who fought with me in Vietnam."

Bill and I talked nonstop for 30 minutes, until it was time to board the plane. I learned that Bill had been in the Special Forces and was blinded in the war. His beautiful wife became too ill to travel with him on this trip. With Bill's positive attitude and his will to spend time with his Special Forces buddies he made the decision to travel alone.

"Who will help you on the plane, pick up your luggage once we arrive in Birmingham, and get you to your hotel?" I asked.

"Someone will help me! God hasn't failed me yet."

Bill shared with me that his faith, family, and friends were responsible for his positive attitude after he lost his sight. Of course, I helped him get to his destination. His positive attitude was the fire that lit our flame of friendship.

My personal relationship with God will empower me to experience the beauty of being an ageless person. God is the life preserver that will keep us from sinking into the sea of aging.

Knowing God through a daily intimate quiet time propels my life into universal and eternal living. It gives me wings to fly through my maturing life and live well. How do we know God? Draw close to him, and he will be near you! Where there is God, there is liberty. Freedom gives wings to fly to our highest dreams! Powered by our dreams, life after 50 has the possibility of being filled with zeal.

I will choose to live fully after 50, dreaming new dreams and investing my energies in others. The words "I have a dream," spoken by Dr. Martin Luther King, burst into our minds like a firecracker on the fourth of July. After his death his wife, Coretta Scott King, continued his legacy of nonviolent social change in the United States. Until her death on January 31, 2006, she devoted her aging life to helping others. She experienced ageless living.

Investing in relationships for eternity gives life depth, breadth, and a reason for living well. The media coverage of President and Laura Bush has given me a new excitement for the possibility of relationships that work. Relationships with a marriage partner, family, friends, coworkers, and soul mates gives life a spicy flavor! Relationships dull the pain of loneliness.

Excellent nutrition energizes me to live agelessly! It is a choice. Eating small meals of a balanced daily diet is the fuel that runs this wonderful machine in which we live. Energy is a hot commodity for fabulous people over 50. Energy yells youth! Energy produces success! Energy is empowering!

With proper exercise, I will re-kindle and re-spark my fire for life. Admiring the star-studded people on the red carpet at the Oscar awards, I observed the results of hard work, exercise, and talent. The reward for exercise is being sexy, savvy, and sassy at any age.

I will open the jaws of menopause with help from my doctor, great habits, and great attitude. Menopause is not a disease—it is a right of passage, a time of renewal and change, and a great time to make life a "bowl of cherries."

To be female, fabulous, and 50, I will make the most of my best. I like who I have become. I am president of my own life. I feel a spirit of aliveness within myself! I say yes to life.

I will dance with anticipation every day of my life as I move toward eternity and my final home! The fountain of youth is overflowing with the sweet fragrance of success for many of the people living the second half of life. It is the grand finale.

ABOUT THE AUTHOR

Shirley W. Mitchell of Alabama is a mother of three and a grandmother of eight. Her mission is to promote positive aging and health. She is the author of five books and a coauthor of three books, a columnist for the "Fabulous after Fifty" weekly newspaper column in the *Sand Mountain Reporter* and for the syndicated on-line column "RE-FIRE not RETIRE," a national speaker, and hostess of the weekly Internet radio show "Aging Outside the Box—Fabulous Women Over 50" on the VoiceAmerica Health and Wellness Channel. Represented by Lighthouse Coastal Literary ((912) 443–9064 orAgent@lighthousecoastalliterary.com). Visit her Web site at http://www.agingoutsidethebox.net.

6

The Anger Diet: How to Be Calm, Balanced, and Positive, No Matter What's Going On

Brenda Shoshanna

Everyone wants to be beautiful, young, healthy, and fit. Available diets and workouts have no end. Yet, the most important diet has been overlooked—this is a diet that releases stress, lets you sleep soundly at night, reduces cravings, makes you feel young, and brings wonderful possibilities into your life. This is a diet that gets rid of the number one toxin that destroys well-being: anger.

Road rage, school shootings, depression, workplace violence, addiction, and even the national obesity epidemic are manifestations of this great problem gripping our society. Anger has many faces. It appears in various forms and creates different consequences. Overt anger is the simplest to deal with and understand, but unfortunately, most anger lurks beneath the surface. As it often does not come to our awareness, it manifests in endless, hidden ways—as depression, anxiety, apathy, or hopelessness, among others.

Today, we fear all kinds of external enemies. It is not so easy to realize, however, that the worst enemy we face is the anger that resides within us, the terror it causes, and the way this poison affects so much of our lives. It is one thing to be told to calm down or to forgive one another. It is another to know how to do this. Even though we may want to forgive, anger can keep arising, disrupting our bodies, minds, and spirits.

However, we can take many specific steps to root this toxin out of our lives. As we do, the results will be reflected not only in our mental and emotional well-being but also in our environment and physical health. Love and forgiveness arise naturally, and our lives and relationships become all they are meant to be.

A Few of the 24 Forms of Anger

The first step in rooting anger out of our lives is to become aware of it. It is crucial that we recognize the many ways in which anger camouflages itself. When anger is allowed to remain camouflaged and hidden, it holds us in its grip. By recognizing the different forms of anger we begin the important step of replacing each one with a healthy antidote, thus letting it go. As we do this, it is easy to see that anger is a choice we make. By choosing to replace our angry responses with life-giving, constructive ones we can stop anger on the spot.

1. **Straightforward anger, attack.** This is anger that is clear-cut and easy to recognize. The anger comes right out. Many regret it afterward, feeling that they couldn't control themselves. This kind of anger has a life of its own; it rises like a flash flood and can easily turn into verbal, emotional, or physical abuse.

2. **Hypocrisy.** You are angry, but you hide it beneath a smile and present a false persona, pretending to be someone that you're not. This behavior evolves into bad faith of all kinds. Although you think that you are fooling others, in truth, you are losing yourself and your own self-respect.

3. **Depression.** Depression is pervasive these days, and it ranges the gamut from mild to severe. Depression is anger and rage turned against oneself. It comes from not being able to identify or appropriately express the anger one is feeling. It then simply turns into depression attacks against the person who is experiencing it.

Steps to Dissolving Anger

Needless to say, we can take many different steps to undo different forms of anger. The important point to realize is that anger can be dissolved in a moment. *We can choose to see things differently. We can choose to have a different response.*

It takes only a moment to escalate a situation, and in that same moment the trouble can be de-escalated. We must stop in the middle of automatic anger that arises and take charge of what is going on. We can and must decide that we will not let anger take over and rule. We have the right and responsibility to choose how we will respond.

1. **Straightforward attack.** Stop in the middle of a situation in which you feel angry or are being attacked. Rather than responding in a knee-jerk manner, say to yourself, "Like me, this person has suffered. Like me, this person wants to be happy. Like me, this person experiences loneliness and loss." As you do this, you are recognizing the similarities and common humanity you share, rather than focusing on the differences. For a moment, allow the person to be right. You have plenty of time to be right later. Ask yourself what is more important to you, to be "right" or to be free of anger? Choose compassion, and see how you feel. See how the other feels as well. Watch new vistas open in your life.

2. **Hypocrisy.** When you notice yourself pretending, lying, exaggerating, or deceiving, stop. Tell the truth at that moment. Be the truth. If you do not know what the truth is, be silent, and become aware of what the deepest truth is for you. This does not mean pouring out negativity or blaming the other. It means taking responsibility for what is real and true for you. This will not only restore goodwill; it will also connect you with what is most meaningful in your life.

3. **Depression.** Make friends with yourself today. When we are depressed, we reject, hate, and blame ourselves. Undo this false state of mind. Find five things you admire and respect about who you are. Focus on sharing your good qualities with another. In depression we are only absorbed with ourselves. A wonderful antidote is to become absorbed with how you can reach out to help another.

As we root anger out of our lives and find meaningful substitutions, not only our lives but the lives of our loved ones, friends, and acquaintances will be lifted and enhanced. Try the full anger diet and see.

ABOUT THE AUTHOR

A psychologist, relationship expert, speaker, and author, Dr. Shoshanna has a therapy practice in Manhattan. This article is based on her most recent book, *The Anger Diet (30 Days To Stress-Free Living)* (http://www.theangerdiet.com). A national speaker, workshop leader, and longtime student and practitioner of meditation, she provides psychological and spiritual guidance for building healthy relationships and becoming all that you are meant to be. Other books include *Zen and the Art of Falling in Love, Zen Miracles, Save Your Relationship*, and *Living By Zen*. In addition, Dr. Shoshanna is a frequent guest on radio and TV and runs workshops for couples on working through difficulty and renewing their love. Visit http://www.brendashoshanna.com, or reach her at topspeaker@yahoo.com.

7

Beating the "What-If" Blues

Deanne Repich

Do you find that a lot of your negative thoughts begin with the words "what if"? Does one anxious thought lead to another, only to become a negative spiral of worry? When this happens, you're probably using what-if thinking.

What Is What-If Thinking?

What-if thinking occurs when you make negative predictions about the future, usually starting with the words "what if." Most of us can relate to Juan's story of what-if thinking: Juan is running a few minutes late to work. The first thought that pops into his head is, "What if I'm late for my nine o'clock meeting?"

His thoughts don't stop there. His negative thoughts start snowballing: "What if I walk in late and everyone looks at me? What if I get nervous, start sweating, and feel embarrassed? What if my boss notices that I can't handle it, and I lose my job? What if I can't afford to feed my family?" His body responds with a host of symptoms: his heart races, it's tough to breathe, and there's a knot in his stomach the size of Texas.

As you can see, when you use what-if thinking, one negative prediction usually leads to another, and another, and another. This negative chain has a snowball effect that leads to intense feelings of anxiety, loss of control, and physical symptoms.

What You Can Do

You have the power to change your thoughts, and studies show that when you change your thoughts, you create biochemical changes in your brain that affect

27

how your body and mind feel and react. In other words, change your thoughts, and you change your reality!

How do you change your what-if thoughts? You do this by using the three R's: Recognize, Replace, and Reinforce.

1. **Recognize.** Keep a small notepad with you. Each time you notice yourself thinking a what-if thought, write it down. Writing things down helps you to slow down and expose habitual negative thoughts to the light of day. If you don't take the time to write down your what-if thoughts, it's easy to miss them because you are so used to them.

The following technique can help you peel off layer after layer of negative thoughts and reach the core negative belief. I call it the "onion technique" because it's like peeling off layer after layer of an onion until you reach the core. Here's how it works: when you are in a fairly relaxed mood, take out your notepad and open it up to the first what-if thought. Read the thought, and then ask yourself, "And what if that did happen? Then what would happen?" Write down your answer. Repeat this process of digging deeper several times.

After several layers you will reach your core belief—the belief that is at the root of your fears. In Juan's case he might reach this core belief: "If I can't feed my family, my wife and kids will be disappointed in me. They'll leave me, and I'll be all alone." His real fear—what is driving his what-if thoughts—is his fear of being rejected, unloved, and all alone if he disappoints the people he loves. That's the belief that Juan needs to replace in order to beat the what-if blues. His worry about arriving a few minutes late to the meeting will fade once he addresses this core issue.

2. **Replace.** Once you've pinpointed the core negative belief, decide what your new belief will be. Adjust the old belief so that it promotes your well-being and reflects the reality you want to create. When creating your new belief, make sure to use the present tense, use "I" statements, and focus on what you want (not on what you don't want).

In Juan's case, here are several new beliefs he may want to use to replace the unhealthy belief.

• "I am worthy of love, even when I disappoint others."

28

- "I am loved for who I am, not how much I earn. I love my family, and we meet life's challenges together."
- "Since I am human, I will disappoint the people I love occasionally. I can be imperfect and still receive love."

When you notice yourself using a what-if thought, stop it in its tracks. It may help to visualize the word "no" or "stop" in big red letters in your mind. This action interrupts the thought. Then, immediately change your focus by replacing the what-if thought with the new, healthier thought you created.

3. **Reinforce.** Once you have chosen your new belief, reinforce it several times a day. Say the new belief with intense positive feeling. Believe that it is true, even if only for a moment. Think it. Say it aloud. Write it down. You can even record yourself saying the belief for several minutes and then play it back every night just as you're drifting off to sleep. Just like any other habit, the more you practice, the sooner it will become second nature to you.

Making the new belief a part of your life takes time and consistent practice, but the results are worth it. You chase away the what-if blues and the physical symptoms that go along with them. Even better, you change the way you look at life!

ABOUT THE AUTHOR

Deanne Repich is the Director of the National Institute of Anxiety and Stress, Inc., an anxiety educator, teacher, and former anxiety sufferer. Deanne created the Conquer Anxiety Success Program, a simple, how-to course that has helped thousands conquer their anxiety. She also conducts seminars, writes articles, and publishes the "Anxiety-Free Living" printed newsletter. Get her free seven-day e-course to conquer anxiety and fears and unleash health, calmness, and confidence at http://www.ConquerAnxiety.com.

8

The Power of Appreciation

Noelle Nelson

You hate your supervisor. There—you finally said it. You've been pussyfooting around it (and her) for long enough now. That's it, you've had it! Let the truth be told—you hate your boss.

Your reflection in the mirror scowls back at you. You sigh, stop waving your toothbrush around, and stick it back in your mouth where it belongs. Fat lot of good that did! You still have to go to work today. You still have to face your supervisor. You still have to go along with whatever she says.

The worst of it is that you love your job! You have no desire to quit. You work for a great company, you enjoy your work, the pay is good, you get along fine with your coworkers—the only downside is your supervisor. But oh, what a downside! Her automatic answer to anything you want is no; her automatic expectation of anything she wants is yes. So, you don't get help when you need it, you don't get a recommendation for that new position, and you don't get vacation when you want it. You *do*, however, have to respond with, "How high?" when she says, "Jump!"

The question is, how do you keep your job without losing your sanity?

Love thine enemy.

No, not "love thine enemy" as in plaster a phony smile on your face and pretend that your supervisor is a great person to work with—she's not! No, this is "love thine enemy" as in *appreciate* your supervisor, *value* something about your supervisor. Deliberately look for one thing, however small, that you find worthwhile about her. Maybe it's that she's always straight with you. Maybe it's that she works as long and as hard as she expects you to. Maybe it's that she challenges you to the very limits of your abilities.

You see, that's the true meaning of appreciation. It's not just another word for gratitude, a polite "thank you" after someone's done something nice for you, but appreciation as valuing. That's actually the basis of how the word appreciate is used in the marketplace: we say that art appreciates in worth, land appreciates, gold appreciates—they all increase in value, and appreciation is first and foremost about valuing. The thoughts you think, when you are appreciating someone or something, are thoughts about their worth, their value to you, what they mean to you, and why they matter.

Back to your supervisor. You know that one thing you found that you can really, truly value about her? Focus on that. For a couple weeks, as best you can, every time you see your supervisor, think about what it is you value about her. If she's been ornery with you, try to let go of your upset feelings as quickly as you can and—you guessed it—focus once again on thoughts of valuing her.

What you think and feel about someone impacts how they think and feel about you. It's actually scientific. Quantum physics teaches us that in the realm of energy, like attracts like. You've felt this yourself many times. When someone's angry and yelling at you, you'll want to snap back in return. When someone is kind and generous toward you, you'll want to be giving toward them. Think of appreciation as a wonderful facilitator of energy. When you genuinely appreciate someone, they become more willing to cooperate with you.

How will this work with your supervisor? Well, the first thing that will happen, as you persistently, consistently value your supervisor, is that your opinion of your supervisor will shift. You'll realize that she rides you hard because she really cares about the success of the company. You'll realize that she doesn't like shifting around vacation schedules because she takes great pride in the smooth running of her department. You'll understand that she doesn't give you that recommendation to a new position because she wants to keep your good work in her department. As you persistently, consistently value your supervisor in this way, she will feel that shift and begin to value you and thus treat your requests differently.

What about in your home life? Would this same concept apply? You betcha!

31

For example, when you first fall in love, you may be delighted by your sweetheart's mellow, easy-going approach to life, which nicely balances out your wired, get-it-done-now approach. Six months down the line, however, when something isn't happening the way you want it to, you redefine his "don't worry, be happy," laid-back attitude as laziness.

Your sweetheart hasn't changed, but how you view him has. In the same way, your "just do it, and do it now" approach was something your mate admired in you—until it meant that you expected him to do something he wasn't in the mood to do (mellow soul that he is), whereupon your decisiveness became "controlling," and you become "bitchy." You haven't changed either, but your sweetheart's perception of you has.

How you view your true love is affected by how you feel in the moment. When you feel wronged, upset, or hurt by your mate, you are likely to forget what endears him to you and focus only on what displeases you. For example, you may ignore how loving your mate is with the kids and focus only on what a slob he is. Both are true. Your sweetheart may ignore how well you handle the family finances and focus only on how you can't stand the sports he loves. Both are true.

When you focus on what you don't like, don't value, or don't cherish about your sweetheart, you feel resentment. With resentment comes a diminishment of love. On the other hand, when you focus on what you do like, do value, and do cherish, you feel love. The love, or lack of it all, stems from what you choose to make significant. That's where appreciation steps in. If you deliberately, proactively choose to focus on what you value about your mate as much and as often as you possibly can, you'll find that the love in your life just grows and grows. Appreciation is a cornerstone of love, one of its most important elements.

Science increasingly shows how interrelated we all are and how we affect each other continuously in both conscious and unconscious ways. Make that interrelatedness work for you. Value everyone in your life, and enjoy the benefits of their valuing you in return.

Ah, the power of appreciation!

ABOUT THE AUTHOR

Dr. Noelle Nelson is a psychologist, best-selling author, and a powerful, passionate speaker. She has empowered countless individuals to be happier, healthier, and more successful at work, at home, and in relationships—drawn from her belief that through the power of appreciation we can accomplish great things. Through her books, articles, seminars, and consulting practice, Dr. Noelle gives the skills and the inspiration to lead rewarding, satisfying lives. Her books include *The Power of Appreciation: The Key to a Vibrant Life* (Beyond Words) and *The Power of Appreciation in Business* (MindLab Publishing). She can be reached at http://www.PowerOfAppreciation.net or at nnelson@dr.noellenelson.com.

9

The 10 Assumptions That Kill Success

Jim M. Allen

One of the biggest factors affecting whether or not a person will fail or succeed at any particular endeavor is the belief he holds in his mind when he embarks on it. My experience as a life coach is that most people have a remarkable knack for making assumptions about their goals that are just incredibly, wildly, mind-bogglingly incorrect. These assumptions, in addition to being incorrect, serve to enhance people's fears and insecurities, deflating their dreams and sounding a death knell for the success they seek.

I've also found that by tackling these assumptions head on and focusing on the truth, people can change their starting beliefs and greatly improve their chances of being successful in everything they do.

Here are the ten deadliest assumptions that I've encountered. Consider this a "most-wanted" list of killer assumptions to avoid.

1. I Know Exactly What's Going On

Warning! If you find yourself saying or thinking this, it's time to stop and ask a few more questions. And then a few more.

Obviously, at some time you have stop asking questions and start taking action, but that should only happen once you have both a respectable level of confidence in what you are about to do *and* an understanding that your knowledge of any situation will always be, in some way, limited.

Invariably, the moment at which you think you see everything is usually the moment at which you have the smallest field of vision. Recheck your facts, get more information, and then proceed.

2. I Have a Foolproof Plan

No plan is foolproof. At best, you might have a plan that is "fool-resistant," and only a fool has just one plan. Chuck this assumption fast, and get to work on plans B, C, and D. Consider worst-case scenarios and as many "what-ifs" as time will allow.

3. I Don't Need (or Can't Get) Help

Success does not occur in a vacuum. Very few truly "solitary" successes (those who created success on their own, without the help of others) can be found in history. A second opinion, a spare set of hands, and a fresh perspective seldom go amiss.

If you think you don't need help, then you probably do (reread assumption 1). If you think you can't get help, I'd encourage you to ask first and then decide. If you're not sure where to go, start by visiting your local library, college, or telephone directory.

4. I Don't Have the Education

Ideas put to action create success, not diplomas. There are plenty of high school and college dropouts who are wildly successful, so stop using this excuse to delay getting started on your endeavors.

If you absolutely must have a formal "education," there are many ways to get one. They may not be traditional means, but they can be just as effective.

5. I Don't Have the Money

Not having the money now does not mean that you cannot get the money in the future. Rather than focusing on what you lack, focus on how you can save, earn, or borrow what you need.

6. I Don't Have the Time

Actually, you have all the time in the world. You may need to reschedule some things, change priorities, and stop doing other things, but you'll never have more time than you do right now. What are you waiting for?

7. I Am Too Old (or Not Old Enough)

You're only "too old" when you're dead. If you're old enough to worry about being old enough, then trust me, you're old enough.

8. I Am Being Unrealistic

Some of the greatest successes ever are the ones that were thought to be the least realistic. Dream big. Be bold. Let the critics debate whether it's realistic or not, while you make it happen.

9. I Don't Deserve to Be Successful

Well, if you don't, who does? And anyway, what if you're wrong? Why not just go ahead and find out? You may just have a surprise (and a success) headed your way.

10. Nobody Understands What I Am Trying to Do

Maybe nobody you know now understands, but look around, and you'll find a world full of wonderful people who, just like you, are each struggling to create success in their own ways. Open up and share your dreams with them, and you'll soon find more supporters than you can count!

ABOUT THE AUTHOR

Jim M. Allen, "The Big Idea Coach," is a professional life and business coach with clients from around the world who are ready to make their small ideas big and their big ideas real. For more information on Jim's coaching and speaking services, or to subscribe to his free Internet newsletter, go to http://www.BigIdeaCoach.com.

10

BEHAVIOR MODIFICATION

Your Most Powerful Tool for Change

Mike Brescia

Ah, today is a wonderful day. It's a great day to be alive—to learn, to give, to grow, and to achieve your dreams.

Did you notice that? Those statements? They are statements of belief and of conviction—of affirmation. I also call them self-instructions because that describes what they do: they instruct us how to feel and how to act. They create who we are at the deepest levels. They are the single most powerful tool for changing your emotions, your actions, and the results you get in your life . . . *if* you use the right self-instructions, and if you use them *a lot*.

You see, every second you are thinking. You can't stop. Even if you were an experienced meditator, it would be difficult to turn off the pictures, sounds, and feelings your mind serves up. Every minute of every day, you are affirming what you believe. You are doing it this very second. If you just thought, "That's not true," you made an affirmation—a statement of belief and conviction. In fact, every thought you've had or ever will have is either a question, an affirmation, or an affirmative command.

So anyone that says affirmations don't work has absolutely no idea what he is talking about. Yours are working on you right now, and they will work on you until you shuffle off these mortal coils.

My point? Since your minute-by-minute thoughts (affirmations) *are* your present and your future, all you need to do is improve your affirmations, and every area of your life will improve right along with them. It is an absolute certainty.

A large part of our research at Think Right Now! International is to discover and compare the beliefs, attitudes, and actions of the world's most successful, happy people to the most unsuccessful, unhappy people. They are always polar opposites.

For example, when the healthiest, oldest living people on the planet feel comfortably full, they typically say to themselves, "I feel just right," and they stop eating, even if a pile of their favorite food is still on their plate.

In contrast, what do people who suffer the most illnesses, pain, and diseases do at the full mark? They often say things like "one more bite won't hurt," and they continue eating.

In fact, we consistently find many hundreds of differences in beliefs between successful people and failures in every discipline of life. And obviously, the longer a person owns a belief (affirms it), the harder it is to change. The old saying that you can't teach an old dog new tricks is an old saying for a good reason. Our minds don't want to change . . . it's uncomfortable. The pain you may feel now, at least, is familiar. When big habit changes happen quickly, it's agony because it's unfamiliar.

That's why when you read a self-help book or go to therapy or attend a seminar, chances are excellent that you will do nothing differently. If you do experience an improvement in your moods or habits, it's usually short-lived because your long-held assumptions, beliefs, and attitudes (affirmations) never changed. You fought it. You found reasons why you couldn't continue, why it was wrong for you, why you couldn't succeed after all.

Information or logic alone usually does not create lasting habit changes. If just knowing what to do guaranteed success, then everyone would get A's in school and would continue to enjoy great accomplishments throughout their lives, but they don't. Out of every 100 students using the same textbook and getting the same lectures from the same teacher, only a few will score above 90 percent, and even fewer will use their knowledge to ensure success in their careers and in life.

Information and logic alone is not enough because we talk to ourselves all day long, and most people have the same failure-oriented self-talk in 2006 that they had in 1996, 1986, and 1976. If something frightened you 10 years ago, it's likely to still make your knees knock today. If you hate exercising now, you probably won't like it much 10 years from now. Why is this so? I call it mental patterns. They are hard wired into you from years of conditioning.

I have many clients whose core mental patterns are so screwed up that they suffer from panic attacks. They lose all control of their minds and bodies, but in most cases, when we aggressively work to alter their moment-by-moment thoughts, thus altering their core assumptions about themselves, their lives, and the world, the panic attacks end. This is true even if decades of therapy have done nothing. Self-instructions *are* powerful.

Think of your usual thoughts (affirmations) as a paintbrush that continues to paint the same colors on the same places on the same canvas . . . for the rest of your life. The longer you paint, the thicker the paint gets. It gets so deep that there comes a point where it feels impossible to alter the picture.

"You make me so mad. I'm too busy to eat healthy. I'll never get this done. I'm depressed. There are no decent men out there. I can't figure this out."

These types of beliefs (affirmations) fill you with anxiety. They make easy decisions hard, suck the joy out of your accomplishments, create illness and disease, and take away your energy and zest for adventure. In any area of life where you cannot seem to succeed no matter what, I guarantee you that your negative beliefs (affirmations) are controlling you every minute of every day— but they don't have to anymore.

Ponder this fact: every sentence you've read here is either a question, an affirmation, or an affirmative command. Check it. Believe in affirmations now? Good. Step 1 is complete.

Now for Step 2: pick any area of your life that doesn't work, where you fail, feel fearful, hopeless, or where your luck is never any good. It could be your diet, fitness level, anxiety or depression, career trouble, social problems, romance, sex, financial woes, poor organization, sports, school, memory, time management . . . any area of life where you are having big troubles.

Then, go somewhere by yourself and think about that topic. Notice your thoughts. When you notice a disempowering thought, if you see a picture of yourself failing or hear yourself saying anything that makes you feel less capable, write down the thought or a description of the picture.

If, for example, you want to improve your financial situation, get by yourself and listen to your inner dialog, and notice your mental pictures about this issue. After you have a few dozen disempowered beliefs and attitudes written down related to money and your lack of it, write opposing statements in affirmation form. So, if you routinely get up late, don't start your daily phone calls until 11 A.M., take long lunches, buy things you can't afford, and never read investment-related books or invest in appreciating assets, turn these beliefs, attitudes, and actions around by writing down opposing first person, present tense statements that affirm that the opposite is true now.

Then, take this new set of desired beliefs, attitudes, and actions and copy each one down on no more than 20 3 × 5 index cards, and live with those cards. Take them everywhere with you, and read them with strong emotion upon waking, at lunchtime, and before you go to bed. Say them aloud whenever possible. Commit to doing this, and soon, you'll be taking positive daily actions that will make all your goals and dreams come true.

If you think this won't work, remember that *that* belief is an affirmation. Suspend your doubt and follow through on this, and you will have taken the most important step in your personal and professional development. Do this, and your confidence will soar. Your motivation will last. Happiness will be your normal mental state. Nothing will be beyond your grasp. These last statements? Just affirmations, right?

ABOUT THE AUTHOR

Mike Brescia is the president and CEO of Think Right Now! International, Inc. Think Right Now! develops thought and behavior modification programs that internalize the 22 core unconscious thought processes of those who are the best at something already. This makes new emotional patterns and behaviors easier to adopt and keep. When you need your emotions, decisions, actions, and results to be like a champion's without patches, powders, or pills, just Think Right Now! Visit our Web site at http://www.thinkrightnow.com.

11

Can You Believe It?

Vic Johnson

> Belief is the basis of all action, and this being so, the belief that dominates the heart or mind is shown in the life.
> —James Allen (*Above Life's Turmoil*)

You will rarely attempt something that you don't believe possible, and you will *never* give 100 percent of your ability to something in which you don't believe.

One of the best known stories about the power of belief concerns Roger Bannister, the first person to run a mile in under four minutes. Before his accomplishment it was generally believed that the human body was incapable of such a feat. Bannister, who was a medical student, held another belief, however. He said, "Fueled by my faith in my training, I will overcome all obstacles. I am brave! I am not afraid to face anyone on the track. I believe this is not a dream. It is my reality."

As soon as he broke the barrier, belief about the feat changed, and his record only lasted 46 days. Within two years, there were nine sub-four-minute miles. Hundreds have done so since. What happened in 1954 that hadn't happened in the previous 6,000 years of human history that allowed Bannister to achieve this? Did the human body change so that this could be done? No, but the human belief system did!

My most favorite story about belief has a twist to it. Cynthia Kersey wrote about George Dantzig in *Unstoppable*. As a college student, George studied very hard and always late into the night, so late, in fact, that he overslept one morning, arriving 20 minutes late for class. He quickly copied the two math problems on the board, assuming that they were the homework assignment. It took him several days to work through the two problems, but finally, he had a breakthrough and dropped the homework on the professor's desk the next day.

Later, on a Sunday morning, George was awoken at six in the morning by his excited professor. Since George had been late for class, he hadn't heard the professor announce that the two unsolvable equations on the board were mathematical mind teasers that even Einstein hadn't been able to answer, but George Dantzig, *believing* that he was working on just ordinary homework problems, had solved not one, but two problems that had stumped mathematicians for thousands of years.

How many great things could you achieve if you just believed that they were as easy as they really are?

Some years ago, I was listening to a friend of mine speak to a business audience, and she quoted a teaching by David Schwartz from *The Magic of Thinking Big* that rocked my life. She said, "The size of your success is determined by the size of your belief." Now, that was the first personal development book I ever read, and I've read it at least 20 times since. I'm sure that I had heard that concept many times before that night, but it so impacted me that I wrote it down and must have looked at it a hundred times or more in the 30 days after that.

I spent the next few months focused on strengthening my belief in myself and in what I wanted to do. I worked each day on my beliefs by constantly affirming myself using written and verbal affirmations. The years since have been an incredible rocket ride.

How do you change your belief system?

- Prepare to win. Nothing will strengthen your belief system more than knowing that you're prepared. His prerace training was the key to Bannister's belief that he could achieve his goal.
- Take control of your thoughts. It's your choice what you think about. Think success, and that's what you'll get; think failure, and that's what you'll attract. To help in controlling your thoughts, make it a habit to affirm yourself. I had a box of business cards with an old address that I was going to discard. Instead, I flipped them over to the blank side and wrote affirmations

on them. I had two identical sets, one for my car and one for my office. Throughout the day I would read my "flash cards" aloud.

- Reevaluate your situation. One of my mentors, Bob Proctor, teaches that "our belief system is based on our evaluation of something. Frequently when we re-evaluate a situation our belief about that situation will change."
- Don't worry about "how to do it." One of my early mistakes was trying to figure out how I was going to do something before I believed that I could do it at all. Start by believing that you can do something, and the "how to" will follow.
- Finally, you must act. Until you act, you're not committed, and belief is not cemented.

What great challenge lies in your path today? Do you sincerely want to overcome or accomplish it? If the answer is yes, then *can you believe it*? Can you believe that the magic is really in you?

Recently, I was dramatically impressed by a passage in *The Message of a Master* by John McDonald. To me, it sums up the reason why most of us don't have the belief to succeed: "The cause of the confusion prevailing in your mind that weakens your thoughts is the false belief that there is a power or powers outside you greater than the power within you."

And that's worth thinking about.

ABOUT THE AUTHOR

Vic Johnson is a popular author, speaker, and founder of four of the hottest personal development sites on the Internet, including http://www.AsAManThinketh.net, where he has given away almost 300,000 e-book copies of James Allen's classic book. He also has several popular blogs, including http://www.VicJohnson.com.

12

BELIEFS

Just Believe

David Neagle

In midwinter of 2000 I was conducting a seminar at a beautiful resort in southern Florida. The focus of the seminar was to break limiting beliefs and create new ones to bring prosperity and abundance into a person's life.

At the end of the last day I went to my hotel room, and as I entered, I noticed that the red message light on my phone was flashing. I called the front desk, and there was only one message: it was from my business partner, telling me that a major snowstorm was developing over the Midwest and that I might not be able to fly back to Chicago the next morning. I was concerned, but I was tired and had to get up early to catch my flight home, so I went to sleep.

The next morning, while I was getting dressed, I turned on the national weather channel. The forecast was indeed for a major snowstorm to hit Chicago. I decided to continue to the airport in the hope of beating the storm. During the ride to the airport I began to think that maybe I should change my belief about this storm delaying my arrival. I was in serious doubt about my chances of making it home. Then, I thought about the snowstorm and laughed because my beliefs certainly couldn't have had any effect on the weather.

When I arrived at the airport, I asked if all flights were still a go. I was told yes, so I boarded my plane, which was bound for a connecting flight in Atlanta. When I arrived in Atlanta, everyone was immediately informed that flights to the Midwest and various other destinations were being cancelled.

I thought it was worth a shot to go see the ticket agent and ask her my options. I was told that I had none and that she was booking me on the next available flight to Chicago, which didn't leave until Wednesday.

"What?" I exclaimed. "Wednesday? It's Monday!"

"Sir, everything is closing—this storm is huge. We will put you up in a hotel."

Disappointed, I agreed and was quickly shuttled off to the hotel. When I arrived, I was appalled. It was the nastiest place I had ever seen, and the room was disgusting. The more I thought about where I was, the more I wanted to get home. I told myself that I was going to believe myself all the way back to Chicago, so I went to the lobby and asked for a ride back to the airport.

When I arrived at the airport, it was filled with people who were desperately stranded. The hotels were full, and there was no place to go. I went to rent a car, only to find that there were no more available.

Believing firmly that I could still make it home that night, I approached the ticket agent and asked if there were any flights left headed for Chicago. Without blinking an eye, she told me that everything had been cancelled. I asked her if she would check her computer again, but she repeated her statement. I calmly but firmly asked her if she would just please check one more time. She wasn't happy about it, but she did.

To her surprise, she found a flight bound for Chicago that night with one open seat, but if I took that seat, I would lose my spot on the Wednesday flight and might not get home until later in the week.

I asked her to give me the seat. She began to protest, but I stopped her midsentence and said, "Please, put me in that seat, I am going home today." She reserved my seat, and I had to wait almost 12 hours to board my plane. During this time I decided that I needed to keep my mind focused on my outcome. I needed to think, feel, and act like I was going home. I needed to expect it with every fiber of my being.

All around me, there were people lying on the floor. People were complaining about being stuck in Atlanta with no place to go. In many cases, tempers began to escalate. I walked around, read for a bit, and had something to eat while continuing to hold the image in my mind of safely landing at O'Hare airport in Chicago.

The hours passed, and every flight on the departure board was cancelled, except for mine. The news on the television was talking about little else other than the massive snowstorm. Then, it happened: the news said that O'Hare airport was officially closed—they had not been able to get any flights in or out all day.

I walked over to the departure board one more time and saw that my flight still had not been cancelled. I held closely to my vision and tightly to my belief that I was going home that night.

As the time for departure approached, I was sitting near the gate and could overhear the ticket agents talking about how strange it was that my flight had not been cancelled. After all, the airport in Chicago was still closed. Then, the pilots showed up and were asking all kinds of questions as to why my flight was still scheduled.

The plane began to board, and as I boarded the plane, I could hear the pilot asking someone on the radio if he was sure they should go. I began to see that my belief was working. I had a bit of a smile on my face as we raced down the runway and became airborne. Soon, the pilots were announcing how amazed they were that we were actually about to land and said that we were the only flight granted permission to land at O'Hare that day.

I have experienced many more events just like this story since that day and so have the people I have taught to "just believe."

ABOUT THE AUTHOR

David Neagle, the "Millionaire Mentor," is an internationally known author, speaker, and master success coach. He is the owner of Life is Now, Inc. Visit his Web site at http://www.DavidNeagle.com.

13

Mind Your Brain™: Three Revolutionary, Recent Brain Research Discoveries You Can Apply to Greatly Advance Your Achievements

Doug Bench

Recently, an explosion of research explaining the intricate workings of the human brain has occurred. Neuroscientists are now able, using advanced equipment, to literally "see" how the brain responds to stimuli as they're happening. This was never before possible and has provided astounding findings about how the brain works. You can now learn to "Mind Your Brain" and apply techniques based on these new discoveries to greatly enhance your brain's performance and create a lifetime of greater achievement.

Thoughts Are Things

Your thoughts are physical things. Your thinking and your thoughts are biological, electrochemical impulses. They can be seen, measured, and examined. They are real. If you understand brain function, you can learn to control your mind and control your thinking. If you control your thinking, you will control your behavior, and your ability to achieve is most affected by your behavior.

Your behavior is controlled by your feelings, and your feelings are created, controlled, or influenced by your attitudes. Your attitudes are the perspective from which you view life. Whatever attitudes have been firing in your brain will create how you feel about stimuli in your life and will always affect how you act.

Your attitudes are created, controlled, and influenced by your beliefs. What you believe about anything will determine your attitudes, which create your feelings, which direct your behavior. Belief neuron patterns are so powerful that they can

47

even make something appear to be different from what it really is. Belief does not require things to be factually true; it only requires us to believe them.

Where do beliefs come from? They come from your thoughts: the interconnections of neurons that fire a given idea. Thoughts that fire the most are relied on the most to create your beliefs. Thoughts are physical things. Every thought that comes into your brain from the outside world and every thought you feed yourself is stored as a neuron pattern in your brain. These neuron pattern firings, these chain reactions, these thoughts, create your beliefs. Learn to control your thoughts, and you will learn to control your behavior.

Brain Plasticity

Your brain is not hardwired! If your brain is stimulated from learning or experiencing, no matter your age, it will physically grow new connections. These new connections will increase the total number of connections within your brain and will increase your brain's capacity for achievement.

This fantastic news means that you and I have only to destroy any neuron patterns that have been firing thoughts saying, "I can't." All those excuses need to go. Scientists have proven that whether you are 6 years old or 60, your brain can form new connections, and the number of new connections you have the capacity to make is greater than the number of molecules in the universe!

It's scientific truth: there is no limit on your capacity to achieve new things. Remember, your beliefs are not necessarily based in reality. It is your perception of reality that ends up controlling your beliefs. If you allow neuron patterns to fire that put limits on your ability to achieve, those limits will become real for you. Stop firing the limiting neuron patterns!

Reticular Activating System

The reticular activating system (RAS) is a bundle of interconnected neurons located near the back of your brain, in the noncortex part, and is not voluntarily controlled by your thoughts. It is an automated system that functions constantly. *All* impulses that enter your brain for interpretation first pass through your RAS. If you are driving and a ball bounces in front of your automobile, you do not have to consciously process thoughts to hit the brake pedal. It happens automatically.

Once the RAS recognizes an impulse coming in, it sends a signal directly to your conscious level, interrupting whatever you are thinking at that moment and bringing you a conscious set of neuron patterns about the stimulus it has observed. You cannot stop it. You cannot keep yourself from thinking about it.

What if you could turn over to your RAS responsibility for taking action toward your goals? Think about how marvelous this would be. If you could turn that over to the automated portion of your brain, procrastination would be eliminated. Stimuli related to your goal would be recognized by your RAS, and you would be forced to respond either in action or reaction to those stimuli automatically.

How can you assign responsibility to your RAS? Repetition makes it your belief. Remember, your thoughts fired over and over again formulate "beliefs." If your beliefs (goals) are on your RAS "important list," then every time an impulse related to that goal enters your brain, it would *automatically* cause an instant message to go to your conscious level.

Think back to when you got a new automobile. Remember how you started seeing that same car everywhere after that? What happens? The car was put on your RAS "important list." Some magical force turns your head and makes you look. You cannot resist it.

This is the power of the RAS. It calls your conscious attention to anything related to neuron patterns that are on your "important list." Determine what's going to be on your "important list" (goals) and get it there! (It takes about 30 days of affirmations to create enough new brain connections to get something onto your "important list.") Then, your RAS will take over and automate your achievements toward those goals.

Mind Your Brain!

So, how do you apply these discoveries to achieve more?

1. Pay attention to your thoughts. Your thoughts are real things, and they create connections in your brain that are forming your beliefs, and your beliefs control your actions. If your thought patterns are negative, they will literally create negative neuron patterns that fire the most (negative beliefs) and create your reality. Keep them positive!

2. Understand the enormity of your brain's capacity to form new connections and to do new things. Your abilities have no limits. Neuroscientists have proven this!

3. Get your positive goals on your RAS "important list." Write them down. Repeat them over and over until they are burned in. Use affirmations to help you. You will have turned action toward your goals over to the automatic portion of your brain and will have achieved "motivation automation." Just watch the action! Before realizing it, your goals will be your achievements . . . automatically!

ABOUT THE AUTHOR

Doug Bench, MS, JD, AAAS, a retired lawyer and former Applied Physiology researcher, has read and researched over 60,000 pages of recent brain research to create what he calls his "Mind Your Brain" Home Study CD Course, which contains all 16 recent revolutionary brain research discoveries, 16 Science-Based Techniques for Success, and over 110 lessons gleaned from brain research that you can apply to greatly improve your achievement skills and your life. Learn more at http://www.scienceforsuccess.com.

14

BULLIES

Taking the Bully by the Horns

Kathy Noll

Bullies are people we deal with 24 hours a day, 7 days a week. They're our coworkers, neighbors, acquaintances, strangers, and, yes, even family and friends slip on their bully masks from time to time. (Some more than others!) No matter who, where, or why, bullies can make you feel *miserable* and about as small as the period at the end of this sentence.

Male or female, young or old, short or tall, fat or thin—I think you see where I'm going with this—bullies aren't easily recognizable by outer appearance. *Anybody* can be a bully. It's what they do, what they say, and their motives behind both that define their bullying behavior.

Has anyone ever made you feel like you're a bad person, not good enough, completely unhappy, scared, angry, anxious, or depressed? Or perhaps he made you feel so bad that you shut yourself off and started believing him? To some degree, most of us have been harassed, picked on, put down, belittled, intimidated, humiliated, criticized, and degraded—in other words, *victimized.* Why do we allow ourselves to be victims? The bully certainly isn't worthy of us bowing down to him.

Bullies are know-it-alls and like to think that they have the answers for everything. Don't be intimidated! They're no better than you, even though they act like they are. Angry most of the time and prone to violent outbursts and destruction of property, bullies thrive on being in control and hurting others with no responsibility or remorse. They believe that their anger and violent behavior are justified.

The best thing that you can do is to stick up for yourself. Before responding to verbal bullying, take a deep breath and think for a moment what you're about to say. Show him that you're strong and can't be taken advantage of or used. Assert yourself. Look the bully in the eye, and explain how he's making you feel. If that doesn't work, firmly tell him to *stop*. If the bully refuses to listen to you or becomes verbally abusive, walk away. Ignoring a bully or nonreacting takes away the power he thinks he has over you. When he sees that he's no longer getting to you, his control game is over. If enough people stand up to a bully, eventually, the bully will be forced to change, but don't expect a bully to change overnight. People change only when they *want* to change.

Bullies need to be in control of situations and enjoy gaining power from inflicting injury on others. How did they get that way? Why do bullies treat us like something they scraped off their shoes? I could simply say because they're jerks, and leave it at that, but to understand their behavior, we have to go deeper. They don't feel good about themselves, and you are their distraction. Arrogance is not high self-esteem. If someone really has good self-esteem, they don't feel the need to control others, and that is what bullying is about—control.

A lot of times, bullies are angry because *they've* been bullied. They started out as victims. I call this the "bully cycle." Don't get sucked in. Powered by all the anger and frustration within their own lives, bullies will try hard to make you think there's something wrong with *you*. Always remember that *you* are okay and that they're the ones who need help.

A young bully may have been exposed to violence in the media. Friends could have been bad influences, or caretakers might have lacked in nurturing, supervision, or the time to teach how wrong it is to hurt others. A spoiled child may think that he can do anything he wants, including bullying.

The recipe for bullying is the same no matter what age: mix what a bully is with why he does it, and add one heapin' cup of what *you* can do about it. These ingredients can also be shared with your children and applied to their bullying dilemmas as well. Children who use violence to resolve conflicts grow up to be adults who use violence to resolve conflicts, so yesterday's school yard bully may now be your boss!

Bullying abuse ranges from physical (a punch to your nose) to emotional (a punch to your self-esteem). Bruises to your self-esteem can last a lifetime, but counseling, knowing your self-worth, and taking back your power are the best medicine to help rebuild it. Never forget that *you* are the only one in charge of you. Nobody can *make* you feel anything. Choose to be happy, and be yourself. Arming yourself with this important knowledge of understanding abusers and how to deal with them will result in a significant change in your life.

The positive, preventative steps we take all add up and along the way help us to improve self-esteem because we feel really good about taking excellent care of ourselves. When we eliminate those bully abusers from our lives, our self-esteem rises and helps us to live guilt-free and in integrity, which is the root to healthiness and happiness.

About the Author

Kathy Noll studied writing and child behavior, won awards for her articles and stories, and authored *Taking the Bully by the Horns* and *Encounters with Every-Day Angels*, self-help books on bullying and character development for school and home. She discusses abusive behavior on radio and TV shows, including *Montel Williams*, with coauthor Dr. Jay Carter (*Nasty People*). She's a consultant for TV news and talk shows, gave expert testimony for a children's literature infomercial (Buena Vista/Disney), is an *NBC News* monitor for classroom bullying, and networks with antiviolence organizations, schools, mental health professionals, and antibullying advocates around the globe, helping children and adults with bullying and self-esteem issues. Free articles and advice, books and videos, and workshop information is available at http://hometown.aol.com/kthynoll.

15

Your Passions and Your Dreams *Can* Make You Money

Lucinda Walters

A lot of people talk about owning their own businesses, working for themselves, or "going out on their own" in the small business world. Few people actually take action to establish a business, and an even smaller number of people sustain a small business past five years.

As I talk with individuals, it seems that three prevailing myths stop people from pursuing their passions to create a thriving business. People believe that they don't have enough money, don't have enough time, or don't know how to get started creating a business. I'd like to destroy the power of these three horrible myths so that *you* can build your dream into a thriving business.

Are you familiar with the idea of a stepping-stone? The phrase comes from placing a stone so that you can cross a body of water or a garden. For our purposes a stepping-stone offers a position for advancement toward a goal. If you start using stepping-stones today, you *will* see results with *consistent* action! Today, you can learn how each stepping-stone will help you to start a business, attract your first client, and improve your life!

Myth #1: You don't have enough money to start your own business. As adults, we seem to identify needless financial barriers for ourselves. It doesn't matter if it's dollars, pounds, euros, yen, or lira—it's all about the money. We fixate on the "if only" way of dreaming about our business ideas: "If only I had more money, then I would do what I really want to do."

If you have a job today, you have money coming into your life *now*. Each day, you choose how to spend that money. To destroy this myth, your stepping-stone action is to spend your money on your dream idea. Choose any amount of money, even if it's just a few dollars, to devote to your passion.

Where you focus your attention, you will see results. If you focus your attention on having the latest fashions, somehow, you "find" the money to buy the latest fashions. Likewise, when you choose to spend money for your dream, you will see results in the oddest and weirdest ways. It doesn't matter what amount you choose. What matters is choosing to put your money where your heart is.

Myth #2: You don't have enough time to start your own business. Our society is paralyzed by the "too much to do" syndrome. We have e-mail, voicemail, mobile phones, pagers, and faxes. We have work, gym and fitness clubs, kids' activities, dates, church, yoga, and all sorts of sports activities. We don't slow down for anything. What I'd like to suggest is that you spend time on what is important: doing what you love.

Every person on the planet gets the same amount of time each day, each week, each month, and each year. Have you ever stopped to figure how you spend your time each week? Every person on the planet has 168 hours each week to do whatever he pleases. Your stepping-stone action for the next three months is to spend one hour each week doing something that makes your heart race and your mind tingle. When you choose to *do* something related to your dream, you will create a new habit, a new pattern of behavior. These new patterns will create a new you and a thriving business.

Myth #3: You don't know how to get started. It's amazing to me how many people with fabulous talent never pursue how to make money with what they were obviously intended to do! One of my girlfriends wants to be the next Mrs. Fields (for those readers who do not live in the United States, Mrs. Fields is a well-known, multimillion-dollar cookie company started in founder Debbie Fields's kitchen). My friend's passion is fudge. She says, "I just don't know what to do first. I'm known as the Fudge Lady to all the beauty salon customers. I made $500 *profit* last Christmas just selling fudge to customers where I get my nails done." I was happy to tell her that she's already in business, and then we talked about how she could expand on her success!

Your stepping-stone action is to identify the person in your life who already believes in your talent and tell that person your heart's dream within the next 48 hours. This action takes a tremendous amount of courage. That is why it is *crucial* to be clear who is the best, most supportive person in your life. It might not be your spouse or your parent. It might be a friend with whom you've lost touch. To destroy the third myth takes a belief in yourself and *one* action.

Now, About That First Client . . .

If you take the stepping-stone actions described above, you will meet new people, behave differently, and create opportunities to attract your first client. Here are some specific stepping-stone actions to build your business.

Open your mouth, and tell people what you are doing! When you speak with passion and enthusiasm, it makes an impression on people. You may not ever sell anything to the person you're telling, however, that person may tell a friend or coworker who needs your product or service. Every time you tell someone what you are doing, you are telling the universe that you are serious about following your heart and making money from what you most enjoy doing.

If you have a product, make a prototype, and ask people's opinions on it. If you have a service, send a postcard to 50 people to offer them the service for a limited time only. When you ask people for their opinions and aren't pushing them to buy something, typically, they will want to help you. Their suggestions can help you to improve your product or service, and they are more likely to tell other people what you're doing after they have experienced it firsthand. People want to see you succeed. After all, your success could inspire them to follow their dreams!

Do not be afraid to try, try, and try again! Most successful businesspeople will tell you that they failed several times before succeeding beyond their wildest dreams. Aren't you worth the effort to improve your life and live your dreams?

It only takes one action, and today is the day to do what you love!

About the Author

Lucinda is an internationally recognized business consultant who believes that *you* can turn your passion into money. If you are ready to design your success and identify *your* next stepping-stone action, call her at (480) 332–7690! To learn the #1 secret for creating success through consistent action, visit http://www.lucinda.biz/steppingstones.htm.

16

BUSINESS WITH HEART

How to Cultivate Invisible Ecology in Your Business

Susan Urquhart-Brown

Have you ever walked into a store and instantly felt a pleasing warmth and friendliness that made your shopping experience wonderful? Did you notice that something special was going on, but you couldn't quite put your finger on it? I call this "something special feeling" the invisible ecology of the business environment.

What Is Invisible Ecology?

Just like it is very important to have balance and harmony in nature for a healthy, thriving physical ecology, it is equally important to have balance and harmony in the invisible ecology, or interior landscape, governing a business owner and employees. When this balance and harmony is present, it breeds teamwork, appreciation, and respect and promotes positive and long-lasting relationships in the workplace and with customers, which is the basis of a successful business. It is this synergy of body, mind, and soul in both the owner and employees that creates positive energy in the business.

This balanced invisible ecology is often what's missing in a business. When you love your work, you pour your heart energy into the office environment, and anyone entering feels it. This pouring of heart energy, just from the sheer joy of sharing, creates the kind of environment that is palpable to customers, and they feel it and respond to it.

Invisible ecology is actually the relationship between your actions and your understanding of what makes you tick. Ask yourself how well you truly know yourself. What motivates you? Do you follow your dreams? Do you find peace and joy in what you do? The more you understand what makes you tick, the more present and available you become to life in general. This presence and availability energizes those around you and produces a harmonious work environment. It also stimulates your inner resources of energy, creativity, cooperation, integrity, and confidence.

What Are the Benefits?

Business is built on relationships. Have you noticed that when the boss is open and happy, the employees tend to be happy, and the customers are happy? Happy customers spend money and come back again and again, and they send their friends. Unhappy customers go elsewhere.

It's not enough to only do good work in your business. Invisible ecology is a new paradigm—one that is value-based and comes from the intention of how you're *being* in your business rather than having total focus on what you're *doing*. It puts human connection and service on an equal footing with business results and profits—and the business thrives. Who are you *being* in business? How is your invisible ecology being expressed? Are you out to get all the business you can, with no regard to whose toes you may be stepping on? Do you create extra problems in your attempt to make budget or hit sales targets? Are you able to see the bigger, long-term picture for your business?

I have found that most successful businesses are about building relationships one to one, season after season. When I connect with a client, they connect with me, and the relationship begins. I have found in my business that when my intention is to serve others, I not only help my clients solve problems, but I learn and feel served in the process—and clients keep showing up!

In today's economy, businesses sell similar products and services. What distinguishes a business today is the quality of the service, and service is expressed through individuals.

How Can You Cultivate Invisible Ecology?

Instead of using attack-defense strategies that raise your blood pressure and increase your lawyer's fees while trying to increase your bottom line, try the following to cultivate and nurture the invisible ecology within you.

1. Accept the challenge and move forward by being open to a variety of possibilities; choose one, and try it. If it doesn't work, try the next possibility. Be like water, which effortlessly changes course to move around obstacles. Stay open.

2. Cultivate your own natural wisdom to solve problems. Have faith in yourself and in your team's good ideas, set a plan, and implement it, trusting that you and your team will be able to handle any and all results. Be sure to start!

3. Let go of past resentments, beliefs, values, judgments, and opinions about products, clients, and especially about yourself that no longer serve you or promote your business. This often is the hardest step to take consistently because we are trained to look at the past to predict the future. Handle what is happening now, and know that the right next step will become clear. Be sure to take it.

4. Approach all business dealings with the attitude of the glass being half full rather than half empty. This is like the difference between greeting a client with a smile rather than a frown!

5. Spend more time asking questions and listening to your clients with the intention of building a relationship, not just selling your service or products. Be present and available to listen to the customers with spaciousness and respect. You will stand out among your competitors by actually delivering what your clients asked for while exceeding their expectations in some special way.

By getting to know yourself a little better and trying some of these ideas you will start to make the shift to seeing the amazing possibilities within your own invisible ecology. You will have greater access to the wealth of natural wisdom that is within you and that guides you on your journey.

ABOUT THE AUTHOR

Susan Urquhart-Brown, top-selling author on Amazon and business success coach, offers individual coaching and Success Mastermind Seminars especially for women business owners who want to attract their ideal clients and build a profitable business. *The Accidental Entrepreneur: Practical Wisdom for People Who Never Expected to Work for Themselves* is like having your own small business mentor 24 hours a day, 7 days a week. It's available on Amazon.com. Visit Susan on the Web at http://www.careersteps123.com.

17

Five Steps For Taking Your Career From Denial to Victory

Deborah Brown-Volkman

Do you have a feeling that something is wrong in your career, yet you have not done anything about it? Do you feel like something is missing in your career, but you'd prefer not to think about it?

This is called denial—when you know something is not right, but you are not acting to change it. Denial in your career can be good: if you focused on every little thing that bothered you such as getting up early every day, dealing with difficult coworkers, or doing work that doesn't thrill you, your career would be hard and not much fun. Denial works *against* you when your career changes for the worse and you do not do anything about it. This is when career distress wins.

When you notice a change in your career and you know in your gut that it's not a good one for you, you have to act and take your career from denial to victory.

Step 1: You Know Something Is Off Course

Your career has veered off course, but you tell yourself that it has not. You want to believe that what you are thinking or experiencing is a mistake. Maybe what is happening is too small to really pinpoint as the beginning of something big, for example, a change is made in your department, you are left out of an important meeting, or there's a rumor about layoffs or outsourcing. You know something is off course, but you hope you are not right about your assessment.

Step 2: Something Goes Wrong

The "something wrongs" are beginning to pile up. You are left out of major decisions that affect you or the people for whom you are responsible. People stop listening to you or coming to you. The politics are getting worse, or your company does something that goes against your values. One thing after another begins to happen. You hope that the "wrongs" will disappear without any effort on your part, but it becomes apparent that this will not happen without your participation.

Step 3: You Begin to Turn Your Wrong into a Right

This requires a shift in attitude. When your attitude gets better, your circumstances get better. This is when you start talking to people about what you want to change. You research different opportunities. You begin to shift your mind-set to make a change. This is a crucial step as most goals are reached in the mind first; the rest is implementation.

Step 4: You Take Action

You put together a plan. You write down your goal along with concrete steps for implementation. You add these steps to your calendar so that there is a timeline for making them happen. When you do not know where to turn or what to do, you write down who could help you—you are not meant to reach your career goals alone. Be clear about what you want and what steps you will take to get there. This is your pathway to victory.

Step 5: You Become Victorious

This is when you become a better person in a better place. You are happier and are enjoying your career. You created a goal and reached it. You achieved your goals because you had the courage to do something about a situation that no longer worked for you. Congratulations!

So, what do you say? You only have one life to live, so it might as well be a life you love!

ABOUT THE AUTHOR

Deborah Brown-Volkman is President of Surpass Your Dreams, Inc., a successful career and mentor coaching company that has been delivering a message of motivation, success, and personal fulfillment since 1998. We work with senior executives, vice presidents, and managers who are out of work or overworked. Deborah is also the creator of the Career Escape Program™ and author of *Coach Yourself to a New Career: A Book to Discover Your Ultimate Profession.*
Deborah Brown-Volkman can be reached at http://www.surpassyourdreams.com, http://www.career-escape-program.com, info@surpassyourdreams.com, or at (631) 874–2877.

18

COACHING

Shopping for a Coach

Bruce Taylor

Imagine a best friend who wants nothing more than your complete success, who always listens with interest to what you have to say, and who gives you the feedback you need to make tough choices and changes. This is the essential job of a personal coach. Coaches believe that you already have the knowledge and skills you need for successful problem resolution and that their job is to help you bring out these skills and use them effectively.

Most coaches work almost exclusively over the telephone, without ever meeting their clients face-to-face. At first, it may seem strange to be working through issues with someone you can't see, but almost everyone gets used to it because coaches are trained to use their voices to communicate more than words. Coaches are also trained to listen to the meaning behind the words you are using and can read the tone of your voice as naturally as you can read someone's face.

What Do You Want to Work On?

It will help your search greatly if you can think about a goal and write it down as clearly as you can. You might start with a general statement such as that your job stinks, but you should try to get clear about why it stinks and what you would like to do about it.

> I've been doing the same job for five years, and I'm getting really bored with it. I want a job that will be more challenging for me and will pay better than this one does. I would rather not leave this employer because I have a lot of seniority, but I would be willing to leave for the perfect job.

Now, you have a clear objective, and you're ready to start shopping for a coach.

How to Find Coaches

If you Google™ "personal coach," you will get thousands and thousands of hits, and you will easily drown in candidates. Instead, try a more targeted approach. Ask your friends if they have had a coach and if they were satisfied—personal recommendation is priceless. Coaches are very big on public speaking as a promotional tool, so if you look in your local paper, you may find someone giving a talk on job stress or beating procrastination: there's a good chance that he is a coach, and you'll have a chance to check him out. The coaching registry at the International Coaching Federation's Web site is a good place to do comparison shopping for coaches—they list coaches' credentials and specialties without elaborate advertising, and you can search for the combination of specialty and price range that you want.

You've Got a List of Candidates—Now What?

When you have a list of four or five coaches that sound suitable, it's time to comparison shop. Every coach in the world will be absolutely delighted to spend half an hour with you to let you get a feel for his style and to see if there's good chemistry between you.

Typically, the coach will ask you a little about yourself and your issue and do about 10 or 15 minutes of real coaching with you. He will also be happy to answer any questions you might have about coaching in general or about his specialties and coaching style. In this time you should trust your instincts: if you feel relaxed talking to the coach and if he seems to understand your issue and is able to help you with it even a little bit, then there's a good chance that he will make a good coach for you.

You don't have to make a decision after the introductory call—it is perfectly all right to try out other coaches and let them know that you will get back to them with a decision in the near future.

Not All Coaches Are Well Qualified

Coaching is not like psychotherapy, with regulations and licensing; anyone can call himself a coach, put up a Web site, and start doing business. Sadly, many people have done just that, and they have no more training in coaching than you do. It's not dangerous to work with an untrained coach, but it's not likely to be very productive either, so you need to ask the coaching candidate some questions. First, find out if they have had specific coaching training, how much they have had, and where they were trained. A coach typically becomes competent after about a year of training and reaches real expertise after about two years. Use your intuition—if you get the feeling that the coach is promising magical solutions to all your problems, you should probably try someone else.

Should My Coach Be Certified?

You will find that many of your coaching candidates use "certified" in their credentials, and you should pay attention to this. Unfortunately, because coaching isn't yet standardized, the term "certified" may mean any of several things. It's all very complicated, but if your coach is certified by the International Coaching Federation or any of its accredited coaching schools, you can assume that he has been trained in coaching, has passed an exam, and has at least two years of actual coaching experience. If he isn't certified, it doesn't mean that he's not competent—he may still be in training or he may be finishing the required coaching experience.

About Fees

You'll find a wide range of coaching fees, from $200 per month to $2000. In my experience, cost is not a good predictor of the coach's talent or effectiveness, so stay within your budget—you should be able to find a good coach in your price range. Finally, if you're really short of cash and really need some coaching, ask the coach if he will reduce his fees for you. Most coaches will accept a few clients at reduced rates or for free, for a good cause—anyway, it can't hurt to ask.

A good coach should be willing to customize his offerings for you. If you can't afford his standard package, you might ask for a reduced rate for a two-per-month package. If you would rather have two hour-long sessions than four half-hour sessions, he should be flexible enough to accommodate you. Within reason, he should adapt his package to your needs, rather than the other way around.

The Final Word

Hiring a coach should be just like buying a car—it's important that you find one that suits your needs, feels comfortable, and is affordable. Most of all, be a good consumer, and shop around until you find just the right coach for you. You'll know when you find him.

ABOUT THE AUTHOR

Bruce Taylor is the owner and principal of Unison coaching, helping people to improve their jobs and create the careers they have always dreamed of. He provides executive coaching for senior managers who are creating superior organizations; management coaching for leaders who are adapting to new practices; and individual coaching for workers who are upgrading their skills. Mr. Taylor has a Master's degree in Community Psychology and a Certificate in Job Stress and Healthy Workplace Design, both from the University of Massachusetts. For more information, visit http://www.unisoncoaching.com.

19

The Alchemy of Commitment: How to Turn Lead into Gold

Molly Gordon

Have you ever had the experience of making promises to yourself that you just didn't keep? Most folks have, and most of us recognize the heaviness, the leaden quality, of the things we say we will do but don't.

Some commitments feel like lead. Something in us simply doesn't believe we can (or want to) follow through. Other commitments are solid gold. They may be difficult and even scary, yet we rise to the occasion with gusto. Finally, there are commitments that fall somewhere in between. These are candidates for a process I call the alchemy of commitment, the process of turning lead into gold.

Separate the Lead from the Gold

1. Write down 10 commitments you want to fulfill in the next six months. Include things you keep saying you want to do but haven't done.

2. Place an "X" next to any item that lacks a specific time of completion.

3. Place an "X" next to anything that depends on someone else's action. (Some items may have more than one "X.")

4. Place an "X" next to any item that you have been meaning to do for more than six months.

5. Review your list. As you read each item, notice what happens in your body. Observe any changes in sensation, such as contractions, shifts in breathing,

changes in posture, or surges or drops in energy. If, on the whole, what you notice feels positive and hopeful, highlight the item. If what you notice feels negative and resistant or frustrated, place an "X" next to the item.

6. Transfer the highlighted items to your Solid Gold Commitments list.

Turning Lead into Gold

Of the items that have an "X" next to them, which ones are necessary to your well-being or that of your family? Highlight these with a different color. These items don't yet quality for your Solid Gold Commitments list because the "X" indicates that there's something missing that will keep you from following through. To close that gap, take the following steps.

1. If you have been putting something off for more than six months, ask yourself if it is absolutely necessary. Odds are that you think you should do it but actually have no intention of following through if you can possibly help it. If you decide it *is* necessary, write down exactly why it is essential for you to carry out this commitment.

2. Chunk down your commitment. Break it into two or three steps (more if necessary) so that each step is manageable. What's manageable? Whatever you can actually see yourself accomplishing in a specific time frame.

3. Get help. Think of two or three people who could help and write down their names along with the contributions you will ask them to make. (Make specific, time-bounded requests, and be equally gracious whether you get a yes or a no. This makes it easy to ask another time.)

4. If your commitment depends on someone else, write down the steps you will take to coordinate with them. (This includes the people you identified in step 4.)

5. Choose a commitment and close your eyes. Breathing easily and fully, imagine that you have met this commitment and are enjoying the results. How do you feel? How has this affected your relationships? Your health? Soak up the sensations of success. Only when you have fully imagined the pleasure of fulfilling the commitment should you transfer it to your Solid Gold Commitments list. Repeat with each commitment.

Sometimes, Lead Is Just Lead

Don't get sidetracked trying to turn all your leaden commitments into gold. Some commitments don't get met because, at the end of the day, they're just not that important. If you have been promising yourself to lose 10 pounds for five years, maybe the truth is that your weight is in line with your real priorities. Let go of half-hearted commitments, and you'll have all the more energy for transmuting lead into gold!

ABOUT THE AUTHOR

Molly Gordon is an internationally recognized Master Certified Coach, writer, and facilitator. She is the author of *Authentic Promotion,* a 12-week audio program and workbook in transformational marketing. Thousands of professionals and organizations from NASA to Lamaze International have used Molly's mind-body-spirit approach to embody a prosperity based on service, purpose, and lifelong learning. A pioneer in establishing a service business online, Molly's e-zine, "Authentic Promotion," is now in its eighth year of publication. Visit Molly's Web sites and blog at http://www.mollygordon.com, http://www.authenticpromotion.com, and http://www.shaboominc.com.

20

COMMUNICATION

Embrace the Four Fundamental Truths of Communication

Mark Susnow

You're on the way to the airport. You get on the plane with a book that you've been planning to read for quite some time. As you open your book, you glance at the person next to you. A few minutes later, you are asked a question, and you reluctantly answer. You lower your book a bit to be polite, and after a few minutes you find yourself putting your book down and engaging in a conversation, although with a lack of enthusiasm. Then, the person next to you, let's call him John, makes an observation about you that's quite perceptive and sensitive. You start to become curious about who John is, and in the course of the conversation he tells you of an experience he has only shared with a few people. You let John know that you have had the same experience. By now, you're totally engaged and listening to every word he says. You notice every nuance in the inflection of his voice and the way he moves. Time seems to stand still, and the next thing you know, the plane lands. You say good-bye to the kindred soul you have just met.

Wouldn't you *love* to have these experiences more often? You feel heard, and everything seems possible. It is communication at its highest level, and it's a lost art. You can have these experiences more often if you embrace the four fundamental truths of communication.

- The first truth is to know that what we all want on a deeper level is the ability to connect with one another, to touch each other's soul. Unfortunately, too many of our conversations are just an exchange of ideas and information, and we very rarely penetrate the surface. Most of our focus is on how we are going to respond to what is being said instead of listening. When we know that what the other person really wants is connection, there is common ground on which to build. With this foundation we can build relationships that can deepen and empower those involved.

- The second truth is to know that listening involves much more than just listening to the words. It is tuning in to the energy beyond the words. It is understanding the needs and feelings of the other person. It is about being totally engaged and at the same time being in the rhythm of life. Yes, it takes a lot of energy, but you will be energized by what you get back. Imagine living in a world where you are truly listening and fully engaged.
- The third truth is to know that you must take responsibility for the quality of your communication. Because we all have long-standing attitudes and beliefs, we sometimes find ourselves trying to convince the other person of our viewpoints. Being right then becomes the goal of the interaction rather than communication, and the next thing you know, you are in a full-fledged argument. Just think of what happens when you discuss politics or religion. Is being right more important than experiencing one of those magical moments?
- The fourth truth is that communication is a process and an art. Being a masterful communicator doesn't happen overnight, but it starts with the intention to experience more connection in your busy life. Just like with other art forms, for example, dancing or music, there is a natural ebb and flow in the learning cycle. As your commitment deepens to this process, you will notice that you are having more frequent glimpses of the magic that is possible in your life. The ultimate communication occurs when you are able to touch each other's soul and share who you are. This newfound magic then becomes the gateway to a more fulfilling life.

At our core level we all have the same human needs and desires. We want to know that we matter and that our life has meaning and purpose. We also have the need to love and to be loved. When we accept and recognize that we all have these human needs and desires, we realize that we are part of one human family. When we work together as one, what is possible in our lives, communities, and the world expands.

Embracing the four fundamental truths of communication and applying them to your daily life is a gift to all involved. It is a way to deepen the connection in your life. As a way of reaching out to others and connecting with them, please share this article with the friends in your circle, and let them know about the advantages of being on the journey. Part of my journey has been listening and

73

learning from all the teachers who have blessed my life. Hopefully, I learn from everyone and every experience that I have. Your suggestions and comments contribute to my learning and help me to expand and evolve. Keep them flowing. Journey on.

ABOUT THE AUTHOR

Mark Susnow is a professional speaker, group facilitator, and coach who brings a balanced and impressive background to his work. A former trial attorney for 30 years and a musician, he integrates what it takes to be successful in the world with the inner wisdom unfolded to him through years of yoga and meditation. He has inspired many leaders and professionals to implement their visions of the future. Mark delivers customized presentations, inspiring others to find more meaning and balance in their lives. To find out more about Mark and his services, be sure to visit his Web site at http://www.inspirepossibility.com, or call (415) 453–5016.

21

CREATIVITY

14 Creativity Tips to Get You Unstuck, Unblocked, Newly Focused, and Passionate About Your Creative Process or Project

Gail McMeekin

You know that you are a creative being. We all have the ability to do original work and to make new connections between ideas, which is the key dynamic of the creative process. Yet, we are also well aware that sometimes, our creativity stalls, plays tricks on us, or appears to have vanished completely. It is at those moments that we need to reconnect with our exuberance for our creative process or project. We need to leverage our inspirational powers to stimulate our ability to innovate. The following tips are meant to arouse your natural creative gifts so that you can surmount the challenges in your creative journey and achieve your best results.

1. Keep a daily excitement list detailing why you are passionate about and committed to your exploration or creative project. What fascinates you and intrigues you about the topic? Why is it compelling to you personally? How does it matter to other people or to the larger world?

2. Visualize your end result, and make a collage of images that support your vision, and then post this collage where you can see it regularly. Let the visual images help you to be as specific as possible in identifying the essence of what you want to invent.

3. Take a field trip relating to your project to explore a particular facet of it. One of my clients was fascinated by gorillas, for some unknown reason, and went to the zoo for a day, without a clue about what she was looking for. While sitting with the gorillas, they reminded her of the power of nonverbal communication—the missing ingredient in her unfinished painting.

4. Collect words that inspire you or relate to your project and write them on note cards so that you can play with them. Move the words around to make designs or sentences that stimulate new linkages. Then, change them as needed to be effective.

5. Start off your creative sessions with inspiring music, selected to reflect the mood of the piece you are working on. Music is a natural high and can inspire your muse. Listening to the same music during an entire project trains your mind to tune in to the content quickly and deeply—almost like in a trance.

6. Exercise regularly to clear your head and stimulate your brain chemistry. Dance, run, walk, or swim—whatever you enjoy most—and reap the benefits of shifting your mental and physical energy. Many creative people get their best ideas while practicing movements.

7. Think of your project as an experiment, and write up three hypotheses. Then, try them on as templates with your content. Often, even the most outlandish ideas can reap new perspectives and clever twists.

8. Experience your project using the three learning styles of visual, auditory, and kinesthetic dimensions.

    a. Draw a picture of it, make a mind-map of it, or take a photo of it, and tinker with it on Photoshop®.

    b. Talk about your project into a tape or video recorder, or teach a real or pretend class on the topic to your friends or to an imaginary audience.

    c. Create a one-scene play, and act it out with props, costumes, and maybe even other characters you invite in to participate with you.

9. Go to a toy store and find a toy that reminds you of your project or process. Spend some time playing with the toy, and write down all the metaphors you discover. A stuffed giant caterpillar once guided me to organize a project into interlocking but flexible sections, similar to the body of a caterpillar.

10. Practice suspension: suspend all judgments, and send your inner critic on vacation. Give yourself the freedom to make mistakes and take positive risks with your work. If you were fearless about your creative process, what "out on a limb" strategies would you try next?

11. Change your location or some aspect of your work environment. Work on your project in bed, outside in nature, or in a museum. Move your desk or easel to a different corner of your office, changing your viewpoint. Write in pen instead of typing, print out your project on wild paper, or gather relevant illustrations and see what they contribute to your conceptualization.

12. Find a symbol of your creativity and keep that object with you when you create. It can be a prosperity stone, a dramatic painting on the wall, or a special jacket that you wear. Draw strength and encouragement from this tangible support.

13. Keep a special journal for each project so that you can capture your new thoughts, emotional traumas and dramas, and trace the key threads of your creative unfolding.

14. If you continue to feel burned out or blocked, you may need a vacation. In my research on creativity, many people have tapped into their creative genius while relaxing. It could be simply lying at the beach or meditating, but for some people it is a total change of scenery. Go someplace that intuitively draws you. As creative conduits, we need to honor our fascinations and follow their lead.

Above all, enjoy your creativity. Regularly tapping into your innovative, uncensored, childlike self is a powerful catalyst against creative blocks of all kinds. Your inner spirit has the answers. Open up your creative window, and invite your inspirations to come in to dance with you!

ABOUT THE AUTHOR

Gail McMeekin, LICSW, is the owner of Creative Success, LLC and the author of *The 12 Secrets of Highly Creative Women* and *The Power of Positive Choices* as well as the monthly, free, e-mail newsletter "Creative Success." She helps clients to discover fulfilling work, activate their creativity, grow their businesses, and restore inner balance, and her information-packed Web site is http://www.creativesuccess.com.

22

CRITICISM

=========================

Go Ahead and Prove All the Naysayers Wrong!

Paul Lawrence

> The strength of criticism lies in the weakness of the
> thing criticized.
> > –Henry Wadsworth Longfellow

Are the people who are close to you—your friends and family—preventing you from going after your dream of starting your own business? If so, you have a problem that is more common than you might think.

It's not that they want to do you harm. It's quite the opposite: they usually have your best interests at heart, but they think it's hard to start a new business, and they don't want to see you fail. As a result, they discourage you from even trying.

For example, one of my early small businesses (one that I operated for quite a while) was a successful ballroom dance instruction studio. While most of my relatives just rolled their eyes when I initially explained my business idea, my grandmother was particularly harsh. She chastised me for wanting to start such a business. She told me that nobody was interested in ballroom dancing anymore and that I simply didn't have any "common sense."

I have to tell you that the scowl she gave me as she belittled my ambitions really gave me some doubts, but I'm sure that she didn't mean to upset me. She probably thought it would be better for me to feel a little hurt at that moment than to go off and start a project doomed for failure.

Is it possible to build your own business without taking enormous risks (like quitting your day job or plunging all your net worth into an unproven new venture)? Absolutely. I've done it myself, and I've shown many other people

78

how to do it. However, what happens when you don't get the support of your family for something that you're excited about doing?

For most people the natural reaction is to become defensive, and in that defensive mode you waste valuable time and energy trying to get the approval of someone who is unlikely to be swayed by anything you say.

Having said that, it is possible to take that criticism and turn it into something positive—something that could help increase your chances of success.

The first thing that you need to do is give yourself a little bit of time to calm down. Once you're feeling rational, objectively analyze the criticism to see if it has any merit—to see if that person may have seen something that you hadn't thought of.

When I started my ballroom dance business (in the early 1990s), my grandmother was certainly correct when she pointed out that ballroom dancing wasn't the latest craze. When I thought about it, I realized that what she was telling me, in her less-than-diplomatic manner, was that she didn't think the market would be big enough for me to earn a good income by teaching people how to do it.

I did some due diligence and researched the matter, and I discovered that virtually every metropolitan area in the country had one or two of the major ballroom franchises as well as some independent operators. That seemed to indicate that, in general, there were enough people interested in taking lessons to sustain a business like mine.

Then, I looked more specifically at my local market. Here in south Florida, there were (and are) many affluent retirees—likely targets for my new business. Also, I learned that there were already about three times more ballroom instruction businesses in this area as there were in other metropolitan areas. A good sign.

Not only had I reassured myself that I had a viable concept, but my grandmother's criticism actually helped make it happen. She'd gotten me to pinpoint my prime marketing target—which is at the heart of any start-up business plan. At this point I was sure that there was a place for me in the marketplace, so I got myself in gear and was able to quickly build up a profitable small business.

Within a short period of time I was making enough money to support myself—much to the surprise of my relatives. Then, I was featured on the front page of the lifestyle section of the area's largest newspaper, and for a brief moment I became a local celebrity.

My grandmother was first in line to say that she always knew I could do it.

ABOUT THE AUTHOR

Paul Lawrence is an entrepreneur and the creator of Early to Rise's exciting new Microbusiness Program. What do you want to do this year? Become wealthier? Get healthier? Read more books, travel the world, and become wiser? Sign up for ETR at http://www.earlytorise.com, and we'll show you how to do all of that and more . . . in just five minutes a day. Paul Lawrence is also a nationally published author, business consultant, and accomplished screenplay writer with a major motion picture featuring name-talent actors and an expected studio-level theatrical release. For his screenwriting Paul is represented in Beverly Hills, California, by Suite A Talent & Literary.

23

DESTRESSORS

The Doer's Guide to Being

Jamee Tenzer

"Nothing is working—what should I do?"

Have you ever had this unsettling thought? What happens when you wake up and nothing seems to be working in your life? There is no immediate crisis, but you feel "out of step." Because you are a doer, you will begin to take a mental inventory of your relationships, your job, your family, and your personal life. You will begin checking to see what has changed. What has caused the life that was fine yesterday to look unappealing today? Your mind is racing, your pulse is rising, and you begin to make a list. "This will solve the problem," you tell yourself between fits of scribbles. "If I make a list and do more, the noise in my mind will stop. I will be satisfied. I will be happy."

As a life coach, I am a great believer in taking action to move forward in life. In fact, I would say that action is one of the most powerful tools that human beings have to change their experience of life. It is the root of progress. There is nothing more powerful than an intention rooted in a personal desire, combined with actions taken in line with that intention. However, there are times when we stop using action as a tool and begin to identify action as the goal itself. In that case, we are not taking action—rather, action is taking *us* where we don't want to go. Too much action for the sake of "doing" can result in fatigue and disillusionment.

The problem that we are having may not be in the realm of doing; the problem may be the microscope through which we view our lives. Are we focusing too closely on each detail? Perhaps the lens is a little dusty. Why does a life that once looked vibrant and colorful become gray? Is there something wrong, or are our doer instincts robbing us of the simple neutrality and rejuvenation that could be found through surrender to these gray moments in life?

In general, doers are not comfortable with a lot of gray in their lives. In fact, by our nature we may see gray as boring, static, listless, and dull. We like to have a plan, a list of things to do, and a well-worn appointment book. We have learned to thrive on the doing of life and to get high on the accomplishment of our goals. Sure, we know how to throw out little pearls like "trust the process" and "smell the roses," but we're not taking any chances. We're hedging our bets by getting out there and making things happen through our ability to do, do, do.

Let's face it: our ability to take action moves the human race along. It took a group of doers to fight for civil rights, and it will take even more doers to solve the problems this world is facing now. However, what happens when our greatest strength is doing, and then one day, doing stops working? We have become so used to the doer mode that we no longer remember that we have options. When faced with challenges or emptiness, we forget that we can take a breath and a break, or if we do stop for even a moment, the stillness makes us anxious. We are afraid that we will be stuck there forever. We do more! Why do we not trust the process of life to help facilitate change?

If you ask for advice from a nondoer, she may suggest that you simply "be." This sounds to the doer like nonsense. The doer may be smiling and nodding in agreement, but inside, she is incredulous. After working with many clients who struggle with this dichotomy of "doing" and "being," I have learned something. When doers are in the gray zone, they can only see through the filter of doing. They need a reminder, in language a doer can understand, that can help them out of the mucky "do." For someone who is most comfortable in the realm of action (even if it means spinning her wheels), "being" is doing something. In fact, it's probably one of the hardest skills the doer will ever learn, and it's one of the most powerful skills if employed at the right time. The following are some ways that I help my doer clients to take a breath and "be."

1. **Take an "action vacation."** Tell yourself that you are not going to work on your weight, job, relationship, or life for one week. When the week is over, you may find that the problem has shifted and that you can attack it with renewed intention.

2. **Tell one person how you are feeling.** A spouse or friend is preferable, but I have found that waiters, bus drivers, and car wash attendants all have the facility to listen. Their reactions don't matter—what is important is that you express the feelings.

3. **Take a walk.** This quiets the mind. I like to listen to music because it shuts out the incessant chatter of my doer brain, but complete silence may be your preference.

4. **Take a long, hot bubbly bath.** This is the oldest trick in the book, and it works.

5. **Write down everything** that is going on in your head, including your fears, anxieties, questions, and thoughts. Read it over and over until you have no reaction to the words or you find yourself laughing uncontrollably.

6. **Read a self-help book.** Some people call them "shelf help" because we buy them and leave them on the shelf. Go to your shelf or your local library to find a book that inspires you when you read the book jacket.

7. **Do something you never allow yourself to do.** Watch TV or take a nap in the middle of the day, skip your exercise class, leave dirty dishes in the sink, or have a triple-scoop ice cream cone.

8. **Visualize.** Use visualization to create what you intend to have in life. Visualizing is very powerful, even if the images are not clear in your mind.

9. **Open a book of prayers, daily thoughts, or meditations** and read the page that you open first.

When you are *not* in the gray zone, add to this list, and delete anything that doesn't work for you. Over time you will create your own personal "doer's guide to being." Remember—it takes practice to shift from "doing" to "being" at will, but even a few moments of "being" will rejuvenate the doer in you.

ABOUT THE AUTHOR

Jamee Tenzer, Founder of Life Works Coaching, is a professional career and life coach specializing in working with women to create a life that works for them. The foundation of Ms. Tenzer's coaching practice is based on the principle that anything is possible through taking action. Ms. Tenzer lives in Los Angeles with her husband and three children. For more information and to schedule a complimentary coaching session, please visit http://lifeworks4ucoaching.com or e-mail tenzer@lifeworks4ucoaching.com.

24

DOUBT

How to Overcome Your "Inner Loser" and Finally Achieve Your Dreams

Craig Perrine

Have you ever started to let yourself dream up something you wanted, only to hear that inner voice tell you all the reasons why you can't get what you want? You say to yourself, "I'd love to start a new business because I just can't afford to take any time off, and I'm sick of my job." Then, that little voice says, "Yeah, but I'm not good at that stuff. I wouldn't know where to start. I'd probably just lose a lot of time and money trying."

Wow . . . who needs enemies when you have stuff like that rattling around in your head? I call the voice our "Inner Loser." Sure, everyone likes to talk about our intuition and our Inner Child, but in my experience the doubts we have that hold us back the most are from a source that sounds suspiciously like our intuition—but it's not.

It's our fear talking—our fear of whatever bad thing we think might happen if we take action on our dreams. It feels easier to make excuses about why we can't make our lives into exactly what we want than to risk really trying with all our heart and face the possible disappointment of failure.

The problem is that our Inner Loser can make us imagine a thousand ways that we might fail. On the very things we most desire we make the most excuses not to try. Sounds like a formula for a pretty miserable life, huh? Well, don't think that this only applies to "miserable" people. Just about every coaching client I've worked with has expressed these Inner Loser thoughts.

These doubts pop up whenever we face an opportunity to grow beyond our current level of achievement. When you are faced with leaving your comfort zone, your Inner Loser will come out and undercut your confidence. You may find your Inner Loser chiming in and reminding you of every blunder you've ever had—just when you need your confidence the most.

To defeat this Inner Loser and break through to the next level, it helps to understand the motivations of your opponent. You don't have to take Psychology 101 to understand that part of you is afraid of failing because of painful memories of past failures. Your Inner Loser is simply trying to keep you from making decisions where the outcome is unknown or beyond your current level of success. If you give in and seek comfort and approval of your Inner Loser, you will inevitably be stuck in a rut and settle for far less than you are capable of in exchange for the false notion that you will avoid pain.

What you have to face is that the cost of never reaching for your dreams or for new opportunities creates a lifetime of loss and pain that is far greater than momentary disappointments from unsuccessful attempts along the way. Once you understand that at a gut level, you can take steps to risk looking foolish or failing in exchange for knowing that you are on the path to your highest potential.

- Step 1: Notice that you are talking to yourself or others about fear of failure. Just catch yourself, and become aware that your Inner Loser is running your thoughts.
- Step 2: Thank your Inner Loser for trying to protect you from pain. You may notice in times of conflict that fighting makes the situation worse, whereas finding common ground can neutralize tense situations. If you deny your fear or talk badly about yourself, you will simply reinforce your fear of taking action. If you can understand your Inner Loser's motivations, you can neutralize the unhelpful dialogue in your head.
- Step 3: Look at what you are afraid of, and ask yourself what the worst thing is that could happen if you took whatever risk you are facing. Compare that with what you stand to gain, and decide if it is worth the risk. Name what you are afraid of out loud, and you'll take your fear from your imagination to the concrete and logical level. That way, if you accept the worst, it is possible that you will be able to handle it. Then, you can proceed to focus on creating a much more positive outcome.

- Step 4: Remind yourself that everything that you don't have and truly want is on the other side of some kind of fear. Any goal worth having is beyond your comfort zone, or you'd already have it. If you do exactly what you fear in the pursuit of a dream or an important goal, you will often find that that is the surest path to success. Successful and brave people achieve so much not because they don't fear, but because they take action anyway and override the fear. Always doing what is comfortable will simply get you what you already have.
- Step 5: Take action, and watch what happens. If you decide to do nothing, that is a decision, too. What is the result? Are you happier? If you do take the risk, what is the result? You will probably find that whatever happens, even failure, is never as bad as the stuff your Inner Loser whipped up for you to fear (and usually, everything turns out far better than the worst case scenario).

Believe it or not, it feels much better to have tried and failed than to know you never tried. Perhaps you can train your Inner Loser to understand that the real pain comes from regretting opportunities not taken and wondering what could have been. Understand that nothing happens without failure at some point in the journey to success, and failure is simply information about how *not* to do something.

Next time you have something you'd like to create in your life, and your Inner Loser pops up with some negative comments, just say, "Thanks, I appreciate your concern," and then, focus on what you want, and go for it. More often than not, your biggest obstacle is your Inner Loser, not the challenge before you.

ABOUT THE AUTHOR

Craig Perrine has helped hundreds of entrepreneurs market their businesses online. He's an author and featured speaker at leading Internet marketing seminars, and he's featured in the best-seller *Online Marketing Superstars*. Craig is recognized as a leading expert on how to build profitable, long-term relationships with a targeted subscriber list. You can see some of his simple yet highly effective methods in a free e-course at http://www.maverickmarketer.com.

25

DREAMS

Transform Your Life through Dreams

Bob Hoss

Dreams bring messages from deep inside, leading to self-understanding and transformation. Although dreams address all levels of consciousness, everyday dreams tend to focus on life's unresolved emotional situations. Many of our emotional difficulties in life result from daily experiences that threaten our inner beliefs, which include our view of ourselves and of what life is all about. Sometimes, these threats are valid, but often, they occur because our internal beliefs have been corrupted by fears and misconceptions and do not match external reality. For example, as we grow up, we may get the idea from others that certain parts of ourselves are acceptable and other parts are unacceptable. Also, early traumatic experiences may grow into general fears. These fears and misconceptions about ourselves stagnate our progress in life and keep us from reaching our full potential. Dreams attempt to reverse this process. They transform us by resolving the differences between inner and outer reality. Dreams do this by "compensating" for our internal misconceptions and guiding us toward healthier alternatives.

If dreams are of such value, then why are they so hard to understand? When we dream, our speech centers are inactive, so dream communications retain only the visual and associative aspects of speech. Whereas waking language uses combinations of words, dream language communicates using combinations of images and symbolic associations. This natural, internal language is bizarre only to the waking mind. Once understood, dream communications, in many ways, appear more truthful and logical than waking thought.

If dreams are visual representations of emotional memories, decoding them should be a simple matter of reversing the process, determining what associations surface when envisioning a dream image. Indeed, that principle is the basis of most dreamworking approaches. Many dreamworking techniques, however, only involve dialogue with the rational mind, where filtering and fear avoidance can hide the emotional memories contained within the dream. In contrast, Image Activation Dreamwork is a simplified, Gestalt-based approach that occupies the rational mind in a role-play fantasy, while permitting the dream centers of the brain to "speak" and reveal emotional content. It uses a simple, scripted role-play technique, affectionately called the "six magic questions," designed to reveal emotional memories within dream images and to associate them with waking feelings and situations.

1. Record the dream as if you are reexperiencing it.

2. Look for obvious dream-life connections. Do any feelings or goals in the dream or statements in the narrative sound like waking feelings and situations?

3. Do some imaginary work (the "six magic questions").

   a. Pick one or more dream elements that feel important, curious, or emotionally significant, perhaps a "thing" or a colored image.

   b. Speak as the dream image. "Become" the dream image. Imagine how it might answer these questions. Speak spontaneously, and answer only in the first person present tense ("I" statements), recording your answers exactly as you speak them.

      i. Who (or what) are you? (Name and describe yourself as the dream image—*I am* . . . .)

      ii. What is your purpose or function? (*My purpose is* . . . .)

      iii. What do you like about what you are?

      iv. What do you dislike about what you are?

      v. What do you fear most?

      vi. What do you desire most?

4. Relate your answers to life. Review each statement and ask, "Does this also sound like a feeling or situation in my waking life?" Review who was involved, your feelings, and any decisions you made. Do the "I am/my purpose" statements sound like a waking role? Do the "I like/I dislike" and the "I fear/I desire" statement pairs sound like waking life conflicts, fears, and desires?

5. You may now understand what the dream is about, but to help bring about transformation, clarifying fears and misconceptions is required. Divide the statements you "connect with" into positives and negatives, for example, "that which I desire or like" (positive) or "that which I dislike, need, or fear" (negative). Contrast the two as conflicting beliefs, for example, "I am/I need/have to _____ because _____, *but* if I _____, then I fear that _____ will happen." Are these logical, healthy, and appropriate beliefs, allowing progress, or are they exaggerations and misconceptions, holding you back?

6. Go back into the dream and review what you were trying to achieve and, specifically, how it ended. How might this be analogous to your waking situation?

   a. **Dream guidance.** Look for an obvious compensating event, which appears in dreams as guidance, surprises, words, reversals, discovery, or a positive ending. Review dream actions and thoughts before the event and how they changed after the event. Dreams rarely provide literal messages. Therefore ask, "How might the event or positive ending be an analogy for a way to deal with my waking situation?"

   b. **New dream ending.** If the dream contained no obvious compensation or ended badly or unresolved, try (a) spontaneously (very first thoughts) imagining a new ending that resolves the dream satisfactorily, (b) filling in imaginary details regarding how it is achieved, or (c) discovering how that new ending might be an analogy for a new way to deal with your waking situation.

   c. **Check it out.** Is it a healthy, appropriate, practical resolution, permitting progress, or does it leave you stuck again?

    d. **Next steps.** If healthy and appropriate, what specific next steps can you take in waking life, and when should you take them, to bring this solution about?

Image Activation Dreamwork also uses a research-based, color questionnaire, designed to trigger your own emotional associations, adding another layer of self-understanding. Using these methods to understand and work with your dreams quickly leads to transformation, allowing you to move more easily through life.

ABOUT THE AUTHOR

Robert Hoss, MS, author of *Dream Language: Self-Understanding through Imagery and Color*, is Executive Officer and former President of the International Association for the Study of Dreams. A frequent guest on radio and TV, he has been an internationally acclaimed instructor on dreams for over 30 years and is presently on the faculty of the Haden Institute for dream leadership training and the adjunct faculty at Scottsdale College in Arizona. For more comprehensive information on dreams and the color questionnaire mentioned above, read the above book, or visit http://www.dreamlanguage.org.

26

EMOTIONAL RELEASE

Free Yourself by Releasing Your Emotions

Hale Dwoskin

One of the ways that we create disappointment and unhappiness is by holding on to limiting thoughts and feelings. When we suppress our emotions rather than experiencing them fully, they linger and make us uncomfortable. Through avoidance, we prevent our emotions from flowing through us, and it doesn't feel good.

Suppression is keeping a lid on our emotions, denying them, repressing them, and pretending that they don't exist. Any emotion that comes into awareness that is not let go of is automatically stored in a part of our mind called the subconscious. We suppress our emotions by escaping them. We take our attention off them long enough so that we can push them back down. You have probably heard the expression "time heals all wounds." It's debatable. For most of us, what that really means is, "Give me enough time, and I can suppress anything."

On the other side of the pendulum is expression. If we are angry, we yell; if we are sad, we cry. We put our emotion into action. We have let off a little steam from the inner emotional pressure cooker, but we have not put out the fire. This often feels better than suppression, particularly if we have blocked our ability to express. Nonetheless, expression also has its drawbacks. For example, what about when we express ourselves inappropriately outside of a therapeutic situation? What about the feelings of the person to whom we have just expressed our emotions? Inappropriate expression can often lead to greater disagreement and conflict and a mutual escalation of emotion that can get out of control.

The balancing point and natural alternative to inappropriate suppression and expression is releasing, or letting go—what we call the Sedona Method®. It is the

91

equivalent of turning down the heat and safely beginning to empty the contents of your inner pressure cooker. Because every feeling that has been suppressed is trying to vent itself, releasing is merely a momentary stopping of the inner action of holding these feelings in so that you can allow them to leave, which you will find they do easily under their own steam. As you use the Sedona Method, you will discover that you will be able to both suppress and express when it's appropriate, and you will find that you often opt for the point of balance, *letting go*.

You Are in Control of Your Emotions

Pick up some small object that you would be willing to drop without giving it a second thought. Now, hold it in front of you and really grip it tightly. Pretend this is one of your limiting feelings and that your hand represents your gut or your consciousness. If you held the object long enough, this would start to feel uncomfortable, yet familiar.

Now, open your hand and roll the object around in it. Notice that you are the one holding on to it; it is not attached to your hand. The same is true with your feelings, too. Your feelings are as attached to you as this object is attached to your hand.

We hold on to our feelings and forget that we are holding on to them. It's even in our language. When we feel angry or sad, we don't usually say, "I feel angry," or, "I feel sad." We say, "I am angry," or, "I am sad." Without realizing it, we are misidentifying that we *are* the feeling. Often, we believe a feeling is holding on to us. This is not true—we are always in control and just don't know it.

Now, let the object go.

What happened? You let go of the object, and it dropped to the floor. Was that hard? Of course not. That's what we mean when we say "let go."

You can do the same thing with any emotion—choose to let it go.

Choosing to Let Go

Make yourself comfortable and focus inwardly. Your eyes may be open or closed.

Step 1: Focus on an issue about which you would like to feel better, and then allow yourself to feel whatever you are feeling in this moment. This doesn't have to be a strong feeling. Just welcome the feeling and allow it to exist, to be, as fully or as best you can.

Step 2: Ask yourself one of the following three questions:

- Could I let this feeling go?
- Could I allow this feeling to be here?
- Could I welcome this feeling?

These questions are merely asking you if it is possible to take action. Yes and no are both acceptable answers. You will often let go even if you say no. As best you can, answer the question that you choose with a minimum of thought, staying away from second-guessing yourself or getting into an internal debate about the merits of that action or its consequences.

Step 3: No matter which question you started with, ask yourself this simple question: "Would I?" In other words, are you willing to let go? Again, stay away from debate as best you can. Also, remember that you are doing this process for yourself—for the purpose of gaining your own freedom and clarity. It doesn't matter whether the feeling is justified, long-standing, or right. If the answer is no, or if you are not sure, ask yourself: "Would I rather have this feeling, or would I rather be free?" Even if the answer is still no, go on to step 4.

Step 4: Ask yourself this simpler question: "When?" This is an invitation to just let it go *now*. You may find yourself easily letting go. Remember that letting go is a decision you can make any time you choose.

Step 5: Repeat the preceding four steps as often as needed until you feel free of that particular feeling. You will probably find yourself letting go a little more on each step of the process. At first, the results may be quite subtle. Very quickly, if you are persistent, the results will get more and more noticeable. You may find that you have layers of feelings about a particular topic. However, what you let go of is gone for good.

As you perfect your use of the Sedona Method, you will find yourself able to let go more and more easily, even on long-standing issues that you were tearing your life apart trying to resolve. You will discover that the answers have been right inside you all along.

About the Author

This chapter has been edited and excerpted from the New York Times Best Seller, *The Sedona Method: Your Key to Lasting Happiness, Success, Peace and Emotional Well-Being* by Hale Dwoskin (Sedona Press, 2003). Hale Dwoskin has been teaching the Sedona Method® to people throughout the world for over 30 years. This unique program helps you to make positive changes in your life by releasing the emotions that block your ability to experience peace and happiness in everyday life. It offers help dealing with fear, anxiety, anger, and depression—emotions that rob you of self-esteem and joy—in order to create a great life for yourself. Visit our Web site at http://www.sedona.com.

27

The Four Emotions That Can Lead to Life Change

Jim Rohn

Emotions are the most powerful forces inside us. Under the power of emotions, human beings can perform the most heroic (as well as barbaric) acts. To a great degree, civilization itself can be defined as the intelligent channeling of human emotion. Emotions are fuel and the mind is the pilot, which together propel the ship of civilized progress.

Which emotions cause people to act? There are four basic ones; each, or a combination of several, can trigger the most incredible activity. The day that you allow these emotions to fuel your desire is the day you'll turn your life around.

Disgust

One does not usually equate the word "disgust" with positive action. And yet, properly channeled, disgust can change a person's life. The person who feels disgusted has reached a point of no return. He is ready to throw down the gauntlet at life and say "I've had it!" That's what I said after many humiliating experiences at age 25. I said, "I don't want to live like this anymore. I've had it with being broke. I've had it with being embarrassed, and I've had it with lying."

Yes, productive feelings of disgust come when a person says "enough is enough."

The "guy" has finally had it with mediocrity. He's had it with those awful sick feelings of fear, pain, and humiliation. He then decides he is not going to live like this anymore. Look out! This could be the day that turns a life around. Call it what you will, the "I've had it" day, the "never again" day, the "enough's enough" day. Whatever you call it, it's powerful! There is nothing so life-changing as gut-wrenching disgust!

Decision

Most of us need to be pushed to the wall to make decisions. And once we reach this point, we have to deal with the conflicting emotions that come with making them. We have reached a fork in the road. Now, this fork can be a two-prong, three-prong, or even a four-prong fork. No wonder that decision-making can create knots in stomachs, keep us awake in the middle of the night, or make us break out in a cold sweat.

Making life-changing decisions can be likened to internal civil war. Conflicting armies of emotions, each with its own arsenal of reasons, battle each other for supremacy of our minds. And our resulting decisions, whether bold or timid, well thought out or impulsive, can either set the course of action or blind it. I don't have much advice to give you about decision-making except this: whatever you do, don't camp at the fork in the road. Decide. It's far better to make a wrong decision than to not make one at all. Each of us must confront our emotional turmoil and sort out our feelings.

Desire

How does one gain desire? I don't think I can answer this directly because there are many ways. But I do know two things about desire: it comes from the inside, not the outside, and it can be triggered by outside forces.

Almost anything can trigger desire. It's a matter of timing as much as preparation. It might be a song that tugs at the heart. It might be a memorable sermon. It might be a movie, a conversation with a friend, a confrontation with the enemy, or a bitter experience. Even a book or an article such as this one can trigger the inner mechanism that will make some people say "I want it now!"

Therefore, while searching for your "hot button" of pure, raw desire, welcome into your life each positive experience. Don't erect a wall to protect you from experiencing life. The same wall that keeps out your disappointment also keeps out the sunlight of enriching experiences. So let life touch you. The next touch could be the one that turns your life around.

Resolve

Resolve says "I will." These two words are among the most potent in the English language. *I will.* Benjamin Disraeli, the great British statesman, once said, "Nothing can resist a human will that will stake even its existence on the extent of its purpose." In other words, when someone resolves to "do or die," nothing can stop him.

The mountain climber says, "I will climb the mountain. They've told me it's too high, it's too far, it's too steep, it's too rocky, it's too difficult. But it's my mountain. I will climb it. You'll soon see me waving from the top, or you'll never see me, because unless I reach the peak, I'm not coming back." Who can argue with such resolve?

When confronted with such iron-will determination, I can see Time, Fate, and Circumstance calling a hasty conference and deciding, "We might as well let him have his dream. He's said he's going to get there or die trying."

The best definition for "resolve" I've ever heard came from a schoolgirl in Foster City, California. As is my custom, I was lecturing about success to a group of bright kids at a junior high school. I asked, "Who can tell me what 'resolve' means?" Several hands went up, and I did get some pretty good definitions. But the last was the best. A shy girl
from the back of the room got up and said with quiet intensity, "I think resolve means promising yourself you will never give up." That's it! That's the best definition I've ever heard: *promise yourself you'll never give up.*

Think about it! How long should a baby try to learn how to walk? How long would you give the average baby before you say, "That's it, you've had your chance"? You say that's crazy? Of course it is. Any mother would say, "My baby is going to keep trying until he learns how to walk!" No wonder everyone walks.

There is a vital lesson in this. Ask yourself, "How long am I going to work to make my dreams come true?" I suggest you answer, "As long as it takes." That's what these four emotions are all about.

To your success,
Jim Rohn

ABOUT THE AUTHOR

Jim Rohn is hailed as one of the most influential thinkers of our time and has helped motivate and train an entire generation of personal development trainers as well as hundreds of executives from America's top corporations. He is one of today's most sought-after success counselors and has addressed over 6,000 audiences and four million people over the past 39 years. Rohn is the author of over 30 best-selling audios, videos, and books and is the 1985 recipient of the National Speakers Association coveted CPAE Award. This article is excerpted from "Seven Strategies for Wealth and Happiness." For more information on Jim Rohn, visit http://www.jimrohn.com.

28

Lies that Prevent Powerful Results

Kathy Gates

Have you ever considered that most of what happens in your life happens because of the way you think? Your thinking directs your emotional reaction, which in turn directs your behavior. The way you react to a situation is not just a representation of the events; your reaction also depends on what you think the events mean.

Everyone has something in his life that he would like to change. Nobody's life circumstances and environment are perfect. What do you tend to tell yourself about these circumstances? Oftentimes, it's easy to fix blame on others. Consider, however, that your feelings are not caused by your cranky boss, or the construction on your street, or your inconsiderate friend, but rather, your feelings are caused by what you *tell* yourself about your circumstances. One writer gives the following example: imagine that a friend is late to meet you for dinner. Depending on what you *think* (for example, she was in an accident; she's rude; I wanted to do something else anyway), you might be worried, annoyed, or relieved. These feelings (ignited by the thoughts) can then dictate how you react, for example, by calling the police, having angry words for her, or being glad that she bailed on you.

What you tell yourself, or what you think about your circumstances, may keep you stuck in a bad situation. For this reason, recognizing the lies that you tell yourself is very important. These lies prevent us from being as powerful as we really are.

It Will Never Happen

It's true, we have all seen our lives change in a heartbeat—sometimes an upturn, and sometimes a downturn. However, generally, success toward any goal is a longer road that takes daily work to make a reality. It will happen. Don't expect it to happen overnight, but expect it to happen. Don't give up. Powerful results come from taking baby steps, one after another, day after day, until you reach your goal.

Complaining Is Okay

The Law of Attraction states that you will attract whatever you put out there. If you have a habit of complaining, you will attract more complainers to you. Life reflects back to you what you expend, or as the Bible puts it, "you reap what you sow." One of my favorite cartoons, "The Far Side," shows the character contemplating spring, and she says, "Time to go out in the garden and see if the bulbs I didn't plant didn't come up." Powerful results come from planting seeds for what you want to grow.

I'll Fix It Later

Winners recognize that it doesn't always matter how the hole got in the boat; it matters that it gets fixed so that you can get on with the fishing. However, it *does* matter if you keep running over the same rock day after day, and you are patching the same hole over and over. It's important to find the *source* of the hole and stop allowing it to happen. Powerful results come from creating a lifestyle that supports your desires.

Having an Idea instead of a Plan

Did you miss becoming a doctor, dancer, chef, actor, or CPA because you were absent the day they were handing out those careers? Of course not. All of those careers require that a person choose to go to school, sometimes for many years. If you don't purposefully choose the path to go down, something else will choose it for you. Those who don't create their future have to endure the future they get. Powerful results come from creating a plan and getting into action.

Ignoring Your Talents

Thomas Leonard, founder of Coach University, suggests that you "customize what you want out of life so that it fits you perfectly." This means using your natural talents in a way that works best for you, in all that you do. So often, we put ourselves into a role or get so busy responding to life's daily crises that we end up frustrated with busy work instead of taking the time to sort out what we're good at, let our strengths help us, and be willing to ask for help with the rest. Powerful results come from customizing whatever you do so that it's a better fit for you.

Having Elusive Goals instead of Doable Goals

An elusive goal is "lose weight." A doable goal is "walk 30 minutes, three times a week," or "stop eating ice cream after dinner." That's a plan of action that has measurable results. Powerful results come from specific actions that have measurable results.

Adopting a "What I Do Doesn't Matter" Attitude

It's easy to say to yourself that other people and circumstances prevent you from doing something. It's easy to think that they are more powerful than you are, so your puny contribution won't matter in the long run. However, this attitude tends to paralyze you and keeps you out of the action of creating better circumstances. Powerful results come from being honest with yourself, listening to yourself, and then doing what needs to be done.

Powerful results come from positive beliefs and emotions, and part of cultivating positive beliefs and emotions is recognizing and eliminating the common lies we all tell ourselves on a daily basis. Keep focused, never give up, have a plan with measurable results, use your talents, define doable goals, and practice self-honesty. If you do, powerful results are sure to follow.

ABOUT THE AUTHOR

Kathy Gates is a professional life coach in Scottsdale, Arizona. She offers traditional coaching as well as a variety of Quick-Results Coaching Calls and coaching programs designed to help you build a life that is happier, more relaxed, and more efficient. Visit http://www.reallifecoach.com today and sign up for the free newsletter!

29

ENERGY

Refilling Your Energy Cup

Sally M. Veillette

A year before I got sick, I'd accumulated 37,888 frequent flier miles, made over 6,500 phone calls, booked $8,103,900 of new business for our company, and received an 18 percent raise. I'd skied 78 hours, hiked 41,420 vertical feet, swam 792 laps, spent 28 hours on the StairMaster®, biked 347 miles, ran 208 miles, and lifted over 485,000 pounds. I'd refinished 28 antique picture frames, took 252 pictures, had 192 friends over for dinner, went on 107 dates, and read over 4,000 pages.

Then, my life changed. Staring out the window of a United Airlines plane, I felt something snap, an inner control break, and I was left with what felt like the start of a flu. Little did I know, it was the sudden onset of something much more severe—chronic fatigue syndrome (CFS)—and little did I know, this very illness that initially took away my drive would eventually show me how to have more energy than ever before.

Each day was a battle inside my own skin. I was bright, but couldn't concentrate, exhausted, but couldn't get a good night's sleep. I'd have energy one minute and lose it the next. When my symptoms were at their worst, I couldn't concentrate enough to add up a simple set of numbers—the very numbers that had controlled my life for so long. I couldn't stand for even five minutes at a time. I remember looking at a simple pile of dishes in the sink and thinking that if someone had offered me a million dollars to wash them, I wouldn't even know how to begin that simple, mundane task.

Winter turned to spring. I hated every minute of it. I wanted my old life back— my energy and drive to accomplish anything I set out to do.

Months later, after my official diagnosis, a friend tried to console me. A confessed adrenaline junkie, I expected him to pity the absence of my beloved overdrive and encourage me to rev up and fight, but he surprised me.

"Come on, Sally," he said. "Don't take this CFS thing so hard. *Relax, you deserve it. Take a break for a while.*"

I was speechless. I'd never even once considered giving in to this thing, but in a wave of emotion even more surprising than his words, tears streamed down my face. Imagine suggesting that *I* relax, that I deserved a break. *Me*, who got up in the morning, turned my engine on high, and played superwoman for the rest of the day. *Me*, who fell exhausted into bed each night, without a drop of energy left to spare. To relax was both unthinkable and, secretly, what I wanted more than anything else in the world.

"*Relax?*" I replied. Even the word sounded funny as it rolled off my tongue.

Again, something clicked, and I could feel a wisp of energy rise up inside my fragile body. I was Alice going down the rabbit hole. Instead of fighting my unstable energy level to regain "control" of it, I realized that only by giving up the fight could I begin to notice what *naturally* caused my energy level to increase on its own and, equally important, what drained it bone dry.

The old Sally gave away energy by the bucketful, gallons and gallons each day. Where did my energy go? That's easy: to everyone around me. To planning. To worrying. It went everywhere except where I needed it to be: *with me*.

Over time, this giving-it-all-away habit caused a large hole to form in what I call my "energy cup." Virtually all of my energy escaped through this hole. I was left with just two drops and an illness called CFS. One drop supported my vital signs; the other was for discretionary use. If I used the latter to do something that was aligned with the real me, a new drop or two would be added to my cup, sometimes more. If, however, I did something that was *against* my natural grain, I would lose all but a single drop of energy and be bedridden until the start of the next day.

Since my energy supply was so low at the time, I could sense the movement of even one drop in or out of my cup. This was the surprise gift of my illness, a kind of spiritual truth serum, a finely tuned energy meter that steered me toward the direction of my heart. I might not have found it otherwise.

It was no wonder that the huge bags of vegetables and megadoses of vitamins that I'd taken the months before had had no lasting effect. Any energy that they'd created had just fallen out of the big "hole" in my cup. I needed to plug the hole by learning how to manage my energy before any type of strength-building techniques could be long lasting.

Over the next months I changed dozens of things about my life—many seemingly insignificant—and the energy gain I experienced was quite significant indeed. One step at a time, I dislodged the heaviness that had obscured my natural light and caused me to become so chronically fatigued that my body broke down under its weight. It wasn't easy, though. I had a lot of habits to break.

After nine months of maintaining a "full" energy cup, my CFS symptoms began to turn around. I felt like Dorothy after the fake wizard had been exposed: the answer had, indeed, been inside of me all along. Yes, I had the brains, heart, and courage to live a life that was truly alive. We all have these things. The only thing I'd ever lacked was an experience to draw these parts of me out, to make me realize that my heart's desire wasn't some big Hollywood dream that took years (or a lifetime) to attain, that it was as simple as following a momentary curiosity, voicing a sudden yearning, pursuing a natural interest, or plugging up an old energy drain.

As I shared my experience, people caught right on.

"A drip, drip, *gush*, happens to me every time I go to the basement and see the boxes of my husband's books and notes from law school. Why does he insist on keeping these things? I know he'll never look at them again," one woman said.

A freelance copywriter began firing clients who didn't pay her promptly (or who were too annoying to be worth the trouble). She concentrated her business on those people and firms who not only brought her business, but positive energy.

The fact is that each of us has all we need to make our way through life, moving with it rather than against it. Within our own bodies we have a friend, an ally, a confidant, a guide. As we learn to trust in this connection, as we open to it and feel its truth, we can draw a pure power from it to steer our future and fuel our days. That's what being real is all about—breathing, smelling, seeing, tasting, touching, and experiencing *yourself*. Your reward? More vitality and satisfaction each step of the way—for you and for everyone you touch.

ABOUT THE AUTHOR

Sally M. Veillette, nicknamed the "Goddess of Glow," is an admitted adrenaline junkie, self-made millionaire, mother of a gorgeous baby girl, business consultant, motivational speaker, and author of award-winning *Coming to Your Senses: Soaring With Your Soul* (2003). An Ivy League electrical engineering degree with top honors launched her career, but her real success came after she got chronic fatigue syndrome, was forced to put her overdrive tendencies on hold, and stumbled on the secrets to unlocking more energy and satisfaction than ever before. Visit her Web site at http://www.gettheglow.com or e-mail her at sally@gettheglow.com.

30

Improving Your Life with Energy Psychology

Lynne McKenna Hoss

Energy psychology is a family of mind/body techniques that offers fast, new methods for reducing stress, achieving goals, and attaining peak performance. The methods are free, noninvasive, and easy to learn. They can benefit adults and children and can be used for self-help or integrated into a therapeutic setting. People often experience change in a single session, with lasting results. Most popular for self-help are Emotional Freedom Techniques® (EFT), founded by Gary Craig, and the Tapas Acupressure Technique (TAT), founded by Tapas Fleming. Each method works with your body's energy system, producing mental shifts that change the way you feel and view life.

Many of our life problems result from early negative experiences that were threatening. These feelings often get programmed into our brains as part of the fight or flight response, our most basic survival mechanism. These old programmed responses and emotions then burst forth in future experiences and relationships, when a current situation reminds you of an earlier one. However, energy psychology can change those programmed emotional responses by actually shifting your neurochemistry, thereby neutralizing the patterns you carry within you.

There are many real-life examples that show that it's possible to easily eliminate negative emotions, thoughts, and behaviors. In *Energy Psychology Interactive* a woman with a terrifying, lifelong fear of snakes attended a personal development workshop at a South African wildlife reserve. Within half an hour of energy treatment her terror was gone, and she walked up to a snake brought in by a handler, touching it with curiosity and interest. Nancy had a strong 20-year fear of heights after being jokingly pushed on the White Cliffs of Dover. After one

EFT session she walked onto a hotel's fourth floor balcony, and the fear was gone. At a two-year follow-up, the results held!

In *The Promise of Energy Psychology*, Vietnam veteran Rich had Post-traumatic Stress Disorder, despite 17 years of treatment. At the VA hospital Gary Craig used EFT on him, and his fear of heights from over 50 parachute jumps cleared within 15 minutes. Within an hour, horrid memories stopped intruding, and within a couple of days he was sleeping through the night. In another example, three-year-old Evan had uncontrollable temper tantrums whenever he couldn't have his way. After a fun hike he didn't want to leave and started screaming, sobbing, and struggling in his caretaker's arms. Although Evan's therapists said that they could let him cry himself out, the caretaker's friend used EFT on him. Within minutes Evan started smiling, wiping away tears, and sitting quietly. His caretaker was dumbstruck. Evan had never reacted that way while in a tantrum.

How are these methods done? They are done by mentally activating the problem state while using a technique to neutralize it, such as tapping or holding acupressure points. They are so simple and effective that many people have a hard time believing that the results are real! However, as they go through their daily lives, they frequently find that the results are real *and* lasting. It's reported in 70–80 percent of cases that delimited fears and issues disappear, specific anxiety goes away, and cravings are eliminated.

Here's an example, including basic steps, of an abbreviated version of the EFT procedure.

- Recall a specific incident when you experienced your problem, such as standing on a 17th floor balcony when you have a fear of heights. Give it a stress rating of 0–10, with 10 being the most stressful.
- Then, write a set-up phrase that pairs the unwanted feeling with a positive affirmation such as, "Even though I have this fear of heights, I deeply and completely accept myself."
- State it out loud three times while rubbing "sore spots" on your chest, which you can find two or three inches in from the point where your arms attach to your chest.
- After that, tap on a standard subset of eight acupuncture points while picturing the stressful scene and saying a reminder phrase such as "fear of heights." Tapping can be done with one or two fingers, on either or both sides of your body. The eight points include the inner edge of the eyebrow,

the bone on the outside of the eye, the bone under the eye, under the nose, the center of the chin, collarbone points, underarm points (three to four inches below the armpit), and the karate chop point (on the little-finger side of the hand).

- Then, picture the scene again, and re-rate your distress level.
- For subsequent rounds, adjust the set-up and reminder phrases to include "still" and "remaining," while rubbing sore spots: "Even though I *still* have this fear of heights, I deeply and completely accept myself." Use the reminder phrase, "Remaining fear."
- Do more tapping rounds, re-rating the level of distress each time until it goes down to zero.

Another simple, effective technique is the Tapas Acupressure Technique, which also mentally activates a problem state while holding acupuncture points. TAT videos show a victim of sexual abuse working with Tapas to clear feelings of negativity and dirtiness, allowing her to feel better about life. Another woman, who was raped as a teenager, was able to clear the trauma with lasting results. TAT (child pose) was used with children who were victims of natural disasters in Mexico and Nicaragua, significantly reducing symptoms of post-traumatic stress.

To do TAT, lightly hold three acupuncture points: one-eighth inch above the inside corner of each eye using your thumb and fourth finger, plus one-half inch above the midpoint between the eyebrows using your third finger (TAT pose). The other hand is placed on the lower back of the head. Hold this pose during each of the procedure's seven steps (one to two minutes), then release. The first four steps include focusing on the problem (a disturbing event, food allergy, etc), focusing on the opposite of the problem (it's over, I survived), healing the origins of the problem, and healing the places in your mind, body, and life where this has been stuck. The method often releases trauma or stress and even sometimes eliminates allergies. However, no self-help method is a substitute for therapy, so seek professional help for serious problems or if any method is unsettling.

Because the methods are quick, easy to learn and use, and have no known side effects, people in Internet energy psychology groups indicate that they are self-applying the methods for lots of emotional and behavioral problems with children, adults, and even with pets! They use the methods for behavior problems in school, autism, heartbreak, old childhood issues, anger, guilt, anxiety, and more. They also use them for physical problems ranging from weight loss to allergies and for achieving goals such as improved eating or exercise habits. In sports psychology they use the techniques to achieve optimal performance by reducing stress and tension and making performance goals more believable to the athlete.

Whether used for problems or goals, energy psychology methods can take down problematic feelings, thoughts, and behaviors one by one, changing how you feel about yourself and others and how you view and experience life. This leads to positive experiences and joyous feelings, improving your life in simple and profound ways!

ABOUT THE AUTHOR

Lynne McKenna Hoss, MA, is Energy Psychology Program Director for Innersource and a former counselor and journalist. She brings the field of energy psychology forward through articles, CE programs, public presentations, and individual instructional sessions on energy psychology methods. Trained in EFT-ADV, EPI Basic & Advanced, Seemorg, REMAP, TAT, Donna Eden's Energy Medicine, and more, she is a member of the Association for Comprehensive Energy Psychology. For more information on energy psychology and home study programs, plus links to Web sites for practitioners and the EFT and TAT methods above (which both have free downloads that fully teach the methods), visit http://www.EnergyPsychEd.com.

31

Choose to Enjoy Life

Ralph Marston

One of the quickest ways to improve your life is to decide that you are going to enjoy it. Enjoyment requires no complicated tools, no special training, and no expensive resources. In fact, enjoyment requires nothing more than your choice to allow it.

The rewards of that choice can be enormous. Think for a moment of the most genuinely and consistently successful person you know. Does that person nearly always seem to be enjoying what he is doing? Most likely, the answer is yes. The fact is that those people who are the most spectacularly successful are the people who most fully enjoy what they are doing.

People who enjoy life are creative, productive, generous, compassionate, and contribute tremendously to the communities in which they live. They are enthusiastic about making a positive difference and work diligently to do so. Where others see only gloom and doom, people who truly enjoy life see valuable, positive opportunities. You can become one of those people right this very minute. As soon as you do, your life will begin to move in a more positive, successful direction.

Perhaps you think that there's nothing enjoyable about your life right now. How, you wonder, can you enjoy life when there are the constant pressures of bills to be paid, health problems, difficult relationships, and a world filled with negativity? The answer is simple and infinitely empowering: you enjoy life by choosing to do so.

If you're not fully enjoying life, the reason is that you've put conditions and restrictions on your enjoyment. You've decided that you cannot possibly enjoy life until you get a better job, or move to a bigger house, or find the perfect partner. You see other people who have accomplished the things you want to accomplish, and those people appear to be enjoying their lives, so you assume that in order to enjoy life, you must first be successful. Have you ever considered that you could have it exactly backward?

Long before Tiger Woods became successful at golf, he enjoyed playing the game. Long before Bill Gates founded the software company that would make him a multibillionaire, he enjoyed programming computers. Long before anyone had ever heard of Lance Armstrong, he enjoyed riding bicycles. Is there a lesson here? You bet there is! Enjoy what you do, and you'll be good at it. Commit your life to doing what you enjoy, and the world will stand up, take notice, cheer you on, and throw roses at your feet as you pass by.

The fact is that every person who is alive is rich beyond all measure. Those who truly enjoy life are able to see and to tap into that richness. By choosing to enjoy this moment you challenge yourself to find the positive value that is most certainly there, and when you find that value, you can nurture it, build on it, and grow it into something even more valuable.

Enjoyment gives you an enormous competitive edge. If you truly love what you're doing, and the person next to you absolutely hates what she is doing, who is going to do the best job? You are, of course. So, what happens when you have to do something that you hate? That's easy—stop hating it, and start finding a way to enjoy it. Realize that enjoyment exists in your mind and that you are in full control of your mind. No outside condition can prevent you from enjoying life when you choose to do so. There is nothing you need for enjoyment other than your own choice.

If you have trouble making that choice, take a step back from yourself and objectively consider the alternatives. At any given time you can choose to be miserable, or you can choose to enjoy the moment. If you choose to be miserable, you'll make more mistakes, you'll drive people away, and you'll have trouble getting anything done. Why would you ever choose to put yourself in that condition?

Certainly, there will be difficult, painful, and unpleasant things coming into your life on a regular basis. Yet, the question you must ask yourself is this: do you really want to add your own negative energy to the pain and difficulties, making them even more burdensome? Or would you rather begin to rise above those difficulties? Choosing to enjoy life will put you in a position to most effectively deal with whatever comes along.

A commitment to enjoyment does not mean pursuing a hedonistic life filled with nothing but empty pleasures. To be sure, many of life's greatest pleasures can be transformed into sheer misery if you become so obsessed with them that they control your life. True enjoyment goes beyond mere pleasure. True enjoyment comes when you choose to be at peace with the moment and with who you are. True enjoyment comes when you value life simply because it is.

Though life is not always enjoyable, you can always enjoy being alive. By allowing yourself to enjoy the moment, whatever the moment may hold, you put yourself in a position to move positively and powerfully forward. The more you enjoy life, the more you'll find to enjoy. Enjoy life, and you can truly make it great.

ABOUT THE AUTHOR

Ralph Marston is the publisher of "The Daily Motivator" on the Web at http://www.DailyMotivator.com. The site features a new positive, daily message every Monday through Saturday and an archive of more than 2,500 previous messages as well as soothing, inspiring photographic presentations set to music. Ralph has published two books, *The Daily Motivator to Go* and *Living the Wonder of It All*, and is finishing another book on the subject of enjoying life that will be published in 2006.

32

I Was So Embarrassed

Michael Angier

In March 1987, I launched a new magazine called *Creating Excellence: Vermont's Journal for People in Growing Businesses.*

It was a very proud moment. The magazine was my baby—a beautiful baby. In fact, the cover of the invitation to the launch party read, "A Magazine is Born."

I'd worked hard for over a year to create it, and the premiere issue was a real success. I did it with only one part-time employee, while contracting with an editor and a design firm for the production.

Shortly after we mailed 25,000 copies of the premiere issue, I received a copy of it in the mail. This one wasn't so beautiful, however. It was all marked up in red ink with corrections of typos and grammatical errors. A very competent proofreader had taken it upon herself to go through the issue with a fine-toothed comb and had found more errors than I could have imagined.

It was a humbling experience. When your masthead says "Creating Excellence," the contents should certainly exemplify excellence. The articles did, but the errors this woman had found showed that we were far from excellent.

I was embarrassed. I was also upset—upset with my editor for not having caught more of the typos and upset with someone I didn't even know who seemed to have taken pleasure in pointing out our errors. Mostly, though, I was upset with myself for not having hired another proofreader to ensure an excellent issue.

It seemed unfair for someone to be so critical. Why couldn't she have cut us some slack? After all, it was our first issue, and I'd never published anything other than a newsletter before.

Somehow, I was able to get over the pain and the defensiveness I felt. I knew I had to admit our errors and to own them. I called the woman who had so pointedly shown us that we were not so excellent. I thanked her for taking the time to so thoroughly go through our magazine. As painful as it was, I took responsibility for it.

Then, I offered her a job. I never asked her if that was her intention, but for the rest of the issues we published, "Wendy" was our proofreader. Before we went to type—yes, that's the way we did it in those days—we sent her a copy of each edited article. She always found mistakes, and we always corrected them before press time.

The result was a far better publication—one in which we could take well-deserved pride.

What did I learn?

I can think of at least three things. First, make a real commitment to excellence. Be willing to do what it takes to put out an excellent product or to provide an excellent service. Second, don't be defensive. Own up to it when you're faced with evidence that you're not as great as you thought you were. Remember, an upset is an opportunity to see the truth. Third, put systems into place to prevent similar errors in the future and to make excellence an ongoing effort.

It's all pretty simple but not always easy. The payoff is, however, well worth it.

ABOUT THE AUTHOR

Michael Angier is the founder and president of SuccessNet. Their mission is to inform, to inspire, and to empower people to be their best—personally and professionally. Download SuccessNet's free e-booklet, "10 ESSENTIAL KEYS TO PERSONAL EFFECTIVENESS," from http://www.SuccessNet.org/keys.htm or by sending a blank e-mail to keys@SuccessNet.org. More free subscriptions, books, and SuccessMark Cards are available at http://www.SuccessNet.org.

33

Expect to Get! A Fail-Safe Formula

Kevin Eikenberry

In school we learn a variety of math formulas. We learn how to convert temperatures from Fahrenheit to Celsius, we learn how to calculate the area of a triangle, and many more. The beauty of these formulas is the certainty that they provide. We know that if we know the formula and have the correct inputs, we can compute the correct answer. Presumably, as adults, we use these formulas to solve problems and to move toward something we desire.

People ask me about unleashing their potential—how to do it and what steps to take. Because of this recurring and important question, I have worked to distill part of the answer into a formula. This formula will help us because if we can identify the inputs and use the formula correctly, we can improve our performance and provide greater service to others as we reach toward our potential.

The Inputs

The inputs to this formula are as follows.

- Expectations: those things we expect of ourselves.
- Beliefs: what we believe to be true about ourselves, our skills, our abilities and potential, and our world.
- Actions: the behaviors we exhibit and the things we do.
- Reality: the result or end point of our efforts.

The Formula

Expectations create beliefs. Beliefs create actions. Actions create realities.

Perhaps you will want to remember this formula as EBA = R. As written, it looks like a formula that uses multiplication. In a way, it does—if you have a zero in any of the first three inputs, there will be no change to your reality (or results). However, as we all learned in math class, in multiplication you can complete the formula by multiplying the factors in any order. In our formula it all starts with expectations; in other words, the multiplication must be done in order to make sense.

Before I go any further, let me say that this formula assumes a desire to reach for new results—without the desire to tap into or discover our potential the formula doesn't even apply.

An Example

Let's say that I see a friend, and they tell me that they just ran a 10K race. I tell myself, "I could do that"—I expect that I am capable of running a 10K race. The more I think about this race, telling myself that I could do it, the more I believe my assertions. My belief and expectations begin to create an excitement that leads me to start running. Even when I realize how out of shape I am, my expectations and belief push me to run a little more every day.

Along with my running, I do some other things. I ask other runners about their preparation plans. I pick up a book at the store or library to learn more about running technique. I ask the knowledgeable salesperson in the store about the proper shoes to buy.

Expectations and belief fueled action, and now the action is reinforcing the belief as well. My running expectation has snowballed! I build a plan to compete in a specific 10K race and then complete it.

At the start of this process, when I put this expectation into my mind, my body wasn't capable of making the 10K—maybe it wasn't capable of making it to the mailbox! However, the potential was there, latent, waiting to be unleashed. I unleashed the potential by having positive expectations, which created belief, which fueled action, which led to me crossing the finish line of the 10K race. EBA = R.

Be Aware

It is important to note that this formula works for any expectation, positive and uplifting or negative and cynical, so be careful what you expect!

It is equally important to recognize that you can use the formula to help others unleash their potential as well. Your positive expectations and encouragement will help them to generate their own expectations, which allow the formula to work.

In Closing

If we fervently expect that something will happen, then we develop a belief, a true expectancy about that event or circumstance. When we believe, we will take action on those beliefs, and the right action, as we all know, is required to create new results. EBA = R.

Use this formula for yourself. Set your expectations higher! Reinforce those expectations by thinking about them regularly. If you couple that with true belief, you are on your way.

Why not start today?

ABOUT THE AUTHOR

Kevin Eikenberry is an expert in helping organizations and individuals reach their potential, a best-selling author and internationally known speaker, and the Chief Potential Officer of the Kevin Eikenberry Group. You can learn more about Kevin and how the Kevin Eikenberry Group can help you at http://KevinEikenberry.com. To receive a free special report on unleashing your potential, go to http://www.KevinEikenberry.com/uypw/index.asp or call (317) 387–1424 or 888–LEARNER.

34

FAILURE

If You Don't Succeed, at Least Fail

Paul Frazer

The generally accepted concept of success and failure is incorrect. People consider success and failure to be opposites. To understand why this is incorrect, consider the concept of failure: for many, failure is when we do not succeed at an assigned task, goal, project, or objective. The reality is that if you look more closely at failure, people often have a number of failures and then still have the success for which they were searching in the first place.

There are many good examples of this, but one is particularly powerful: Abraham Lincoln is considered to be a success, right? Well, here's a portion of his track record:

> 1831: failed in business
> 1832: defeated for legislature
> 1833: failed in business again
> 1836: suffered a nervous breakdown
> 1838: defeated for speaker
> 1840: defeated for elector
> 1843: lost his bid for Congress
> 1855: lost his run for Senate
> 1856: defeated for Vice President
> 1858: lost another run for Senate
> 1860: was elected President . . . *finally*

What can we interpret from an example like Abraham Lincoln's? One common perspective is that he persevered through his failures until he ultimately succeeded. This suggests that the failures were the opposite of the success he wanted. It also suggests that his string of failures was a struggle that he needed to endure. Let's look at the situation more closely. Without all of his failure (also

119

note the period of time) Mr. Lincoln would likely not have had the experience and perspective to become such a great and successful leader. Did Mr. Lincoln see each "setback" as a failure or as another successful attempt at striving for his personal and professional vision? Did he see his life as a struggle through failure or as an ongoing reflection of his mission and vision?

Consider that Mr. Lincoln learned from each failure. He learned more about what he needed to do to drive his personal and professional vision forward. He also learned from his successes. Both success and failure are learning events in life. From this standpoint, both success and failure are needed to drive your vision forward. In essence, success and failure are really more similar than they are different. This is where common thinking needs to change. Success and failure are not at opposite ends of a spectrum but at the same end. From this you can see that failure is not the opposite to success but a component of success. You need failure to learn and to be able to redefine your focus toward success.

Okay, failure is just a component of success, so what is the opposite of success? Consider that success and failure both require action. You must be pushing forward, striving or acting to be succeeding (or, as discussed, failing). Therefore the opposite of success is inaction. Isn't this absolutely true? The greatest threat we have to succeeding isn't failing—it is inaction.

In our efforts to succeed we need to embrace failure as part of the process, and we need to remove inaction.

To embrace failure requires a new way of thinking. You need to stop worrying about failure and accept it, learn from it, and continue to push forward on your vision. Your vision will change and adapt as you gain more information, but you should not stop pushing forward. Looking at failure in this way is something that is challenging at first, but ultimately, it is empowering.

To remove inaction from your environment, you first need to understand it. Where does it come from? Why does it exist? Most inaction comes from hesitation, lack of confidence, and, yes, procrastination. Inaction does not really come from fatigue or laziness. All people have varying energies and will be able to at least work toward their goals, although perhaps at different speeds. Also, people are not lazy. They may not be motivated or you may not understand their motivations, but people are not lazy. This also applies to you.

How do we remove our hesitation, lack of confidence, and procrastination? Hesitation is just that. You need to cultivate a culture of being bold and decisive. This is learned behavior. It is also very helpful to understand how you make decisions and then to learn how to make better decisions more quickly and more consistently.

Confidence comes from self-esteem and knowledge. As your self-esteem and your knowledge of the environment around you grow, so will your ability to act.

Procrastination is prevalent for many people. The first thing that you need to understand is that it is not the problem. Procrastination is only the coping mechanism for some other issue. It is best for you to try to understand what is driving your procrastination. Is it fear of failure, fear of success, or fear of losing someone or something? Perhaps it is not even fear—it may be a true lack of interest in the work required to achieve your goals. Once you have a better idea of what is driving your procrastination, you can then look at removing the cause. You can also take a more action-oriented position to the tasks that you need to do. Sometimes, all that you need to do to break your procrastination is to do something, anything, even if it is a small task or a task not even related to the work that you are doing. This tends to get you back on track. Finally, understand how you need to approach your tasks. Do you need to look at them as time-oriented or task-oriented? In other words, will you get more accomplished if you say that you will work on this task, followed by another task, followed by another and then be done? Or, will you get more done if you say you will work on these tasks for three hours and then be done?

As a final thought on success, failure, and inaction, people do not look down on those who fail. When people succeed, everyone celebrates their success and completely forgets their failures. Most importantly, the failures that you do notice the most are your own failures. This is where the largest change in common thinking has to happen.

Here's to celebrating your successes . . . and your failures!

ABOUT THE AUTHOR

Ignite your success by developing a mind-set and strategies for peak performance. Paul founded Mindscape as a company dedicated to researching and sharing information on human performance and success. He is passionate about people and what makes us "tick." To have Paul Frazer speak to your organization or for more information on Paul Frazer or Mindscape, his speaking programs, his book, *Stop, Drop & Re-Balance: A Self Renewal Manual*, his newsletter, "Food For Thought," or just to contact Paul, please visit his Web site at http://www.mindscape.ca, send an e-mail to info@mindscape.ca, or call (613) 264–3791.

35

The Fairest One of All:
Breaking the Bonds of Female Competition

Rebecca Grado & Christy Whitman

It happens between mothers and daughters, female coworkers, sisters and gal pals—women constantly comparing themselves to others. Whether consciously or unconsciously, most women question who is more beautiful, more successful, or has the most possessions.

At the root of a woman's misguided beliefs lies female competition. While the idea of competition among women might bring to mind the dramatic makings of a Hollywood soap opera—complete with hair-pulling, name-calling, and catfights—in reality, female competition is quite different from the stereotypes.

Female competition is actually a very subtle and insidious thought process that seduces many women into judging themselves and questioning their worth. A woman may be feeling beautiful and strong until another attractive woman crosses her path; then, a slight shift occurs within. She begins to feel inadequate and to find fault with her own appearance. When the game of competition is present within us, we are directed away from ourselves, from our inner worth and value, and are focused outward on the beauty and success of others.

Female competition is not a concept that most would identify as a problem in their lives. It is so engrained in our belief systems that few see the subtle ways in which we undermine one another and harm ourselves, but as we come to understand and recognize the core beliefs attached to a competitive mind-set and the misguided actions taken when in competition mode, we can begin to see the damaging consequences to our self-esteem and self-worth.

As women, we are conditioned to compare and compete on many levels. On a physical level we begin at an early age to identify our worth through our looks. We learn to value the "thinnest" or the "prettiest" girl. On a social level we learn to compete for possessions: the biggest house, the most expensive car, the best clothes. We compete in our careers through promotions, titles, and positions. We compete through our children: the cutest, the most successful, and the best athletically or academically. We also compete emotionally for the affection and attention of our husbands, children, parents, friends, and coworkers. We compare everything from bodies to boyfriends, bank accounts to bra sizes.

When did we learn to turn away from our own truths and look to others for our validation and worth? One answer may lie in the conditioning we received as young girls to live the perfect, fairy tale life. Most little girls were read the popular tales as they were growing up. These stories typically ended with only *one* very lucky maiden winning the heart of the noble prince and living "happily ever after." It was very clear in the stories that there was only one Snow White who would have all her dreams come true, one Sleeping Beauty who would marry Prince Charming, or one Cinderella whose perfect foot would fit the coveted glass slipper. Oh, how we longed to be the "fairest one of all," that one special maiden who would be held above all others, the one who would be recognized and adored for her beauty and goodness, the one who would receive all the adulation and live in a castle filled with riches.

As we listened to these tales, we were told that happiness and fulfillment were things found outside of ourselves (in the love of the handsome prince, the admiration of others, and the riches and possessions of the kingdom), and we realized that these rewards could only be obtained through victory over another. We learned that "happily ever after" was bestowed on only one woman, and in order for us to reap this reward, we would need to outdo all other women.

When women compete among themselves, they hold the false belief that their feelings of success and worthiness come only at the defeat or devaluation of another woman. In the constant comparison to be the prettiest, the most accomplished, or the wealthiest, women often treat each other as though they were sworn enemies. This game of female competition, which ultimately defeats our best efforts and sabotages our greatest desires, also isolates us and prevents us from accessing all that is loving and supportive in our relationships with other women.

When we are caught up in female competition, we are constantly ranking everything about ourselves. This scorecard mentality is extremely self-defeating. There will always be someone with longer legs, a more prestigious and successful job, a cuter boyfriend, a bigger house, or smarter kids. Striving to be the best, constantly comparing ourselves to others, struggling to defend and maintain our victories, acquiring, accumulating, and achieving all exact a huge price on us physically, emotionally, and energetically.

By becoming aware of the destructive effects of female competition, we can move beyond it. Recognizing the cues and clues of a competitive mind-set is the first step in freeing ourselves from the fairy tale illusion and reclaiming our power.

- A friend's success evokes anxiety, bitterness, resentment, or fear.
- You secretly hope that your coworker will fail.
- You feel small, intimidated, or unworthy in the presence of an accomplished woman.
- There is a constant scorecard in your head of wins and losses for yourself and others.
- You are overly critical and judgmental of yourself and others.
- You do not allow yourself to make mistakes or to be less than perfect.
- You spend a majority of your time thinking about your girlfriends and their accomplishments.
- Hopelessness, sadness, or self-defeat plague you when others succeed.
- Being the best consumes your thoughts.

As we become more aware of the many ways in which we compare and compete, we will then begin to identify within ourselves the effects this mind-set may be having on us. For some, female competition may evoke a simple shift in confidence or a minor decrease in energy and vitality. We may not even recognize the subtle feelings of self-doubt or the self-deprecating thoughts that quietly whisper to us of our perceived inadequacies. For other women, or in other situations, the effect of competition may be overwhelming. We may experience tremendous anxiety at the thought of being in the presence of other successful and attractive women, or we may feel ourselves sliding into depression and apathy because we do not believe that we can "keep up" with those around us.

Transforming female competition occurs when we stop looking outside ourselves for love, validation, and admiration and begin finding it within. When we look to the wisdom and strength that resides deep within each of us and when we direct our attention and affection back to ourselves, we cultivate a deeper relationship with the most essential, important, vital, and trustworthy person we will ever know—ourselves.

When our eyes remain focused on the magnificence and beauty that rests at our core, or our essential self, we will finally find the love that we desire and deserve. This love is not the love that comes from Prince Charming or from the admiration and adulation of others. It is love that comes from the knowledge and recognition of each one of us as a unique, glorious, and remarkable woman.

ABOUT THE AUTHORS

Christy Whitman is a personal empowerment coach and the best-selling author of *Perfect Pictures*. Rebecca Grado is an MFT. For a free bonus meditation (valued at $29) to reclaim your self-worth and cultivate self-love, visit http://www.christywhitman.com and sign up for "The Quarterly Newsletter."

36

Letting Go of Stuff

Darren L. Johnson

Have you ever lain awake at two o'clock in the morning, feeling stressed and overwhelmed because your dreams are not being accomplished? Do you constantly remind yourself that you have made mistakes in the past? Do you worry about whether or not you are making the right decisions about your life? You can spend hours writing down desires and wants. You can tell friends about your dreams. However, until you change your internal conversation and create a clear picture of your future, until you are prepared to let go of the stuff that keeps you stuck in a rut, the outcome will remain the same.

What is "stuff"? Stuff is dwelling on mistakes you have made in the past, being angry at someone who did something to you in the past, being afraid to enter into a new relationship because you got hurt in a previous one, worrying about your health at age 50 while you are still 35 . . . I could go on and on. Stuff is the unspecified, intangible, often negative element we introduce into our minds through our words, thoughts, or some other outside stimulation. When we don't focus our thoughts effectively, they can become scattered, miscellaneous, and fixated on stuff that can lead to negative notions, toxic relationships, and fear of taking risks. Stuff will find its way into your life regardless of who you are, how much money you make, and what your status is in life. This stuff keeps us from moving forward with our lives. This is the stuff that we need to let go, and quickly.

How do you let go of stuff? It begins with a commitment to yourself, a commitment to your dreams, and a belief that you deserve to have what you want out of life. That having been said, please remember the old adage that you don't get what you want out of life, you get what you are out of life. Therefore letting go begins with deciding who you want to be, then creating a plan to be that person—no matter what! Making that commitment is critical.

Many people believe that changing hairstyles, clothes, jewelry, and the like will make a significant difference in their unwanted habits. Some people think that changing jobs, moving from city to city, and making new friends will bring long-term internal change. These kinds of activities will make some difference, but any difference will be short-lived. In order to make long-lasting changes and to effectively let go of stuff in your life that keeps you from moving forward, an inside out approach to letting go is necessary, along with two important tools: the mirror and time.

In order to let go of unwanted habits and actions, it is important to take the time to get to know yourself. Until you take that genuine look in the mirror and recognize yourself, it will be difficult to let go of those unwanted habits and actions. Time is your friend when it comes to letting go of stuff in your life. As long as you realize that it will take time, and you have a plan, then letting go and moving forward can happen for you.

The first step in the process of letting go of stuff is to acknowledge that you have stuff. Acceptance of the stuff in your life is key, just as is acceptance of anything you want to change. Before remodeling a home, for example, you must first accept its current condition. After taking inventory, you can then make plans to remodel. The same is true for making long-lasting, inside out changes in your life: you must first take inventory of the stuff that is keeping you from making those changes. Taking inventory will help you to bring about acceptance of the stuff in your life.

To gain acceptance, we must be willing to do something else that is critical—forgive. Forgiveness is what lies between acknowledging and accepting the stuff in your life. One key to forgiveness is to identify the perpetrator and the victim, who are often one and the same because we are often our own worst enemy. Once you have forgiven yourself, it makes it easier to continue the process of letting go. Forgiveness allows you to be able to move from a place of pain and suffering to one of peace and harmony. Have you ever actually forgiven yourself?

Here are a few questions and actions to assist with the process of forgiveness as you begin to let go of stuff.

1. Make a list of those you need and would like to forgive (don't be afraid to include yourself on the list).

2. Give yourself permission to forgive by making a claim that you can forgive those listed.

3. Forgive yourself! The process of forgiving must begin with forgiving yourself.

4. Contact each person on your list, and genuinely say, "I forgive you for what happened in the past." By forgiving them you release yourself.

5. Ask them to forgive you, and accept their responses regardless. It does not matter whether or not you agree with them. You must be willing to simply accept where they are right now when it comes to them forgiving you. They may not be ready, and remember, you must accept this.

Now that you know where to put your energy, focus your efforts, and how to begin to choose to let go of the stuff that interferes with moving forward in life, I challenge you to get started today. Your destiny is in your hands. Creating the life you want is totally up to you. Letting go of stuff will put you on the path to redesigning your life. Best of luck to you, and remember that long-lasting change and truly letting go only happen when done from the inside out.

ABOUT THE AUTHOR

Darren L. Johnson, MSOD, is an organization development consultant and author of *Letting Go of Stuff: Powerful Secrets to Simplify Your Life* (InsideOut Learning, Inc.). Using researched theory on change and various philosophies as a foundation for a step-by-step process for letting go, he also offers one-on-one coaching for those interested in successfully letting go of stuff in their lives and has helped thousands since 1994. To learn more, visit the publisher's Web site at http://www.LettingGoOfStuff.com.

37

FREE WILL

Goal-Free Living©

Stephen Shapiro

Success and happiness are unarguably our Holy Grails, but the standards taught to find them are all wrong. We have been brainwashed into believing that the only way to achieve this elusive combination of success and happiness is through setting goals. This is simply not true. In fact, goal-setting is often the shortest route to discontentment. Fifty eight percent of those I surveyed say that they are consciously sacrificing today's happiness in the belief that achieving their goals will bring fulfillment. Sadly, 41 percent say that each goal achieved brings little, if any, satisfaction, despite all the hard work. So, what do they do? They set another goal. This creates a perpetual cycle of sacrifice and disillusionment. What is the solution?

After interviewing hundreds of people and surveying thousands I discovered that the most passionate, creative, and sometimes wealthiest people live free from the burden of traditional goals. Instead, they have mastered the rare skill of enjoying "now" rather than delaying gratification until the future.

Goals are not inherently bad, but many individuals have an unhealthy relationship with their goals, distorting this potentially helpful tool into a surefire recipe for failure. Why?

- Quite often, the goals we chase are not our own. Fifty three percent of those I surveyed feel that they are living their lives in a way that satisfies others more than themselves. Whose life are *you* living?
- Goals can cause you to lose your peripheral vision. When you focus on your goals, you are cutting off potentially greater opportunities from emerging.
- Goals set you up for failure, say 74 percent of those surveyed, conceding to disappointment and dissatisfaction when they are unsuccessful in achieving

their goals. In fact, 92 percent fail to achieve their New Year's resolutions. That is a lot of discontentment.

Goal-Free Living is liberating. It opens new possibilities typically hidden from sight.

We often associate goals with our career. While that is a big aspect of our lives, Goal-Free Living applies to all areas of life, from dating to business.

- **Dating.** When you are on a date, do not worry about the next date. Instead, just enjoy the other person's company . . . for that moment. You will come across as being more genuine and less desperate, and ironically, this increases your chances of getting that second date.
- **Vacationing.** When on a vacation, instead of planning every minute of every day, try venturing out into an area not in your guidebook. You may discover some hidden gems. You will feel less hurried and more relaxed. Isn't that what a vacation is all about?
- **Meetings.** When you attend a business conference, stop focusing on what you will get out of it and how you will use it. Rather, concentrate on just being there and soaking in as much as possible. Incredible opportunities show up when you are unburdened and blinded by myopic goals.

When you are doing something, ask yourself "Why am I doing this?" If you have a reason—other than just to be there—then you may have a goal. While is it quite acceptable to have a particular interest in an outcome, do not let that specific focus become so dominant that it blinds you to other opportunities.

How does one embark on a more goal-free life? During my travels around the world and after hundreds of interviews I discovered eight secrets for living goal-free.

1. Use a compass, not a map—have a sense of direction (not a specific destination), and then "meander with purpose."

2. Trust that you are never lost—every seemingly wrong turn is an opportunity to learn and experience new things.

3. Remember that opportunity knocks often but sometimes softly—while blindly pursuing our goals, we often miss unexpected and wonderful possibilities.

4. Want what you have—measure your life by your own yardstick and appreciate who you are, what you do, and what you have . . . now.

5. Seek out adventure—treat your life like a one-time-only journey, and revel in new and different experiences.

6. Become a people magnet—constantly attract, build, and nurture relationships with new people so that you always have the support and camaraderie of others.

7. Embrace your limits—transform your inadequacies and boundaries into unique qualities that you can use to your advantage.

8. Remain detached—focus on the present, act with a commitment to the future, and avoid worrying about how things will turn out.

For each of these secrets, there are a number of tips for implementing the concept. Here are a few you can try today.

- Set "themes," not "resolutions"—rather than set a resolution (i.e., a goal), choose one word to describe your next year. Choose something that is bold and inspires you. Instead of losing 10 pounds, you could choose "health." "Relationships"—in the broadest sense—may work better for you than "finding a boyfriend." Any word will do: "grace," "adventure," "serenity," "play."
- Use "could do" lists rather than "to do" lists—"to do" lists tend to be draining as they are the things you feel you must do. "Could do" lists contain those things that you want to do that inspire you. They keep possibility in front of you. Keep your list of "could do" items large and your list of "to do" items small.
- Change your filter. One creative way to "seek out adventure" is to make believe you are another person—an artist, a musician, or a doctor. It doesn't matter, as long as it is someone other than you. When you live your normal day standing in the shoes of someone else, you will see things you have never seen before.

- Appreciate the whole spectrum of life. Create contrasts to help you appreciate where you are right now. Sleep in a tent and sleeping bag versus always staying in a five-star hotel. Volunteer for a charity. Take the bus to work. Eat at a greasy spoon diner. Swap jobs with someone with a less glamorous assignment for a week. Experience the whole spectrum of life.

The origin of the word "goal" comes from the Old English word for "obstacles" or "a hindrance." In order to achieve a goal, you must work hard to overcome these barriers and roadblocks. Conversely, the origin of the word "aspiration" is the same as the Latin word for "spirit" and "inspire," which means "to breathe into" or "panting with desire." Barriers or inspiration. Which would you prefer?

ABOUT THE AUTHOR

Stephen Shapiro has inspired hundreds of thousands of people in 27 countries with his speeches on creativity and innovation. During a 15-year tenure with the international consulting firm Accenture he established and led their Global Process Excellence Practice. His first book, *24/7 Innovation* (McGraw-Hill), has been featured in *Investor's Business Daily* and the *New York Times*. His latest book, *Goal-Free Living: How to Have the Life You Want NOW!* (Wiley), became the #1 Amazon.com "Business Inspiration" book, was featured on TomPeters.com, and was the cover story in *O, The Oprah Magazine*. Go to http://www.GoalFree.com and http://www.24-7Innovation.com for more information.

38

The Company We Keep

Greg Reid

At 8 A.M. the phone rings, right on schedule. The call is not an appointment I've made, but I'm expecting it all the same.

Owing to being known as the Millionaire Mentor, I receive calls daily from people around the world, all with the same question: "What is the one thing I could do right now, at this very moment, to dramatically improve my current situation?"

"The answer," I say, "is simple—change the five people you associate with most."

I can imagine your reaction now. You're thinking, "I'm not going to write off my lifelong friends!"

Don't worry, I wouldn't ask that of you. You don't have to cut your ties to the family and friends that you spend time with now; however, I *am* suggesting that if you truly wish to change your life, this single step could be the first on a path toward success!

Let me explain how this works. Think back to when you were in school—it probably doesn't seem like that long ago, right? Now, in school, if you hung out with the kids who smoked, more than likely, who would you be? A smoker. If you hung out with the jocks on campus, you probably played sports, and if you wanted to get straight A's, would it have made sense to surround yourself with the D students? Of course not! You would only find yourself attracting other people with a negative attitude and poor grades.

The same principle that applied back in high school still applies to the grown-up you today. If you want to become a powerful and top-producing salesperson, hang out with the top five salespeople. If you want to write a book, seek out best-selling authors, and you will learn how to duplicate the steps that led them to success. If your desire is to become a gourmet chef, learn everything you can from those who are already excelling in this field.

I told you it was simple.

You can still play poker, golf, and spend social time with your old friends, yet if you really want to make dramatic progress in moving forward, you need to stop asking for uninformed advice and approval and start hanging out with those who are already succeeding in the direction you wish to venture.

The truth is that we are a *direct reflection* of the five people we hang around the most, and our income is the average of those five people.

Not convinced? Look around. If everyone at the backyard barbecue this weekend is in law enforcement, more than likely, you are too. Now insert electrician, teacher, or whatever your current profession is in the place of law enforcement, and see how this rule applies to you.

Imagine how your life could improve and be positively impacted by associating with five other like-minded people—friends who think just like you, read the same books, share the same attitude, and act as a support group to assist you along your journey. How would your chances of success change? They would skyrocket!

When you hang out with five other positive role models and work together toward making your lives better and more productive, it's called a Mastermind group. On the flip side, when five other non-like-minded people get together and hold each other back for fear of stretching their own comfort zones, it's called a Land Mine group. This group explodes your dreams and desires, telling you all the reasons why you'll fail and never make it out of their own ignorance and self-imposed limitations.

So what do we do? Where do we start? Where do we find these other five like-minded people? Here's a suggestion: start your own Mastermind group! Yes, *you* can do it! Take out an ad in the local paper or on the Internet announcing that you are seeking five other commonly focused individuals who have the desire to grow personally and professionally. Be clear when discussing what your expectations are and any requirements that you have set forth when you meet potential members.

Once your group is formed, meet once a month. At each meeting, share your goals from the previous session, what you did to achieve them, and any obstacles you encountered. Ask the other members for their input, suggestions, and for any assistance you need from them. Lastly, set your new goal to be achieved by the next meeting. Continue on with the next person in the group until all members have shared and set new goals.

By sharing your goals you will become *accountable* for them. Group members also serve as a sounding board for new ideas and will help each other progress at lightning speeds.

There is one catch! If someone does not follow through, they have to *leave the group*. The purpose of the organization is for winners to win; this is not the place for negativity, excuses, or complaints. Meetings are not a time for members to dump on the others about how they cannot catch a break. A member who does this will only weaken the integrity of the group and slow down your progress. In other words, practice "tough love." By doing so you will be helping those who fail see what they are doing to themselves by sabotaging their own success as well as letting the others in the group know that what they are working toward is important and that you are working together as a supportive team.

My favorite quote of all time is, "Many receive great advice, yet few actually profit from it." Now that you know the answer to the one thing we can do right now, at this moment, to make a positive change in our lives, please allow me to ask a question of my own: what are you going to do with it?

ABOUT THE AUTHOR

Gregory Scott Reid is a master speaker, radio personality, the best-selling author of *The Millionaire Mentor* and *Positive Impact*, and the best-selling coauthor of *Wake Up, Live the Life You Love*. Visit his Web site at http://www.AlwaysGood.com.

39

The Secret Power of Giving

Warren Whitlock

You can get anything you want out of life if you see
that enough other people get what they want.
–Zig Ziglar

In the 30 years I've been studying self-improvement I've seen this principle proven time and time again. I've been most successful myself when I find out what other people want and then get it for them. When I need to find new customers, improve sales, sell an idea, or even help a family member, I have found that it's much easier to focus on serving the needs of that prospect, client, friend, or relative. I learn their core desires, then I try to make sure that those desires are filled. One way or another, my needs are always taken care of.

The Law of Reciprocity states that once you give something to someone, they are far more likely to respond favorably to you. Usually, you'll get what you need from the same relationship you build by giving. Other times, you give and don't see a quick return, but sooner or later, often in ways you'd never expect, it all balances out.

I've made *giving* my mantra, my core philosophy. On occasion I still have a bad day, worrying about *my* problems, screaming to get my own needs filled. Focusing on yourself is hard work. It is much easier to focus on others. You'll get better results and have a lot more fun.

Giving has always worked for me. The moment I switch my focus from myself, options open up, and it's easier to solve any problem or obtain any goal. It's as simple as this: *stop focusing on yourself.* We were taught to set goals, focus on achievement, develop good habits, and strive to improve ourselves to get the best results. It's true, when you're motivated, anything is possible. Striving, pushing, struggling, and working hard will get results. You will achieve your goals and likely some negative side effects. Hard work will get you somewhere . . . but where? Sometimes, you'll wind up learning that you were working on the wrong goal.

If you use this universal principle and switch your focus to getting other people what they want, you'll find that you always end up with what you want . . . with a lot less struggle. Things just work out.

Billionaires know this. More than one has taught this simple formula for success:

1. Find out what people what.
2. Get it for them.

The natural outcome of focusing on yourself will usually leave you selfish— putting yourself before others. We don't mean to be self-centered, but when we think about our own desires, that's what happens.

With the best of intentions a person of integrity tries to be fair, to establish a *quid pro quo*, where he balances what he can get with what he gives. "I'll scratch your back if you scratch mine." That's a fair, honest way to do business . . . but there is something better.

It's Better to Give Than to Receive

From the Golden Rule through all great spiritual teachings we are encouraged to *give*, to be charitable. No mention is given of *quid pro quo*. We are instructed to give service without seeking a reward, not to "give unto others if they give unto you." Give up the struggle for *quid pro quo*, and you'll unleash the power of the Law of Reciprocity. It's more than a moral or religious teaching. It's just good marketing sense.

In *Influence: The Psychology of Persuasion* Robert Caldini describes an experiment where a person is put in a room for a research experiment, not knowing that the other person (Joe) performing the same task is in fact the researcher's assistant. Joe leaves the room during a rest period and returns with two sodas, giving one to the research subject. Later, the subject is asked for a small favor: Joe needs to sell some raffle tickets. The study concluded that Joe would sell twice as many tickets to subjects that had received the coke—a 200 percent improvement when a small gift was given.

We know that samples, gifts, and promotional items increase sales, but there's a bigger point here. Would Joe have doubled his sales if he had brought in the soda and said, "I'll give you this if you buy tickets"? Probably not.

I've used the power of giving at my ZeroCostPromotions.com Web site. We give away dozens of gifts during our promotions, all provided by people who have learned the power of the Law of Reciprocity. If you have a sample of true value, you can give it away to let people learn about what you do. Thanks to the Internet, there is no cost to being generous.

Giving something with the expectation of an immediate return works, but giving a *real gift*, forgetting your needs and focusing on what other people want, will give you a much better return. The universe will not stay out of balance. You will get everything you desire and more. All you have to do is *give*, and the Law of Reciprocity will always pay.

True joy comes from love and service to others, so follow the billionaire's advice, find out what people want, and see that they get it. You'll feel great, and you'll always get back more than you give.

ABOUT THE AUTHOR

Warren Whitlock (http://MarketingResultsCoach.com) helps business owners exponentially grow their profits and income with proven direct marketing campaigns. Whitlock is a #1 best-selling author, publisher, and entrepreneur. His focus on "getting people what they want" extends to clients in retail, publishing, media, Internet, and real estate and to professionals of all kinds. Readers of this book are entitled to a *free gift* at http://MarketingResultsCoach.com/101.

40

GOAL SETTING

How to Set and Achieve Goals and Inspire Others

Matt Bacak

The ability to set and reach our goals and to inspire others is not an elusive one. You have within you everything you need to realize your goals, while at the same time inspiring others to follow your example. Even if you do not intentionally set out to inspire someone else, it happens naturally as you achieve your own success.

Think about the people who have realized their goals and have inspired you at the same time. Oprah Winfrey is an inspiration for millions, and she has earned this status primarily by following her dreams, by setting goals, and then by taking the necessary steps to achieve them. Paul Newman also inspires many people with his yearly charitable contributions amounting to millions. Every time you buy his popcorn or any other item in his product line, others are helped, and the giving inspires many. Yet, it all started after Newman had achieved his goal of becoming a successful actor.

These people can serve as our mentors, and while we may not aspire to do things on such a grand scale, in our everyday, ordinary lives we all have the power to be mentors for others while setting, planning, and reaching our own goals.

- Read. It may not follow that all readers are leaders, but certainly, all leaders are readers. Stay informed. Share what you read with others. Tell people about books that have inspired you. Share your knowledge; to give is to receive.
- Be a good communicator. Increasing your ability to communicate effectively is a critical element for inspiring others. Watch how you speak and what you say. Take the time to improve your communication skills.

- Share from your own experience. You have more to share than you realize. Recall the rich learning experiences of your life, and share your wisdom from your unique point of view. You may be the only one who can touch someone with your personal message.
- Care about others. People don't care about how much you know until they know how much you care. Take a genuine interest in people.
- Be a good example. People watch what you do more than they listen to what you say. Be someone worth imitating.
- Be inspired yourself. Look for people, ideas, situations, and knowledge that you find inspiring and motivating. Share them.

In order to inspire others, though, our primary task is to achieve our goals. Thinking but not acting on your thoughts can be habit-forming and often leads to what I call "chronic procrastination." This leads to always being late, often being behind, and being in a constant state of trying to catch up. Here are some steps to take to help you go from thinking to doing.

- Get in the habit of writing down those things you want to accomplish. Keep a pad with you wherever you go, and write down all those small goals you mentally set for yourself each day.
- Review this list at least once each week, and remove any items that no longer appeal to you.
- Choose an item from the list, and make a plan for how you will get it done. Set a timeline, and make notes about those things you will need to do to realize the goal.
- Don't be afraid to cross items off the list if they cease to appeal to you over time.
- After a few weeks you will begin to see a pattern as you get a sense of what is really worth your thought and planning. Look for any connection that might exist between the thoughts you have collected.

After some time has passed, if you are faithful to this process, you will find that you are actually spending more time doing than thinking. Over the weeks you will have disciplined yourself and taught yourself to organize your thoughts and to create a plan of action. You will be amazed at how much you are getting done. You will find that procrastination is much less of an issue for you because you will know what to do and when. You will be surprised by how productive you can be and how much time you will have for other things. Analyzing the items you cross off the list and the items for which you don't write a plan of action will help you to determine what is really important in your life. Concentrate on the things that matter, and you will become motivated to set goals, plan for them, and carry them out.

You can go from thinking to doing, and in so doing you can become a mentor and an inspiration for others. Your thoughts today can become your successes tomorrow. Take some time now, find your inspiration, set goals, find an appropriate mentor, and take *action*!

ABOUT THE AUTHOR

Matt Bacak, the Powerful Promoter and *Entrepreneur Magazine* e-Biz radio show host, became a "#1 Best Selling Author" in just a few short hours. He has helped a number of clients target his specialty, opt-in e-mail direct marketing systems. The Powerful Promoter is not only a sought-after Internet marketer but has also marketed for some of the world's top experts, whose reputations would shrivel if their followers ever found out that someone else coached them on their online marketing strategies. For more information, visit Bacak's site at http://www.powerfulpromoter.com or sign up for his Powerful Promoting Tips at http://www.promotingtips.com.

41

Transforming Dreams, Creating Goals

Diana Robinson

What is the difference between having a dream and having a goal? A dream is a goal without legs. It is a wonderful thing to have and can be the guiding passion of your life, but unless you give it the legs to move, getting there is going to be very much a matter of luck.

To transform a dream into a reachable goal, clarify it, provide the details, and make it so clear that you can see it, feel it, and know what you will feel like when you get there. This works for you in many ways.

- It clarifies what you want to the point that you will always be attuned to anything that is relevant. Opportunities will not pass you by unnoticed.
- It shows you what you need to do to get there, step by action step.
- It makes false detours and dead ends less likely to distract you.
- Perhaps the images you carry in your mind and heart will echo out to the universe for manifestation.

The clearer and more vivid the image, the more likely are all of these things to happen. As an illustration, I will use a dream someone might have regarding a career, but the principle remains the same, whatever the nature of your dream.

Let's suppose that you yearn to work outdoors and close to nature. Someone asks you to tell them more, but you can't. You don't know. All you know is that you want to work outdoors and close to nature. This is a dream. Why is it not a goal? Because it is not specific. That description could fit many occupations, including park ranger, beach bum, safari tour guide, farmer, landscape gardener, migrant worker, beekeeper, or many more. There is a saying, "Be careful what you pray for because you will surely get it, but not necessarily in the form and at the time that you expected." This applies particularly when your thoughts are not specific. Imagine putting out a prayer and a wish to the universe that you find a job that involves being in the outdoors and close to nature and having your prayer answered by falling into a job as a beekeeper—when you are truly terrified of insects!

This is not bad luck, it is bad management—bad management of your own desires and intentions. Both your own unconscious and the universe need clear direction before they can begin to manifest a path, let alone get results. If you are to harness your own energy and that of the universe so as to bring your dream into reality, you need first to create it in imagination.

Okay, let's start again. You want a job working in the outdoors and close to nature. Buy yourself one of the many books on the subject of career choice that will help you to *clarify*. Ask yourself those annoying questions that any career counselor would ask you. What sort of work do you want to be doing? Do you like people? Do you like animals? What kinds of animals? Do you enjoy structure or freedom?

For every image that comes to you, follow it, ask yourself how it fits, how you will work with it, and what comes next until your dream is as vivid and enthralling as a blockbuster movie. Know in your heart that this is what you want to be doing with your life, that it is a job you will enjoy so much that you'd love to do it even if you didn't have to earn a living. Then, put *that* image out there for manifestation. This time, there will be no mistakes.

When I say to put it out there for manifestation, I am not saying that you then sit back and wait. One of my mother's sayings is, "Pray as if it all depends on God, and then work as if it all depends on you." This is good advice, but now, with your mental picture in place, you have the guidance of a vivid image toward which to work.

What you *don't* need to put out to the universe is exactly how this manifestation has to happen. If you do, then you are limiting the way in which you and your goal can come together. In truth, there are more paths to your goal than you can imagine. Whatever it is that you seek, it may be manifested in ways beyond your wildest dreams.

ABOUT THE AUTHOR

Diana Robinson, PhD, is a life coach, a writer, and a college professor. Originally from England, she now lives in Rochester, New York, and has an international coaching practice. She may be reached at diana@ChoiceCoach.com or visited on the Web at http://ChoiceCoach.com.

42

GUILT

Break the Chains by Zapping the Guilt

Lori Radun

My first conscious and vivid encounter with guilt was when I was about 13 years old. It was the day of my parents' official divorce. We were in the courthouse and, because of my age, I was assigned my own attorney. I had no idea why I had an attorney or even what was going on. My attorney was there for one reason only—to ask me which parent I wanted to live with. I had no idea I was going to be asked this question and had little time to think about my answer. I went with my gut and chose my father. I thought that was the best choice for me at the time. After the divorce proceedings my mother told me that I had humiliated her in front of everyone.

Now that I am a mother, I understand how hurt she must have felt. However, as a child, I just remember feeling that I had done something horribly wrong. I was overwhelmed with guilt. What I have learned is that the cycle of guilt starts early in life and, if not broken, will continue to affect your life.

The chains of guilt, like many negative emotions, take a toll on our physical, emotional, spiritual, and relational health. The physical manifestations of guilt include headaches, stomach disorders, lethargy, and even exhaustion. Emotionally, guilt may lead to depression and anger, causing us to lash out inappropriately. Guilt has a tendency to make us think we are inadequate in some way, impairing our self-esteem. This can affect every aspect of our lives. A by-product of guilt may be self-pity, which, in turn, can lead to a lack of motivation; we feel powerless to change our lives.

Unresolved guilt impacts relationships in many ways. We may feel irritable or angry. We may find it hard to enjoy our lives, which may make it difficult for others to enjoy us. When we don't feel good about ourselves, we feel emotionally sensitive. This sensitivity can lead to a distorted perspective and cause harmful emotional reactions. Extreme guilt may even cause a withdrawal from loved ones, resulting in unmet needs and strained relationships. The spiritual repercussions of guilt can be an alienation from God, robbing us of the joy we deserve to feel in life. Guilt fills us with negative feelings and thoughts; it counteracts and destroys feelings of happiness. In order to move forward and enjoy life, we must release guilt and break the patterns that bind us to the cycle.

In order to eliminate guilty feelings, it is important to understand guilt. We have been taught to feel guilt when we do something "wrong." Herein lies the problem: wrong by whose standards? Everyone seems more than ready to judge us: our friends, family, spouse, the experts, society. Many times, we pass judgment on ourselves, but who is "right"? There are moral, ethical, and legal standards that most people agree should be obeyed. However, after those standards are met, each of us must decide how to determine right from wrong in our lives. Ultimately, each of us determines what guidelines we choose to live by.

Guilt comes when we veer from the rules we have chosen to follow. When we believe we have disobeyed those rules, guilt becomes the signal for us to redirect our behavior. Guilt should be no more than that. Guilt does not determine one's self-worth. "Valid guilt" should only be used to evaluate actions and make decisions on future behavior.

To illustrate, each person must evaluate whether a rule is valid and whether breaking the rule should result in guilt. When a mother decides to breast-feed her child until the age of three, she may feel the disapproval of people who disagree with that behavior. However, if she believes her decision is right for her and for her child, she must resist feeling guilty about her decision.

In summary, valid guilt comes when we behave in a way that does not support a rule or value that we fully embrace. Breaking rules we do not value or embrace may result in invalid guilt as we allow ourselves to be pressured by others in society. The true challenge is to understand our guilt and determine whether it is, indeed, valid.

All of us deserve to live free of guilty feelings. To do this, we must first recognize and challenge feelings that trigger guilt. We must then sort out the triggers that come from breaking rules we are invested in personally from those that have been imposed upon us by others. To do this, we must truly understand and honor those things that are important to us, and we must be willing to stop the unhealthy patterns that allow others to impose guilt upon us.

Following are some tips that may help break the chains and zap the guilt.

- If the guilt is valid, pray and ask for forgiveness.
- If the guilt is valid, apologize to any injured party.
- If the guilt is valid, forgive yourself.
- If the guilt is valid, take steps to change your behavior.
- If the guilt is invalid, let it go immediately.
- Tell yourself that it's okay to make mistakes.
- Write your guilty feelings down on paper, and burn the paper.
- Journal your feelings until you have released the guilt.
- Talk to a trusted friend about your feelings.
- Accept your limitations as real and okay.
- Believe that you are worthy and lovable.
- Trust yourself.
- Ask God for help.
- Give yourself permission to say no.
- Weigh outside opinions lightly.
- Acknowledge and celebrate your gifts.
- Stop justifying your behavior.
- Stop apologizing when you haven't done anything wrong.
- Take responsibility for your behavior only.
- Walk away or stand up to people who instill guilt.

By using these tips you will be better able to analyze your guilt and decide if the guilt is valid or invalid and will be able to take steps to conquer your guilt in the long term.

ABOUT THE AUTHOR

Lori Radun, CEC, is a certified life coach and founder of True to You Life Coaching. She is also the mother of two boys. Lori's coaching practice is centered on mothers and is focused on helping them to live fulfilling lives while they raise their children to be happy, healthy, and well-adjusted adults. Lori does this through speaking engagements, personal coaching, and other coaching products. More about Lori, her free newsletter, and the special report, "155 Things Moms Can Do to Raise Great Children," are available on her Web site at http://www.true2youlifecoaching.com.

43

HABITS

Positive Habits: The Key to Improving Your Life

Dan Robey

Did you know that habits are incredibly powerful tools for personal growth and success?

Think about the habits you have now and how they affect virtually every aspect of your life. Your weight and health are determined by your eating habits. Your relationships with people are determined by your social habits. Your success at work is determined by your work habits. You even have buying habits—just take a look around your house, and you will quickly see them. Our character, health, and virtually every aspect of our lives are indeed determined by our habits.

If you ask 10 people on the street what the word habit means, nine will tell you that a habit is a negative action that people do over and over again. Bad habits get all the press. Let's look at the results of just one bad habit: smoking. Every year, over 400,000 people lose their lives to smoking-related illnesses in the United States. Imagine, then, the negative power that exists in just that one bad habit. It is staggering.

Now, I want you think about an even greater power, a power that can bring you success, health, and happiness, a power for positive, permanent, and automatic personal growth: the power of positive habits. Let's look a little closer at the meaning of the word "habit," according to *Random House Dictionary*:

> An acquired behavior pattern regularly followed until
> it has become almost involuntary.

Let me ask you a question: when is the last time you sat down and said to yourself, "Today, I am going to add a new habit to my life?" You have probably never said those words. As you read this article, you will see how easy it is to add positive habits to your life and the great power they have to improve it. Think about the words "almost involuntary." This means that the habit is so powerful in your mind that it is almost unstoppable! With respect to bad habits like smoking, procrastination, and overeating, this is very bad. But with positive habits, this is very, very good.

Habits are Knowledge in Action

All of your habits are knowledge in action. You are probably saying, "That's crazy. When I smoke a cigarette, it's just because I want to." Look a little closer. You will see that you smoked the cigarette because you had the knowledge that it would make you feel more calm. The key to improving your life is to acquire new knowledge that can be actionized into new positive habits.

What is a positive habit? A positive habit is simply a habit that produces positive benefits, actions, and attitudes that you want to acquire and make a part of your life. Why is there such great power in positive habits to effect change? Because habits, by their very nature, are automatic. After a period of time they can become permanent.

How do we go about adding new positive habits to our lives? It's really quite easy. You simply begin repeating an action, attitude, or thought process every day for at least 21 days. Research has shown that an action that is repeated for a minimum of 21 days is likely to become a permanent habit. Remember that positive habits have positive benefits, and you will reap those benefits for as long as you maintain that habit. So, now that we know what positive habits are and how to acquire them, let's look at some simple positive habits that will help you to improve your life right now!

Keep a Daily Journal

Keeping a daily journal is an extremely powerful, positive habit that will allow you to quickly track your daily progress toward reaching important goals in your life. It is amazing how quickly we forget things. If I asked you to describe detailed information about your health and activities from last Tuesday, chances are that you would be hard pressed to remember much. Can you remember what you ate? How many hours of sleep did you get? How much did you weigh on that day?

Why is a daily journal so important? Here are just a few of the benefits the positive habit of keeping a daily journal will provide:

- It reminds you of your goals and the actions you are taking toward them every day.
- It allows you to factually track your progress in reaching your goals.
- It provides detailed information such as dietary changes, calorie reductions, fat reduction, and so on.
- It helps build your self-esteem because you are able to see your progress as you get closer to your goals.
- It helps to paint the picture every day of who you are becoming.
- You can learn from your failures and turn them into opportunities if you can look back and see how you handled them.

To create an effective daily journal, keep a simple, short log of your daily activities, either on a notepad or using a word processing program on your computer. Each day, make short entries into your log: list such things as your attitude, emotions, diet, weight, goals, and responses to situations and conditions in your life. For example, if having a healthy heart is one of your goals, you will want to keep track of your cholesterol levels, your blood pressure, your diet, and your weight. More than likely, you can complete writing down the information in your daily log in one minute or less. Yet, in that one minute you created an important snapshot of data in your life. You see where you have been and how quickly you are moving toward your goals, and you can estimate when you will reach your goals. You now have important historical data that you can refer to as time goes by to help you track your progress.

The 4-D Habit

Another positive habit you can acquire that will make you instantly more productive is the 4-D habit. The 4-D habit increases your productivity by helping you prioritize daily tasks and get more done in a shorter period of time.

Each day, we are faced with new tasks that must be acted upon. Your boss calls you and asks you to prepare a sales report; your child calls and asks you to help with homework. There is a very simple formula to help you prevent work overload. Every time you are faced with a new task to perform, apply the four Ds, as listed below. You will find that your workload will be reduced as you apply this screening and decision making tool to each task. Decide on the most appropriate choice, and take action.

- Do It Now: take immediate action, do the task right away, and don't procrastinate.
- Dump It Now: make a quick decision, and dump the task.
- Delegate It: give the task to someone else. Your time is valuable; make it a habit to work on tasks that you do best, and delegate the tasks that can be performed by someone else.
- Defer the Task: make an immediate decision to postpone the task to a later time. Make sure to schedule a time to complete it.

Remember, it only takes 21 days to acquire a new positive habit that can dramatically improve your life!

ABOUT THE AUTHOR

Dan Robey is the author of the best-selling book *The Power of Positive Habits*, which is published in 22 countries worldwide. This article is an excerpt from the book. To learn more about how positive habits can change your life and to sign up for a free 21-day e-course on positive habits, visit http://www.thepowerofpositivehabits.com.

44

Yes, Virginia, There Is a Secret to Happiness

David Leonhardt

Is there a secret to happiness? You probably are expecting me to say that no, there is no secret. While it is true that there are many factors that affect our happiness, I believe that there is one secret that determines whether those factors will work for you, and that is the secret to happiness.

But first, a few words of background. In 2001 I published a book concerning the nine habits toward achieving maximum happiness. I did all the things authors do, right up to getting myself some media interviews. Being an old hand at media relations, you would think that I would have been superbly prepared for the question that almost every journalist would ask me: "So, which of the nine habits is most important?"

What?! Which one is most important? Why, they are all important, of course. That's why I wrote about them all. I was obviously too close to the forest to see the trees, or, in this case, the tree.

After being asked this question a few times I was forced to think, and think hard. Out of nowhere, I had an "Aha!" moment that stands the test of time five years later.

One of the nine habits about which I wrote *is* more important than the others. One of my nine habits *activates* all the others. One of my habits *is* the secret to happiness.

Count Your Blessings

It sounds so simple, and so, well, almost corny, but let me give you a concrete example of how this works.

Have you ever bought a new car? Remember the pride you felt and the excitement when you made the choice? When you signed the papers? When you drove it off the lot? Do you remember that "new car smell"?

Then, something happened. Where is that pride today? Where is that excitement now? What happened to that "new car smell"?

Simple: you stopped counting your blessings. When you bought the car, it was a step up. Perhaps it was a better car, or a bigger car, or simply a car that would spend less days on the hoist. You were grateful. You were appreciative. You were counting this blessing.

It doesn't take long for a new blessing to be taken for granted, and the new car becomes just another thing in your life that you take for granted. Consider this incredible set of statistics:

- 99 percent of people in the developed world take shelter for granted.
- 99 percent of people in the developed world take breakfast for granted.
- 99 percent of people in the developed world take lunch for granted.
- 99 percent of people in the developed world take dinner for granted.
- 99 percent of people in the developed world take clothing for granted.

At the risk of sounding trite or glib, most people in the developed world take cars, televisions, computers, vacations, toasters, freedom of speech, paper clips, and thousands of other conveniences for granted. In fact, a TV remote control that requires a battery change or a Web page that takes more than five seconds to load are considered serious irritations.

Who is happier, the person grateful to be able to change those batteries and wait for that Web page, or the person grumbling about the time it takes and the inconvenience and the bother, and why can't things work better? (Why don't they make things like they used to? Why does the lineup have to be so long? Why is it so cold outside? Why do I have to go to work today?)

155

Of course, you have every right to complain anytime you choose. Nobody wants to take away your right to be unhappy, but I would love to take away your unhappiness, if *you* are willing to take action.

This is where "counting your blessings," simple and even corny, is not as easy as it sounds. Our knee-jerk reaction is to complain, to grumble, to be frustrated, to feel almost offended when things don't work out perfectly, just the way we want them to. Imagine poor God, sifting through the millions of prayers he receives daily. Despite the cornucopia of blessings we receive, I am willing to bet that he receives 10 times more "gimme" prayers than "thank you" prayers.

Counting our blessings in this day and age of entitlement is not as simple as it sounds, and it sure is not easy to do. In fact, billions of dollars of advertising conspire to reinforce the belief that whatever we have is not good enough and that we deserve better. Who is there to tell us we have enough? Who can help us feel happy with what we have?

You. Only you. Are you ready to give up your own natural knee-jerk reaction and choose to be happy?

You can have all the confidence in the world, but if you do not actively feel grateful for the fruits of your confidence, it will not bring you happiness. You can have immaculate health, but if you do not think about how wonderful that is, it will not bring you happiness. You can smile, build friendships, achieve success, win the lottery, or do whatever you desire, but if you are not saying every day, "Wow! This is wonderful. This is grand. I am the luckiest man (or woman) alive because of this," don't expect it to bring you happiness.

Yes, there is a secret to happiness. The secret is gratitude. The secret is appreciation. The secret is to count your blessings.

ABOUT THE AUTHOR

David Leonhardt, the Happy Guy, is the author of *Climb Your Stairway to Heaven: The 9 Habits of Maximum Happiness*, publishes "A Daily Dose of Happiness," an e-mail newsletter available at http://www.thehappyguy. com, and runs a ghostwriting service at http://www.seo-writer.net.

45

HEROES

10 Life and Leadership Lessons I Learned from Superman (and How They Changed My Life Forever)

Eric Taylor

For many, the actor who epitomized the character "Superman" is Christopher Reeve, and as millions know, at the height of his career he suffered a tragic accident that left him totally paralyzed, unable to care for himself or, initially, even to breathe unassisted.

With the support of his wife, Dana, Chris persevered and battled back, becoming a vigorous advocate and the public face for research that develops treatments and cures for paralysis caused by spinal cord injury and other central nervous system disorders. The foundation that now bears his name has awarded over $55 million in research grants to the world's best neuroscientists and Quality of Life grants worth over $7 million to nonprofit organizations that help improve the daily lives of people living with paralysis, particularly spinal cord injuries.

Christopher Reeve redefined courage and hope. His strength, determination, and compassion inspired the world, but what I think is the superhuman part of the story has not been fully told. There's more to this story for me and greater lessons for us all—in fact, 10 of them.

It was my distinct privilege to produce Chris's last public appearance in New Jersey, where he filled a baseball stadium. I'll never forget it—or him. He died 10 days later. He is my hero.

Chris Reeve taught me 10 lessons on that day. I know that they apply to you, and when you decide to take them to heart and act on them, they will change your life, too.

1. Empower yourself first! The only way to truly connect with another human is to connect with yourself first. Compassion, rapport, and caring all come from allowing, understanding, and knowing yourself first.

    Action Idea: Take time out of each day (even if by self-appointment) to reflect on the day, week, month, or year, evaluate the words you chose to speak and the actions you chose to take, and ask yourself the critical question, "Am I being congruent with what I truly believe and value?"

2. Refuse absolutes. There are no absolutes! Anyone who says "that will never happen" doesn't understand faith, persistence, and belief. The world was once thought to be flat; Christopher Columbus debunked that myth and created a paradigm shift for mankind. Christopher Reeve should not have survived as long as he did and accomplished as much as he did after his accident.

    Action Idea: Have you embraced false absolutes with "security thinking," believing that absolutes actually exist? Remove all self-imposed limitations and boundaries that you or someone else have placed in your mind.

3. Become a respected and feared competitor. Both are equally important. Have the respect of your peers, but be sure that they are aware that you are playing to win every time!

    Action Idea: Get close to your competitors, and let them get close to you— but only in physical proximity! Treat them with kindness and respect, but keep your eye on the prize.

4. Get moving as soon as possible. There is never time to get ready. When you set a goal, make a decision, or experience adversity, get moving on it immediately! Christopher's tragedy was something for which he could not have prepared. Chris knew that if he didn't take action immediately to find a cure and to move toward walking again, he might begin to think that death was a better alternative.

Action Idea: Decide! Once you make up your mind to achieve a desired outcome or goal, never let anything or anyone stop you.

5. You have more talent and gifts than you realize. You possess all of the resources to lead an extraordinary life. Accept the gifts, and use them to serve.
   Action Idea: Ask "what if" questions. "What if I could discover the cure for AIDS?" "What if I could run a three-minute mile?" "What if I give love first without expecting anything in return?"

6. Give yourself a chance—you are worthy. Let the people who love you, love you. Share your dreams and desires with those who can, will, and want to help you. Don't beat yourself up when you fail or create an undesirable outcome.

   Action Idea: Everything is an experience, not a test. The events that take place in our lives are not a thermometer to gauge our self-worth. The most important opinion you must possess in your life is the opinion you have of you!

7. Nothing is impossible—use your personal power, and have faith that you can overcome and achieve anything you set your mind to. The phrase "nothing is impossible" is a mind-set each of us should embrace.

   Action Idea: Faith equals persistence. If you believe you can, you can. Walt Disney said, "You will see it when you believe it."

8. Ignore your own feelings of inadequacy. There is always someone doing better than you are. What's more important is what you are doing and what your goals are. The grass always looks greener on the other side, and it is almost always a false assumption. If you honor self-promises and stick to your dreams and goals, your time will come. Beware of negative self-talk and negative thinking. The real truth is that the glass is always half full, and it is always partly sunny. These small distinctions can pay huge dividends in your life.

   Action Idea: Protect your mind and your body and what you allow to enter it; they are your most prized possessions.

9. Negativity will kill empowerment. Avoid negativity at all costs: negative people, negative news, negative thoughts, and all the things and people in your life that are dream-stealers. You are a leader. Become a leader in your life first.

    Action Idea: Just as empowerment begins with you, positivism in your world begins with you as well. Negativity drains energy, diminishes hope, blocks creativity, and steals faith and one's ability to persist. Surround yourself with everything and everyone that makes you feel good. Life is too short not to be happy.

10. Giving up is not an option. After Dana told Chris, "I still love you, you are still you," his giving up was not an option. He knew that he had only one choice and one life to leave his legacy. Quitting does last forever—quitters never win, and winners never quit. You are not automatically entitled to everything in this life, but you are entitled to become your personal best. What will your legacy be? What will you create? What is your purpose for being here?

    Action Idea: If you have yet to discover your calling, get excited! It is about to be discovered. If you know your calling, go there with passion and serve!

Those, in a nutshell, are the 10 life and leadership lessons I learned from Superman—my real-life hero, Christopher Reeve. I strive to live them every day.

There's one more quote from Chris that takes a bit of thinking to understand, but I'd like you to consider it.

> If there is no great glorious end to all this, if nothing
> we do matters, then all that matters is what we do.

Now, go forward!

ABOUT THE AUTHOR

The mission of Eric Taylor's Empowerment Group is to enrich the lives of its clients and prospects by providing extraordinary personal and professional development seminars, business training, resources, and relationship-building opportunities. Eric Taylor, known as "Mr. Energy," is frequently called upon by some of the most respected companies in the country for motivational speaking, training, and consulting. He walks his talk every day, speaking to business professionals in corporations, organizations, and associations on the topics about which he is most passionate—sales, leadership, presentation skills, and personal development. For more information, visit http://www.empowermentgroup.com.

46

Life with the Greatest of Ease

Kristy Iris

You can recreate your life through making simple physical changes in your home or office that can enhance your execution in expanding your personal and business purpose. You can *literally live in your intentions.* Look around you. What do you see, and more importantly, what is it saying to you? Is it positive or negative? Let's explore a few ways that you can empower your surroundings to help you out.

Focal Points

The first thing you see when you enter a room sets the intention for that room and its purpose. It is usually the wall opposite the door. Stand in the doorway. Notice the first thing that catches your attention when you enter the room. This is your focal point—is it a positive image or message? Is it in alignment with your dreams, values, and passions and the specific use of the room? For example, a master bedroom is about the couple that shares it, so make it a place to celebrate your union. Use only images of couples, or better yet, of the two of you on your wedding day and doing what you love together. There are plenty of places in other parts of the house for pictures of the family. Use your imagination! The focal point acts as the title page for the room. What is the title for each room in your home?

Flow

How does each room flow? We naturally feel better when we flow in a clockwise direction. Is your home allowing that? Are there sharp angles that are not comfortable to walk around? Are there piles that block walkways and stuff behind doors that prevents you from entering a room with ease? If there is something that just doesn't feel right, move it, or let it go. Don't struggle against any area of your environment. Those little annoyances, whether you are conscious of them or not, really do deeply affect your quality of life. Imagine how much all the little expenditures of energy over those annoyances are costing your well-being. Couldn't your energy be better spent toward what makes you happy?

Clutter

Okay. Breathe. There is hope, I promise. As a "sentimental saver," first, stop beating yourself up over having clutter and being powerless over it. This only creates more clutter—in your thoughts and emotions. Everything that you see has an association, a memory and emotion you process subconsciously and, at times, consciously. This makes clutter exhausting as there is a finite amount of space in your life—whether it be physical, temporal, or mental.

Be gentle with yourself in letting clutter go. Make this fun—don't focus on the letting go but on making room for your dreams and goals. You will find that you have room for a new hobby or business with the space that you create when you let go. You will find that your energy level increases, stress subsides, and productivity increases when you let go of the clutter that you do not need.

Commanding Position

This is such a subtle foundation of being a comfortable human being. We naturally feel empowered when we are in a commanding position, and this means simply always sitting and sleeping facing the door. For example, positioning your bed to be able to face the door is a key aspect of having a great night's sleep. I have seen many people with home offices skyrocket in their prosperity and productivity when we move their desks from facing the wall with their backs to the door, as if they work in a cubicle. We turn the desk around with the added intention that they are giving themselves a promotion to CEO. This radically alters the whole mind-set of their approach to their workspace and, in turn, their success.

Here is an exercise to try:

Stand in a room with your back to the door. Close your eyes, and observe your comfort level.

Turn around and face the door. Close your eyes, and observe how you feel. In which direction did you feel best? Facing the door, right? Can you see how this is an important element to positioning yourself, literally, for success?

Receive

Now, let it go. You've put out your intentions. Let them come to you. A little goes a long way. Your intention is far more powerful than anything you can do. In fact, this external process is more internal because if at your core you don't believe that you deserve miracles, you will block them. Influencing your surroundings to manifest your goals is paramount in achieving your success. Even if right this moment you don't think you deserve all that you dream of, I do. *I know you deserve it!*

You will find that this process becomes a great creative outlet to expressing who you are and what you love. It will open up new levels of your quality of life. As your life progresses, you will find that your home will change with you and keep cheering you on and reflecting where you are going. You will create a dynamic conversation between your inner and outer worlds.

Be open to opportunities and gifts of which you had previously never thought. Be receptive to getting exactly what you want, just not the way you imagined it, but better. Have fun with this! Let your surroundings be your call to action, your reminder to take the steps needed to live in your dreams while awake. Remember: you deserve it!

ABOUT THE AUTHOR

Kristy Iris, MFA, founder of *fizom*, a system for self-improvement meeting home improvement, offers consultations, seminars, tele-classes, home study programs, artwork, and a free Friday fiztip e-zine. She has used her Masters in Fine Art from NYU in theater design and extensive professional experience in designing "make-believe worlds" for "make-believe people," added a deep spiritual essence, and transformed that into *fizom*, helping real people create a sacred setting and script for their dreams. Kristy has been called "a fusion of the best of Oprah and Martha Stewart." Visit her to learn more at http://fizom.com.

47

You Are Your Own President

John Di Lemme

Congratulations! You are the president of your own nation, and it's called Imagination. This particular nation is the driving force behind your life and is the underlying factor of your future. You have an enormous responsibility as President of this nation. You must always focus on the future, internalize the power that you have as President, and strive to have the ultimate nation. As President, you also have the power to choose and consider. For example, you are the one that holds the votes on who is allowed to live in your nation. These people are considered your mastermind team and will determine if your nation succeeds or fails.

You must create and begin to maximize your mastermind team. This team will empower you to build an unreal Imagination and cause others to wonder how and why you are achieving such an awesome level of success. As President, you will inspire others to create phenomenal imaginations of their own. The world needs many people that are proud of their own imaginations!

Each of us has the ability to imagine such powerful dreams for our future, which can ultimately change the destinies of millions of people. Let's think about a few people that had unreal imaginations: Henry Ford imagined an eight-cylinder car and then achieved it. The Wright Brothers imagined that men could fly and then discovered a way to make that possible. John F. Kennedy said that we would have a man on the moon and then realized that dream. Ask yourself, "Where did these people first dream of those achievements?" The answer is that they did their dreaming in their own nation called Imagination.

You need to take some personal time to evaluate how you are handling your nation. Are you proud of what you are imagining you can be or what you can do?

165

If you answer that question truthfully, you will either be enthused or disillusioned. You truly need to reexamine your nation. I suggest that you brainstorm, which means to take some time for yourself and write down all of your dreams that you've never written down before. Write down 25 dreams, and then put them away for two days so that they can sink in a little. When you go back and reread them, your inner spirit will direct you to the dream that you need to focus on the most, and you can begin to design that dream with your own imagination. Each of us is empowered to create wealth for ourselves in every aspect of life—spiritually, physically, and financially—and it all starts with a simple dream.

I challenge you to utilize your God-given imagination to visualize your ultimate dream, and then you will become empowered to run your nation in the most productive means possible. This alone will entirely change your life because you will have a responsibility as President of a nation—your very own Imagination.

Find Your Why and Fly!

ABOUT THE AUTHOR

John Di Lemme, a former clinically diagnosed stutterer and now the world's leading motivational expert, shocks millions globally by exposing the truth for which they've been searching in order to achieve monumental life success through his award-winning live seminars, power-packed training programs, live tele-classes, motivational club, and weekly e-zine. Take action now and join thousands of others that have used John's proven methods to live their lives to the maximum! Visit http://www.FindYourWhy.com, and discover how you can finally create monumental success in your life today.

48

What Makes You Different?

Frank Traditi

What makes you different? It's a good bet you've been asked this question before.

Prospects, hiring managers, and people with influence frequently ask this question when making a buying or hiring decision. Each day, we are bombarded with opportunities, advertisements, messages, and people trying to sell us something or to convince us to hire them. A hiring manager scans through hundreds of résumés, only to conclude that nobody stands out in the crowd. A decision maker sits through four presentations and can't decide which service is the best fit. After a while, everything looks and sounds the same.

The average person is exposed to *over 2000 impressions* a day. During the last hour, how many of those impressions do you remember? In the last day? In the last week? Are there certain messages that stand out from the thousands of impressions, or do they all start to look and sound the same?

Companies spend tens of millions delivering these messages, some subtle and some not so subtle, every day of the week. A few of these communication methods actually work, but most don't. What did you hear today that made you sit up and take notice? Most likely, you felt like that message was directed at you personally. Something was different in the presentation of the message that spoke to your needs, problems, ideas, challenges, and personal situation. Now, you want to learn more.

Let's make this personal for you. What makes *you* different compared to the thousands of people with similar backgrounds, skills, and experience who are delivering the same message? You don't have the budget to spend millions on delivering your message like big companies do, but you can stand out from the crowd. What are you communicating to people to get them to stand up and listen? Regardless of your profession, you are tested every day on your communication skills. Whether you are in an interview, sales presentation, or manager conference or are even just dealing with day-to-day issues, people will pay attention to you because you said something different.

Let's take a look at three key reasons why people will want to sit up and take notice of you. These three reasons can work for you in any setting—an interview, a sales call, a meeting with your manager, or just plain small talk with your colleagues.

1. **You offer ideas to solve a problem.** We all have problems to solve, whether it's making the perfect pancake or creating the perfect Web site. The message your audience hears loud and clear when you communicate with them says, "That will solve my problem." Businesses large and small manage a daily set of challenges. It's a good day if at the end, more problems got solved than didn't. There's no substitute for solving people's problems. Any time you hear someone describing his problems, start thinking of solutions. Comments like "that's a good idea" or "I hadn't thought of that" indicate that you've made a special connection.

2. **You fit in.** While your experience, education, and other qualifications play a significant role, the hiring decision is still very much based on the personal opinion of the decision maker. He will decide whether or not to hire you based not only on your qualifications, but on how well your personality fits in at his company. Often, his instinct decides who will get the job or project. You don't have to go through a personality transplant in order to deliver the message that you fit in. A sincere, professional conversational style is a great place to start: smile, look your interviewer or contact in the eye, and engage in a two-way conversation; listen carefully, respond thoughtfully, and don't digress into personal details.

3. **You bring value to the relationship.** Think of the people in your life who you respect most and who stand out from the rest of the crowd. What happens when you engage in conversation with them? Chances are that you usually hear something of value. They go out of their way to listen and to understand your situation and offer a kind word, praise, empathy, a helpful tip, a great idea, or maybe just a shoulder to lean on. Conversely, think of

people you know that drain your energy just by being in their presence. Most everything they say has a negative tone, and you have that heavy feeling after you've walked away from them. When you assess that conversation, you find that there was no value whatsoever for either of you. Putting all this into a business relationship, potential hiring managers can easily connect with someone who brings value and recognize those who don't. In an interview, demonstrate your experience and knowledge as significant value to the team, and you will get the attention of the person across the desk.

Listen to yourself carefully now as you go back out into the crowded world. Put your words and actions to the test. Ask yourself if you're thinking of ways to solve people's problems. Ask yourself if you're engaged in a professional and personable conversation that connects with your audience and if you bring value to every relationship. Don't stop asking until you can honestly answer yes to each question.

Here's to being that one in a million.

ABOUT THE AUTHOR

Frank Traditi is the coauthor of *Get Hired NOW!: A 28-Day Program for Landing the Job You Want*, a motivational speaker, an executive career coach, and a small business marketing specialist. Frank has more than 20 years of experience in management, sales, and marketing for Fortune 500 companies. His expertise is helping talented people create an extraordinary career and teaching the one thing we never learned in school: how to market yourself. Learn more about Frank at http://www.coachfrank.com or http://www.gethirednow.com.

49

INDIVIDUALITY

Just Like Chicken

Laura Lallone

Give up.

Yes, give up trying to be something streamlined, tucked, professional, more of something, less of something. It's over. It's done. It's so last year.

Be yourself. All of yourself. The world needs more of *you*.

Under the layers we all speak different languages. We see, feel, and experience different worlds, and, my goodness, we are all a bit sideways. It's a lesson to learn over and over. I learned it loud and clear last Friday night in a very unlikely place.

It was 10 o'clock, and I was doing sit-ups on a bench at the gym—not just any gym, but the original Gold's Gym in Venice, California, the celebrity and body building Mecca made famous by the Arnold Schwarzenegger classic film *Pumping Iron*. Already weird, right?

When I rolled off the sit-up bench, I immediately saw that my sweat had made a perfect pattern, like feathers on a rooster. What the heck? My sweatshirt must have folded under me in just the right way. Amazing! It was like finding a French fry that looks like Mother Theresa at a Wendy's in Mobile, Alabama.

A pair of eyes burned through the back of my head. Why not? I was staring and smiling at an empty bench. I slowly turned to find a remarkably handsome man on a bicep machine about 10 feet away. Awestruck about the bench and a bit delirious from the week behind me, I walked over to the man and said, "I know it's strange, but . . . my sweat left a really beautiful mark on the bench." (Gong!

Bring in the hook!) The very exotic-looking man tilted his head and sort of nodded. Not knowing what to do and feeling quite ridiculous, I said, "Do you want to see it?" I pointed at the bench. He nodded, said "okay," and walked over to the bench with me.

Of course, thanks to evaporation, there were no signs of my sweat miracle. Smiling and stammering, I said, "Oh . . . I . . . it disappeared. It looked like a rooster." He smiled and said, "Okay, okay . . . I don't speak English that good." (Perfect.)

Most people would have given up. Not me. I was in too deep. I said, "Like a rooster," and made a motion over my head like a rooster's feathers. He nodded and said, "Okay, okay." Then, before I could stop myself I was flapping my arms like wings and clucking like a chicken.

In response to my clucking he just repeated, "I don't know English very good."

He *really* didn't know English! I was clucking like a chicken at this man in the gym, taking him away from his bicep workout to do heaven knows what. He probably thought he was coming over to the bench to help me move it or fix it or spot me while I was doing sit-ups!

That was my cue, my closing. My work was done. I said "it's okay" about 17 times, smiled, and gathered up my belongings and backed out of the room. The man looked on, seeming very confused as he walked back to his bicep machine.

Lest you think that there *was* a miraculous sighting that day, I must tell you that I later realized that underneath my sweatshirt I had on a t-shirt with a big decal on the back—which, in reverse, looked like a rooster.

Here's the bottom line.

1. **People speak different languages.** Okay, sometimes the difference is more subtle than others. When was the last time you misinterpreted someone? How about the last time someone misinterpreted you? It happens all the time. Sometimes, you get really flustered or mad because of the way you're reading someone, only to learn later that he was stressed about getting evicted from his apartment. It had nothing to do with you.

Sometimes, it's *you* who's misunderstood.

It's easier to stay grounded and neutral if you remember that you're seeing the interaction through your own lens—*your* own experience, *your* internal makeup, using *your* personal history to create the reality. Another person's reality may be, and probably is, really different—not better or worse, just different.

What if you didn't have to change anyone or convince people that your version of the world is *more* right? What if *you* were more curious and asked questions to find out where the other person is coming from? What would happen then?

2. **Popeye said it best: "I y'am who I y'am."** And you are who you are. Yes, it's true. Among all my other qualities, sometimes I'm really "train-wreck" goofy. There, I said it.

Why is this important? Because a couple years ago, I would have tortured myself about how ridiculous I was, clucking like a chicken to a gorgeous man in an oh-so-hip LA hot spot. This time, I just laughed and laughed the whole way home. The interaction was a real marker for me, evidence that I've grown to accept and appreciate more of myself and to accept that I'm human.

What are your markers? How have you grown? Think back 1, 2, 5, or even 10 years. How are you different now? How are you being more yourself?

Now, there *is* another perspective to consider. What was the man in the gym thinking? Well, he may have been thinking that I was out of my mind. That's always a possibility. He may have been thinking that he *really* should learn better English. But my guess is that he was thinking that it was refreshing to see someone having a good time, letting down her guard, and being herself in a place that is usually so slick and image-conscious.

At the very least, he has a great story to share over dinner. That is, of course, a chicken dinner. (Gong.)

Have fun. Be yourself. It makes all the difference.

ABOUT THE AUTHOR

Laura Lallone is a professional coach, speaker, and writer based in Southern California. She offers insight with empathy and humor, opening up new perspectives and possibilities to an international following. Strikingly straightforward and very compassionate, she is talented at "listening between the lines" and helping women and men connect with each other to achieve their aspirations more quickly and thoroughly. With a "think fast" background as VP of Employee Communications at one of the nation's fastest-growing brokerage firms, Laura has a deep understanding of what makes people tick and how to get "stuff" done. Visit Laura at http://www.lauralallone.com.

50

INNER SERENITY

A Really Great Place to Live

Carolyn Porter

Much has been said about ways to improve your life; you're reading some in this book. Perhaps you've already tried different approaches, some that helped and others that didn't. One thing that is irrevocably true is this: anything utilized to improve your life must have its origin in love because love is all there is! I have discovered one empowering tool that is required for life to flow in perfect harmony, no matter what happens in your external realm. It can literally transform your life into one of abundance and continuous bliss because it resides in the arms of love, a really great place to live.

For many decades I lived my life through the eyes of lack, believing there was never enough: not enough money, love, happiness, time, energy, and so forth. Lack is simply a by-product of fear (the opposite of love), although I didn't realize it then. I noticed that most individuals who crossed my path lived through the same mind-set, and there seemed to be so much negativity in everyone's life, which was downright depressing. However, like most people, I fell into the trap of pushing and driving myself to achieve and produce more so that I could have what I thought I lacked. That process tore down my health and created an insatiable thirst for what I didn't have, leaving me miserably unhappy.

My life journey continued in the search for the missing things in my life, yet I wondered if I'd ever find them. I learned how to make more money, but somehow, it was never enough. I tried for years to "fix" my marriage, but that didn't work either. I changed careers, introduced healthy alternatives, researched and studied many new ideas, and decided to be a more loving person. I introduced time management and added a "things to do list" to my daily routine in the attempt to reduce stress and accomplish more, but no matter what I did to enhance my life, that inner despair that told me something was lacking still existed. These things did help in external ways to improve my life, but I later learned that the problem was with my internal self.

One day, I began to see a faint glimmer of light as teachers appeared because I, the student, was now ready. New ways of thinking were introduced that began a tremendous shift in my very foundation. An expansive metamorphosis took place, and my life opened up in ways that were mind-boggling. I learned that happiness came from within me and wasn't anybody else's job to create but mine. I discovered my true life purpose and began to live it. My health improved, and I made changes that supported me rather than someone else. Yet, negativity remained in my life because I knew deep inside that something was still missing.

Several years later, the awareness of what was missing in my life was revealed to me through meditation, prayer, and study, and it was so simple that it surprised me. One feeling, once taken deep within so that it becomes part of you, will literally change everything in your life so that your entire perception of life shifts for the better. What is this feeling? Gratitude. I mean gratitude for everything, not just the good things but also the things that appear as challenges. Everything in your life is a gift, a truly marvelous gift that helps you grow. When you actually see life through the eyes of gratitude, it raises you up beyond what was envisioned before in truly miraculous ways.

Gratitude is an expression of love and is a top-of-the-list tool for empowerment. In fact, without the comprehension and acceptance of gratitude it is impossible to be empowered. The universe provides unlimited abundance, but if you don't believe this, you actually push it away. Beginning with gratitude for all you presently have and are opens the channels of love to embrace you. This isn't merely the use of the words; it literally means pulling the feeling of gratitude inside so that your life begins and ends through gratitude. In this place it doesn't matter what appears in life because you can gratefully accept it and trust the universe to provide the resolution. Gratitude means that there is always enough, and when your truth is gratitude in all things, it emanates outward to all who are in your presence because you *feel* it within you.

How does living through gratitude affect your life? It allows you total freedom to be love. In this place you are already okay, a masterpiece from the designer of the universe, which makes you magnificent right now, just as you are. The beauty of living in gratitude is that as you focus in this energy, you continually expand it to create more of the same. Thoughts are pure energy, and whatever is your focus shows up in your life. As you express your thoughts and feelings from the higher elements of love, only more of the same comes back to you. Gratitude expresses through the essence of love. As Plato once said, "A grateful mind is a great mind that eventually attracts great things."

My truth says that in order to improve your life on all levels, simply develop the attitude of gratitude, but go a little deeper, and develop an *aptitude* for gratitude. It then becomes more than just a thought or behavior and actually becomes who you are. Amazing miracles will appear in your life that will continuously keep you in awe of the power available to you when you live through gratitude. While many things can assist you on your path, gratitude is of God as an expression of love, your true essence.

Begin and end each day by thanking your Creator for everything: your life, home, material possessions, all relationships, internal gifts, capabilities, your body, and so on. Write them down, speak them, think them, live them. Even if there isn't enough money to pay your bills at the moment, be thankful for the amount you have to pay the ones you can, then be openly thankful to the universe for bringing you the rest you need *even though it isn't seen yet*. When a challenge shows up, say "thank you," and know that there is a gift in it. Also, know that you are greater than the challenge, and expect the universe to resolve the situation. Surrender the challenge, and go about your life. *It will be resolved effortlessly* because you are in a space of love when you are grateful for it and know the answer is on the way. Living in the state of gratitude generates continuous abundance and bliss—no stress, no worries, no lack, no fear—and a deep internal knowing that all is in divine order. Try it out, and I guarantee that you'll like living there! One more benefit—you'll smile a lot!

ABOUT THE AUTHOR

Carolyn Porter, DDiv, is an inspirational speaker, trainer, wholeness coach, energy facilitator, and an author of multiple books, audios, and e-books as well as coowner of a health store. For more than two decades Carolyn has helped individuals improve their lives in many ways. Her passion is to empower individuals with their own magnificence and to know that the power to create their lives as they desire is within them. We invite you to visit www.drcarolynporter.com for more about Carolyn.

51

INSTANT LEARNING STRATEGIES ®

Instant Learning Strategies®: The Top Five Secrets You Need to Learn Anything *Fast*

Pat Wyman

In your ever-busy, "on demand" life, have you ever wondered how it would feel to be able to learn twice as much in half the time? Life changes in an instant, so here is a proven, Instant Learning® formula that will give you the learning edge you need.

Whether you are a CEO, an employee in job training, a student, or a parent, did you know that a baby learning to walk uses the same techniques that are key to your Instant Learning® ability? The baby practices but really learns to walk in an "instant" once he unlocks the code I share in my Instant Learning® seminars—"learning is not about being smart; it's about strategy!"

Curious? Read on, put your eyebrows on relax, and you will remember everything you read in this chapter. Here are five proven strategies that neuroscientists, psychologists, and learning experts say anyone can use to confidently learn anything new. I call this Instant Learning® formula BBAPI.

1. **Belief.** You already believe that you can learn in an instant because you've been doing it your whole life. When you were younger, you learned thousands of new things, firm in the belief that you would succeed. You simply tried new strategies until you mastered the task. As Henry Ford said, "If you think you can do a thing, or think you can't do a thing, you're right."

Right now, give yourself permission to believe that you can learn anything based solely on the information you receive from your actions. Adjust your learning strategies as you read this chapter, and do things differently until you get the result you want. Remember, your belief and strategies together are so strong that they inspire the highest vision of what is possible.

2. **Body.** Your body movements are a reflection of what is going on in your brain. If you lie on the couch in a dimly lit room and say self-defeating things to yourself while deciding that you're going to learn something new, you will simply end up on the couch. This is information that you're not highly motivated to learn anything new.

Do this: change your body position as if you are perfectly successful and record how you feel. When you are ready to learn something new, put yourself into your "success position." Next, do what experts do with their bodies: I call it "Brain Smart, Body Smart™." Make sure you get any "body or brain" roadblocks to learning out of the way. Have your eyes checked by a developmental optometrist to make sure that you see the printed page the same way others do; make sure you are hearing properly; exercise, love your body enough to put nourishing foods into it, and explore why supplements like omega 3s, which are proven to help you think faster and remember longer, are the very best strategies to enhance your body and brain.

3. **Association.** Have you ever met someone and liked them right away, even though you did not actually know the person? The reason is called association, which neuroscientists say is created from connections in your brain that remind you of someone else you already know and like.

To make learning faster, connect it with something you already know because your brain craves patterns. To cement the learning, add more connections like humor, uniqueness, emotion, and visual, auditory, and tactile modalities. Psychologists report that you can learn something new the very first time, if the associations you make along with it are strong enough. When I teach medical students how to recall complicated medical terms, we use humorous letters, pictures, and words connected with things they already know. Their learning is stress-free and virtually "instant"!

4. **Pictures**. Have you ever read sections of a book and then forgot what you just read? After you see a movie, do you notice that it seems easier to remember the pictures?

Picture recall has much more meaning across many parts of the brain, so the saying "one picture is worth a thousand words" really is true. Whenever you are reading something new, put your body into success position and become a filmmaker in your mind. Read something, look up, and make a movie from the words. Then, add your own, personalized version of something familiar in your picture. Connect the two images, and when you look up at your images again, you'll easily be able to learn and remember whatever you want. This is called the eye-brain connection.

5.   **Match Input, Storage, and Output.** If you wanted to find out whether a baseball player had the skills to make the team, would you give the person a written test? Sounds silly, but the mismatch between learning and testing styles is a major reason people wonder about whether they can learn new things.

One of the best-kept learning secrets that you'll never hear in school is how to match learning styles with testing styles for effortless learning. Discover your preferred learning style (visual, auditory, or tactile), and ask yourself what style will be used to test your knowledge. Match your learning style (input), memory style (storage), and testing style (output), and learning becomes a breeze.

Remember, *learning is not about being smart*. It is only about strategy, and once you know the strategies, you can choose to learn anything at any time. Learning how to learn is your key to Instant Learning® for a lifetime of learning success.

ABOUT THE AUTHOR

Pat Wyman is known as America's Most Trusted Learning Expert. She is a best-selling author, international consultant, and corporate spokesperson. She conducts seminars on her Instant Learning® strategies for corporations, schools, parents, teachers, and medical schools. Her work has been featured in such publications as *Family Circle Magazine*, *Woman's World*, and *Nickelodeon Family Magazine*. Wyman is also an Instructor of Continuing Education at California State University, East Bay, a regular media guest on radio and TV, Director of the nonprofit organization I Read I Succeed, and founder of the award-winning Web site http://www.HowToLearn.com.

52

INTEGRITY

Becoming a Person of Integrity

Brian Tracy

Integrity is a value, like persistence, courage, and industriousness. Even more than that, it is the value that guarantees all the other values. You are a good person to the degree to which you live your life consistently with the highest values that you espouse. Integrity is the quality that locks in your values and causes you to live consistently with them.

Integrity is the foundation of character, and character development is one of the most important activities you can engage in. Working on your character means disciplining yourself to do more and more of those things that a thoroughly honest person would do, under all circumstances.

To be impeccably honest with others, you must first be impeccably honest with yourself. You must be true to yourself. You must be true to the very best that is in you, to the very best that you know. Only a person who is living consistently with his highest values and virtues is really living a life of integrity, and when you commit to living this kind of life, you will find yourself continually raising your own standards, continually refining your definition of integrity and honesty.

You can tell how high your level of integrity is by simply looking at the things you do in your day-to-day life. You can look at your reactions and responses to the inevitable ups and downs of life. You can observe the behaviors you typically engage in, and you will then know the person you are.

The external manifestation of high integrity is high-quality work. A person who is totally honest with himself will be someone who does, or strives to do, excellent work on every occasion. The totally honest person recognizes, sometimes unconsciously, that everything he does is a statement about who he really is as a person.

When you start a little earlier, work a little harder, stay a little later, and concentrate on every detail, you are practicing integrity in your work. And whether you know it or not, your true level of integrity is apparent and obvious to everyone around you.

Perhaps the most important rule you will ever learn is that your life only becomes better when you become better.

All of life is lived from the inside out. At the very core of your personality lie your values about yourself and life in general. Your values determine the kind of person you really are, what you believe has defined your character and your personality. It is what you stand for, and what you won't stand for, that tells you and the world the kind of person you have become.

Ask yourself this question: what are your five most important values in life? Your answer will reveal an enormous amount about you. What would you pay for, sacrifice for, suffer for, and even die for? What would you stand up for or refuse to lie down for? What are the values that you hold most dear? Think these questions through carefully and, when you get a chance, write down your answers. Here's another way of asking that question: what men and women, living or dead, do you most admire? Once you pick three or four men or women, the next question is, why do you admire them? What values, qualities, or virtues do they have that you respect and look up to? Can you articulate those qualities? What is a quality possessed by human beings in general that you most respect? This is the starting point for determining your values. The answers to these questions form the foundation of your character and your personality.

Once you have determined your five major values, you should now organize them in order of importance. What is your first, most important value? What is your second value? What is your third value? And so on. Ranking your values is one of the very best and fastest ways to define your character.

Remember, a higher-order value will always take precedence over a lower-order value. Whenever you are forced to choose between acting on one value or another, you always choose the value that is the highest on your own personal hierarchy.

Who you are, in your heart, is evidenced by what you do on a day-to-day basis, especially when you are pushed into a position where you have to make a choice between two values or alternatives. Ralph Waldo Emerson said, "Guard your integrity as a sacred thing." In study after study the quality of integrity, or a person's adherence to values, ranks as the number one quality sought in every field. When it comes to determining with whom they will do business, customers rank the honesty of a salesperson as the most important single quality. Even if they feel that a salesperson's product, quality, and price is superior, customers will not buy from that salesperson if they feel that he or she is lacking in honesty and character.

Likewise, integrity is the number one quality of leadership. Integrity in leadership is expressed in terms of constancy and consistency. It is manifested in an absolute devotion to keeping one's word. The glue that holds all relationships together—including the relationship between the leader and the led—is trust, and trust is based on integrity.

Integrity is so important that functioning in our society would be impossible without it. We could not make even a simple purchase without a high level of confidence that the price was honest and that the change was correct. The most successful individuals and companies in America are those with reputations of high integrity among everyone they deal with. This level of integrity builds the confidence that others have in them and enables them to do more business than their competitors, whose ethics may be a little shaky. Earl Nightingale once wrote, "If honesty did not exist, it would have to be invented, as it is the surest way of getting rich." A study at Harvard University concluded that the most valuable asset that a company has is how it is known to its customers: its reputation.

By the same token, your greatest personal asset is the way that you are known to your customers. It is your personal reputation for keeping your word and fulfilling your commitments. Your integrity precedes you and affects all of your interactions with other people. There are several things you can do to move you more rapidly toward becoming the kind of person that you know you are capable of becoming. The first, as I mentioned, is to decide upon your five most important values in life. Organize them in order of priority. Then, write a brief paragraph defining what each of those values means to you. A value combined with a definition becomes an organizing principle, a statement that you can use to help you make better decisions. It is a measure and standard which enables you to know how closely you are adhering to your innermost beliefs and convictions.

The second step to developing integrity and character in yourself is to study men and women of great character. Study the lives and stories of people like George Washington, Abraham Lincoln, Winston Churchill, Florence Nightingale, Susan B. Anthony, and Margaret Thatcher. Study the people whose strength of character enabled them to change their world. As you read, think about how they would behave if they were facing the difficulties that you face.

Napoleon Hill, in his book *The Master Key to Riches*, tells about how he created an imaginary board of personal advisors made up of great figures of history. He chose people like Napoleon, Lincoln, Jesus, and Alexander the Great. Whenever he had to make a decision, he would relax deeply and then imagine that the members of his advisory council were sitting at a large table in front of him. He would then ask them what he should do to deal effectively with a particular situation. In time, they would begin to give him answers, observations, and insights that helped him to see more clearly and act more effectively.

You can do the same thing. Select someone that you very much admire for his qualities of courage, tenacity, honesty, or wisdom. Ask yourself "What would Jesus do in my situation?" or "What would Lincoln do if he were here at this time?" You will find yourself with guidance that enables you to be the very best person that you can possibly be.

The third and most important step in building your integrity has to do with formulating your approach based on the psychology of human behavior. We know that if you feel a particular way, you will act in a manner consistent with that feeling. For example, if you feel happy, you will act happily. If you feel angry, you will act angrily. If you feel courageous, you will act courageously.

But we also know that you don't always start off feeling the way you want to. However, because of the Law of Reversibility, if you act as if you had a particular feeling, the action will generate the feeling consistent with it. You can, in effect, act your way into feeling. You can "fake it until you make it."

You can become a superior human being by consciously acting exactly as the kind of person that you would most like to become. If you behave like an individual of integrity, courage, resolution, persistence, and character, you will soon create within yourself the mental structure and habits of such a person. Your actions will become your reality. You will create a personality that is consistent with your highest aspirations.

The more you walk, talk, and behave consistently with your highest values, the more you will like yourself and the better you will feel about yourself. Your self-image will improve, and your level of self-acceptance will go up. You will feel stronger, bolder, and more capable of facing any challenge.

There are three primary areas of your life where acting with integrity is crucial. These are the three areas of greatest temptation for forsaking your integrity as well as the areas of greatest opportunity for building your integrity. When you listen to your inner voice and do what you know to be the right thing in each of these areas, you will have a sense of peace and satisfaction that will lead you on to success and high achievement.

The first area of integrity has to do with your relationships with your family and your friends, the people close to you. Being true to yourself means living in truth with each person in your life. It means refusing to say or do something that you don't believe is right. Living in truth with other people means that you refuse to stay in any situation where you are unhappy with the behavior of another person. You refuse to tolerate it. You refuse to compromise. Psychologists have determined that most stress and negativity come from attempting to live in a way that is not congruent with your highest values. It is when your life is out of alignment, when you are doing and saying one thing on the outside but really feeling and believing something different on the inside, that you feel most unhappy. When you decide to become an individual of character and integrity, your first action will be to neutralize or remove all difficult relationships from your life.

This doesn't mean that you have to go and hit somebody over the head with a stick. It simply means that you honestly confront another person and tell him that you are not happy. Tell him that you would like to reorganize this relationship so that you feel more content and satisfied. If the other person is not willing to make adjustments so that you can be happy, it should be clear to you that you don't want to be in this relationship much longer anyway. The second area of integrity has to do with your attitude and behavior toward money. Casualness toward money brings casualties in your financial life. You must be fastidious about your treatment of money, especially other people's money. You must guard your credit rating the same way you would guard your honor. You must pay your bills

184

punctually, or even early. You must keep your promises with regard to your financial commitments.

The third area of integrity has to do with your commitments to others, especially in your business, your work, and your sales activities. Always keep your word. Be a man or a woman of honor. If you say that you will do something, do it. If you make a promise, keep it. If you make a commitment, fulfill it. Be known as the kind of person that can be trusted absolutely, no matter what the circumstances.

Your integrity is manifested in your willingness to adhere to the values you hold most dear. It's easy to make promises and hard to keep them, but if you do, every single act of integrity will make your character a little stronger. And as you improve the quality and strength of your character, every other part of your life will improve as well.

ABOUT THE AUTHOR

Brian Tracy is Chairman and CEO of Brian Tracy International, a human resources company specializing in the training and development of individuals and organizations. Brian is the best-selling author of more than 40 books and has written and produced more than 300 audio and video learning programs. Brian addresses more than 250,000 people each year and has spoken in more than 40 countries worldwide. He speaks to corporate and public audiences, including the executives and staffs of many of America's largest corporations, on the subjects of personal and professional development. To learn more about Brian Tracy, please visit his Web site at http://www.briantracy.com.

53

Take Advantage of the Internet

Scott Martineau

We live in a glorious time.

The world's entire body of knowledge is easily accessible and readily available to anyone who cares. A mere 100 years ago, the information now available at your fingertips was reserved only for kings and scholars, for the rich and the titled. One generation ago, only credentialed journalists and university researchers could access information that can now be accessed by literally anyone with an interest and an Internet connection.

This new age of information provides all of us with infinite possibilities. The ability to discover, examine, experience, and connect with our passions has never been easier. The road to your self-improvement, personal growth, and enlightened spirituality has never been more smoothly paved.

The Road To Discovery

One of the keys to improving your life is to be able access a feeling, thought, or action that gives you a sense of passion—something that inspires you. It doesn't matter what it is. Here's a powerful exercise: make a list of 100 things you love to do, without censoring yourself. Just write them down on a piece of paper. Pick your top three—those that excite you the most and those that actually give you energy when you think about them or say them out loud. Now, it's time to take action.

Take those three items and enter them into a search engine on the Internet. You'll be amazed at how much you'll find out. If you have an interest in a career in one of your top choices, type in the word "career" along with each of your top three items. It's so easy, you'll be amazed. You can quickly and easily research a subject that is near and dear to your heart.

Still unclear about what your passion is? Type in "find your passion" in Google™, and watch what happens. You'll be floored. Ten minutes later, you will have an answer. Congratulations—welcome to Discovery Road.

The Examination

Now that you've discovered your passion, or at least three items you'd love to do, it's time for an examination of the content you might find. Some of it will resonate immediately. Part of it will prove irrelevant. Review each site and quickly decide if it relates to your passion or interest and if it resonates for you. If not, move on.

The Experience

The results of your discovery and examination should give you a sense of whether you are on the right path. The information available should align directly with your interest. The sites should create excitement as they match your interest. You should experience the content on the site and know immediately if it is worthy of further pursuit. Look for sites where you can see, hear, and read free content before making any purchase decisions. Make sure it's a good fit. If it is, take the plunge, and get involved. Make use of the content in pursuit of your interest.

The Connection

One of the greatest ways to improve your life is to find others who are in pursuit of exactly the same interests. The Internet does that better than any tool available. If your interest or passion is self-esteem, you can find endless material on the subject. With a little discovery and experience you can drill down and find numerous Web sites that have groups discussing self-esteem.

Look for sites that have chat rooms or content groups so that you can share your interests with others. You'll be humbled by how quickly your requests will be answered. Whatever your interest, whatever way you want to improve your life, you can drill down and make that connection—the one that could change your life.

ABOUT THE AUTHOR

Conscious One began with an idea: what would happen if we formed a company based on our own passion for personal growth? Could we create an enterprise with a mission to develop programs that help people step out of their comfort zones and express their fullest potential as a human beings? Scott Martineau and Steve Amos, Co-Founders of Conscious One, birthed this idyllic dream and went to work. From no more than an inspired thought, Conscious One has become the number one producer of personal development courses on the Internet and one of the top 20,000 Web sites in the world. You can visit their site at http://www.ConsciousOne.com.

54

Judgment Day

Michelle C. Ustaszeski

As I walked out of a convenience store with my cup of coffee one late October evening, I noticed an older woman standing next to a pay phone. She was wearing a weathered hat, pink leg warmers that have been out of style for at least 10 years, a black miniskirt with gray stockings, what used to be white sneakers, a brown, tattered coat, and frayed gloves. Stereotypically speaking, she seemed to be homeless. As I waited for my friend to come out of another store, I nonchalantly sipped my coffee from inside my car and watched her rummage through her bag for some change in order to make a call. My compassion for her grew when I noticed how upset she seemed, aggravated at her disposition and frustrated with where her life had led. At least, that is the way she appeared to me as I watched her surrender in her search for change and then slide down the side of the store wall in order to rest.

She looked exhausted. I couldn't help but wonder what trials had led her to this day. With another sip of coffee I thought about what decisions she may have made. I considered different childhood and young adult scenarios she could have suffered. Perhaps she was emotionally mistreated or physically abused. I considered the possibility of her choosing this lifestyle since surrendering when times become insufferable can feel like the most direct route to relief. Regardless of how hard the times she endured must have been and their cause, I wanted to do something to help.

Just as I was about to rummage through my own bag and offer change for her phone call, a Lexus pulled up alongside of me. Surprisingly enough, I watched her jump to her feet, walk up to it . . . and get in. At that very moment a young girl, about the age of 10, stepped out from the back seat wearing a cat costume. I overheard the homeless woman telling the driver, whose devil horns were perfectly placed, that he was late and that she had been waiting for over a half hour. It was then that I realized Halloween was just a week away and that they were probably on their way to a Halloween party. Since I hadn't yet prepared for the holiday myself, being consumed in my own world, it was not a determining factor.

We make false judgments about people every day, without knowing what is happening in their lives. We often subconsciously judge people based on their appearance and not on that of which they are made up. We judge their actions based on what we would do given our own personal experiences. We judge based on the information that we have been provided up to that point and given the environment in which we were raised and now live.

It takes a lot of practice to learn how to put yourself in another person's shoes. I don't even believe that it is completely possible, but we can begin by realizing that our thoughts, opinions, beliefs, and ultimate actions are based on a combination of all the experiences that we have had throughout our lives. Every person experiences his own reality, and that reality, regardless how different from our own, creates who he becomes and how he will react.

The next time you find yourself judging a stranger, take a moment to realize that they are acting perfectly within their own world, and then smile at them as you carry on perfectly within your own.

ABOUT THE AUTHOR

Michelle C. Ustaszeski is a writer and photographer of inspirational and motivational art. She believes that if you can prematurely feel the emotions of your desired outcome, your reservations have been made and reaching your destination is simply a matter of time. In 1998 Michelle created Sam-n-Nick's Inspirations (http://soulfuel.com), named after her two sons, when she combined her love of writing together with the digital camera. Sam-n-Nick's Inspirations produces and sells scenic and enlightening framed art, bookmarks, stationary, music, books, candles, bath products, and other comforting gifts to warm the hearts and souls of her customers through private home parties.

55

KNOWLEDGE

The Power of Ignorance

Blair Warren

Knowledge is power.

How many times have we heard this one? It's one of the battle cries of our society. It's an idea so obvious, so undeniable, that few ever give it a second thought. We don't just seek knowledge, we worship it. Even Socrates, a wise man if ever there was one, said, "There is only one good, knowledge, and one evil, ignorance."

If only it were that simple. The truth is that Socrates was wrong, and here's why. First, the pursuit of knowledge often becomes an end in itself. Too many people are living their lives as if they're just "one secret away" from being able to take action. One secret, one book, one seminar, one whatever away from having the knowledge it's going to take for them to succeed. Then, and only then, will they attempt to do the things they wish to do with their lives. Of course, they never quite achieve the state of knowledge they're seeking. Why? Because it doesn't exist.

In his book *If You Meet the Buddha on the Road, Kill Him* Sheldon Kopp points out that "All important decisions must be made on the basis of insufficient data." Notice that he said *all* important decisions, not some, many, or even most. All of them. If we take this reasoning a step further, we can easily infer that all *endeavors* we undertake must be made in the same way—based on insufficient data. In other words, no matter how much we study, prepare, or practice, some degree of ignorance is unavoidable, and accepting this is what separates those who overcome their ignorance from those who are eaten up by it.

Second, knowledge can actually destroy your power. Yes, *destroy* it. A few years ago, I had a conversation with a very successful entrepreneur. When I asked him to what he attributed his success, he said, without hesitation, "Ignorance." Yes, ignorance. He said that he was grateful he didn't know how difficult his climb to the top was going to be before he began. If he had known, he would have never begun. For him, knowledge isn't power. Ignorance is. He's not alone. I've asked the same question of other successful people, and almost without fail, ignorance ranks high on their lists of success attributes. Whether they knew it explicitly or not from the onset of their endeavors, on some level these people understood that "too much knowledge" could destroy their will to act. If they had entertained all the negative possibilities that could have befallen them before taking action, they would never have taken action.

Third, knowledge isn't the sole, or even primary, determining factor in man's ability to succeed in life. To elevate knowledge above such qualities as drive, resilience, awareness, cunning, and the like is, ironically, the height of ignorance. Dr. Christopher Hyatt, in the introduction to his deliciously irreverent book, *The Psychopath's Bible*, puts it this way:

> There is a lot of slop in life. You can make a ton of mistakes, be the biggest screwup and still survive and even succeed. Don't let anyone fool you about this. There are millions-billions-of people who believe all kinds of lies and still do well. Some people believe the truth and are utter failures. Life is tolerant, even stupidly so.

You might want to read that one again, maybe even put it in a frame above your desk as I have done, because it's a lot closer to reality than Socrates's pithy quote. Where does this leave us? How do we satisfy our desire "to know" without losing the inherent power our ignorance often provides us?

Here's how I do it: I remind myself that no matter how certain I may feel before making a decision, it doesn't negate the fact that I'm basing it on insufficient data, and then, I make it anyway. When others question my decisions and ask how I intend to achieve something I set out to do, I reply, "I don't know. Let's find out."

In other words, I practice making commitments *with full awareness* that I'm making them without any promise that my decision is sound or that my desired outcome is certain.

I am not suggesting that we abandon our quest for knowledge, but I am suggesting that we do not make our *quest for knowledge* replace our *quest for achievement*. To do so does not empower us; it cripples us. No, knowledge is *not* power. Neither is ignorance. There is, however, a balance between the two, and our power lies in finding it. The surest way to do that is not to delay taking action until one is "wise" enough to succeed but to act now and learn along the way. After all, if there is something we *must* learn in order to succeed, we are more apt to learn it by living life and making mistakes than by preparing to live life and hoping to avoid them.

ABOUT THE AUTHOR

Blair Warren is a television producer, writer, marketing consultant, and voracious student of human nature. He is the creator of "The Forbidden Keys to Persuasion" e-class, the author of *The No-Nonsense Guide to Enlightenment*, and is currently working on his next book, *Spontaneous Persuasion: Getting What You Want By Simply Being Who You Are*. To read more of Blair's material and to get more information on his work, visit his Web site at http://www.blairwarren.com.

56

LIFE BALANCE

Unplug Your Life:
Short-Circuit "Infowhelm"
and Recharge Your Life Energy

Barbara Schiffman

Do you

- spend hours surfing the Web, answering e-mails, instant messaging, or blogging?
- take calls on your cell phone no matter where you are or who you're with?
- listen to tunes or podcasts on your audio player from breakfast to bedtime?

If you answered yes to at least one of these questions but often feel wired, frustrated, exhausted, or overwhelmed, you may be suffering from "infowhelm." I've coined this term to describe being overwhelmed by the abundance of information and stimulation in our constantly busy and plugged-in lives.

It's no surprise that many people feel infowhelmed today. Marketing expert Dave Lakhani reports that we receive more mental and visual stimulation in one day than our great-grandparents in 1900 absorbed in a year. The constant demands on our attention by advertising, music, movies, the Internet, and other people have increased dramatically since the 1950s, while TV has also evolved from a three-channel world to a 200-channel universe.

Time Magazine's 2006 "Mind-Body Issue" (January 16, 2006) notes that e-mail and cell phones may make people more productive, but they also "drive us to distraction." We spend too much time "frazzing" (doing frantic, inefficient multitasking with the delusion that we're getting things done) and "screen sucking" (wasting time online) according to psychiatrist and ADD expert Edward

Hallowell, author of *CrazyBusy* and *Driven to Distraction*. Many people are also addicted to "infosnacking"—randomly nibbling bytes of news, e-mails, and Web information throughout the day—which was 2005's Word of the Year per *Webster's New World College Dictionary*.

I realized that I suffer from infowhelm after I avoided checking my e-mail for nearly two weeks. When I finally and reluctantly went online, it took a whole day to wade through them. My experience was recently echoed by law professor Rosa Brooks in her *LA Times* op-ed essay about her love-hate relationship with e-mail (January 13, 2006). Rosa once thought that e-mail would "bring absent friends closer and enable us all to communicate so much more efficiently, quickly and deeply," but she's now inundated with over 200 e-mails a day, mostly spam and lawyer jokes sent by friends who incorrectly think that she enjoys them.

In addition to answering e-mails only when I feel like it, I try to control the tsunami of information by choosing to keep my cell phone off unless I'm expecting an urgent call. Cell phones are great for emergencies and while traveling, but interaction by computer and cell phone has replaced the art of talking with people face-to-face. Our conversation styles have become fast and furious as people rush around chatting on their cells, but they seem unaware that others don't enjoy listening to their one-sided conversations. This is also true of iPod™ addicts who ignore the people around them while listening to their favorite tunes.

Our attention spans have also diminished due to online chats and the preference for brief e-mails. In *Driven to Distraction* Hallowell points out that in 1994 Americans were beginning to exhibit ADT, or attention deficit trait. This is similar to ADD but only makes people frantic in certain situations or places— like at the office for stressed-out corporate executives or at home for exhausted stay-at-home moms. Being interrupted by the demands of others or by high-tech devices also drains our adrenaline and locks us into a state of fight or flight.

Our obsession with high-tech toys and tools seems to have unbalanced our lives instead of giving us more freedom and time to enjoy ourselves. By plugging in we've lost touch with the natural world of our slower-paced but less-overwhelmed ancestors. We're now paying the price of choosing "high tech" over "high touch" in deeper levels of anxiety and a continual sense of being off-balance. By listening primarily to loud sounds through our iPods and cell phones we've stopped hearing the natural symphony of wind, birds, and crickets. By focusing on TV, computers, and cell phone screens we've stopped gazing out windows to watch the world around us or the clouds drifting by.

Unfortunately, our sense of infowhelm is likely to increase as commercials are beamed to our iPods and cell phones in the near future. Then, we won't even be able to turn off the flood of unwanted messages . . . *unless we unplug!*

I don't advocate trashing our computers or tossing our cell phones away forever, but I do urge you to seek the right balance of high tech and high touch for your life before it becomes even harder to stop and smell the roses or gaze at the moon.

The concept of high tech/high touch was originally posed by author and researcher John Naisbitt in his 1982 best seller *Megatrends*. According to a *Publishers' Weekly* review, "Naisbitt sees Americans trapped in what he calls a 'Technology Intoxication Zone,' and he urges people to unplug their laptops long enough to rediscover the simplicity of starry nights and snowfalls, and remember what it means to be human." I emphatically agree. As a life balance coach, I invite you to unplug long enough to regain your balance by recharging drained energy at least once a week.

How? Try spending face time with people you care about. If you can't get together in person, at least call them instead of e-mailing—even if you must use your cell phone. Listen to their voices, and let them hear yours. You can also balance infowhelm by tuning in to nature. Walk on the beach, or take a hike in the woods. Notice the moon's phases each month as it evolves from new to full and back again. Treat the new moon as a time of new beginnings; at the full moon, stop and review how far you've come since the last new moon, then reflect on what you want to accomplish before the next one.

Also, tune in to the earth's seasons plus the four elements of earth, air, water, and fire. We forget that the natural energy of the world and our lives flows in cycles and that each natural element helps balance the others. Our energy flow is not just mental or "on" all the time like the Internet. Humans weren't designed to be plugged in to machines 24 hours a day, 7 days a week. We need regular downtime to rejuvenate, relax, and recharge.

I've found that tuning in to natural energy patterns is especially effective as an antidote for infowhelm. When we unplug for a while, we can remember how to move at a more peaceful pace—to communicate with more emotional depth and to pay attention to what we see and feel. Imagine how energizing, balanced, and peaceful our lives can be if we all consciously tune in to each other and the world around us again!

ABOUT THE AUTHOR

Barbara Schiffman is a life balance and personal evolution coach in Burbank, California. As an author, speaker, publisher, Hollywood script consultant, life and career breakthrough trainer, wife, and mother, Barbara's a first-hand life balance expert. She brings fresh perspectives to living in tune with the universe, and her EvoLuminus Coaching tele-classes, workshops, and guided meditation CD Kits include "New Moon. New Beginnings," "Life Energy Tune-Up," and "The EnergiFlow Process." Barbara's also published in *Inspiration to Realization*, an anthology of women's wisdom. For information, call (818) 846–3043 or (800) 306–8290, e-mail fullspectrum@charter.net, or visit http://www.barbaraschiffman.com.

57

Five Simple Strategies for Keeping Your Life Stuck

Mary Ann Bailey

One of the most common complaints I hear when I talk with potential clients is that they feel "stuck." They may be in relationships that are no longer working, but they don't know how to leave. They may have dreams of starting their own businesses, but they aren't sure where to begin. They may want to incorporate more fun into their lives, but they aren't sure how to make that happen.

The feeling of being stuck is very familiar for most of us. Even though our lives seem to be in constant motion, very little of that motion actually moves us forward. We are similar to a logjam in a river: the river is rushing all around us, but we aren't going anywhere. Why is it so easy for us to lose life's flow? What is it about the way we live our lives that leads us toward being stuck?

Many different answers to these questions could be offered, but here are five of the most common behaviors I have observed that hold us back from living the lives we really want to live.

Believing What You Think

The average mind has about 60,000 thoughts a day, and most of us believe about 99 percent of what we think. Some of our thoughts are products of how we were raised and the culture in which we live. Others are the products of our mind synthesizing our observations into our own brilliant deductions about the world. Our thoughts help us to make sense of our world and our lives, so it is only logical that we hold our thoughts to be the truth.

198

This, however, is where we can get into trouble: we cling to beliefs that may no longer serve us. How many of you know for certain that you are not good at art, sports, or math? Most of us left elementary school having gotten at least some negative feedback in one of these three areas.

What beliefs are you still hanging on to that may be keeping your life stuck? What things do you think you will never be able to do? What things shouldn't be the way they are? Who would be very upset if you were to follow your heart? It might be time to examine your belief system and determine which thoughts are holding your life hostage.

Blaming Others for Our Circumstances

We all have things in our lives that are not going as well as we would like. Life is always presenting us with new challenges, and our job is to figure out the best way to deal with them. Some people defer to these challenges. They step back and wait for the challenge to go away or to work itself out; they ignore it. Meanwhile, life continues on, and after a while these people find themselves still standing in the corner feeling stalled.

Another approach would be to face that challenge head on. Realize that you are the only one who can truly take charge of the situation. What would it take for you to face that challenge? A good place to start would be putting together a game plan that includes intention, determination, and lots of practice. Your first few tries might not be successful, but eventually, you will perfect your approach, and you will begin knocking down those challenges. You will begin to see that the more you step into your life, the less stuck you will feel.

Taking Life (and Yourself) Too Seriously

Most of us were raised to believe that the key to success is hard work. Recently, that belief has been revised to include hard work and very long hours. I would like to challenge that belief with an old adage: "All work and no play makes Jack a dull boy."

To keep our lives flowing, we need to intersperse fun, laughter, and creativity with our work. We need to be able to take time to enjoy our lives and reenergize ourselves without feeling guilty or irresponsible. During these times of rest and fun, our minds are free to dream and imagine. This is when we very often come up with solutions to our problems and new strategies to enliven and enrich our lives.

Living Life from the Middle

One of the easiest ways to keep our lives stuck is to live them from the middle rather than closer to the edge. Living life from the middle means to remain safely in your comfort zone, to do things the same way, avoiding change at all costs and eliminating all spontaneity. As boring as this may sound, it is the way a majority of people live. As a result, the middle is an extremely crowded place, and it is very easy to feel stuck when you are there.

By encouraging yourself to take small, yet consistent steps toward the "edge," you will find that life has much more room in which to move around. The edge is not as scary as you might think. As you begin to try new things, new perspectives will open up, and you will begin to see more possibilities and opportunities. You will meet people who are also stepping outside their comfort zones and who can offer you support in your journey. As your life begins to open and flow, you will wonder how you ever lived in the middle.

Falling Prey to the Fear of the Unknown

Fear is a powerful emotion. It protects us and keeps us from doing dangerous things, yet it can also keep us from doing new and wonderful things. Most of us get a little nervous when we are not sure about what is around the corner. Yet, sometimes getting our lives unstuck takes a leap of faith.

Have you always dreamed about starting your own business, becoming a sculptor, or sailing around the world? To give any chance to those dreams coming true, you must face the fears that are holding you back head on and put your trust in you and your dream. Will you be successful? Maybe yes, maybe no, but at least you will have opened the door to the possibility of your dream coming true.

Our lives, like rivers, will always experience a few logjams. The issue is not whether we get stuck, but rather, it is how we extricate ourselves from the flotsam and get our lives flowing again. Becoming more aware of those behavior patterns that are responsible for keeping us stuck is a great way to start that process.

ABOUT THE AUTHOR

Mary Ann Bailey, MC, is a life coach who specializes in working with people going through midlife career transitions. She is also the author of the recently published book *Changing Course, Changing Careers*. Visit her Web site at http://www.baileycoaching.com to read more of her articles and to learn how coaching can help you make the changes you want to make in your life.

58

Assimilation Versus Accumulation: The Practice of Getting Full Nourishment from Everything in Your Life

Steve Davis

The wealth of material and information available to the modern world has reached a level greater than at any other time in history. Now at the pinnacle of our ability to manipulate our environment and produce all the things we need, and many that we don't, it's entirely possibly that many of our ills are arising as a result of our inability to handle this incredible glut of input, in all of its forms.

Prior to the recent age, when resources and information were scarce, we would never have thought of turning either of these away. The arrival of this incredible abundance is relatively recent, in the past 50 years or so, with the refinement of industry and the emergence of the information age and the Internet. It has come upon us so quickly that most of us haven't learned to handle this new level of abundance, if indeed it is possible to adapt to this onslaught at all.

Adaptation starts by asking ourselves the right questions. We seldom ask ourselves, "How much is enough?" and "What do I value over everything else?" We just cannot say no to available things that meet our fancy. In some ways we crave each new thing with the hope that it will somehow set us free. Consequently, we are literally dying from overconsumption in one form or another.

For example, more than half the U.S. population is now considered obese, while people are starving for renewal of spirit and soul in their lives and work. People are busier, have less time, and often feel overwhelmed, surrounded by too much stuff and stressed out under the growing burden of too much information.

What Can You Do about It?

How do we cope with the temptation to consume ourselves into oblivion? Our proposal is simple. First, we suggest that you begin replacing the habit of "accumulating" with the practice of "assimilating." Second, make sure that what you ingest in any form is of the highest quality possible. Let's first quickly define these words.

> **Accumulate**: To heap up in a mass; to pile up; to increase; to collect or bring together; to amass; as, to accumulate a sum of money.

> **Assimilate**: To appropriate and transform or incorporate into the substance of the assimilating body; to absorb or appropriate, as nourishment; as food is assimilated and converted into organic tissue.

Proper assimilation and digestion of food, experience, and information allows us to extract their full benefits and put them to good use, whereas overstuffing ourselves in any of these arenas will cause a buildup of unsightly fat, waste, stress, toxicity, confusion, and unease, often fueling an unconscious compulsion for more. All of us know how much better we feel when we push ourselves away from the table before we're full and the satisfied feeling we get when we give ourselves a little time for our systems to "assimilate" what we've taken in.

Satisfaction comes from fully digesting and extracting the fine nutrients from what we already have and making choices for new input based on our true values and passions, not on our casual likes and vague interests. Unconscious compulsions for more input seldom satisfy our true needs, nor will having piles of unread books and magazines ringing our desks reduce the nagging sense that there is some piece of information that will really change everything for us. Saying yes only to what most serves our needs and resonates with our deepest sense of self will go a long way to lessen the burden.

How to Facilitate Assimilation

Of Information

We often spend a great deal of time looking for that special piece of information or that magical answer to our current problem when more often than not, the answer we seek is right in front of us. However, unless we slow down to see, hear, and process what's already in our world, we may miss these gifts. Try to assimilate fully the meaning and consequences of every activity you undertake.

Of Relationships

We often rush around so focused on getting stuff done that we sometimes neglect our most precious resources: our friends, associates, coworkers, and family. The benefits of goodwill, emotional support, and new connections and ideas very often offset the time spent cultivating and maintaining these existing relationships.

Of Ideas

You might be an avid reader of personal growth books. If so, just imagine what might happen if instead of picking up yet another new title to read, you were to study the principles from just one chapter of a favorite you've already read and actually apply them for the next 30 days. Create a learning plan with specific goals for the next six months. Include both informational and learning goals in this plan, and only include that which you know you can assimilate with minimum effort so that you have time to really make the information a part of your very being.

Of Food

During at least one meal this week, try eating more slowly than usual. Chew your food just a little bit longer. When you're talking or listening to someone, stop eating. Take time to really assimilate your food, and experience it with family. Try doing just one thing at a time. Enjoy the rainbow of flavors and textures, each bite a miniature world of experience.

Of Experience

We're all tempted to accelerate our pace of life to match that of our increasingly frenetic culture, but this is a personal choice. Most of the time, we can choose to slow down and carefully select our inputs and experiences and the speed at which we subject ourselves to them. There are ways to help make this choice easier. Commit to a practice of being "fully present" for a few minutes each day. Use whatever method appeals to you. Some choices are meditation, yoga, quiet walks, prayer, tai chi, martial arts, sitting alone quietly, journaling, etc. Alternatively, just look out the window with all your senses. Focus on what is before you, and allow it to really enter your being.

These kinds of practices are more and more important as the world accelerates around you. They give your inner self time catch up with, reconnect with, and properly assimilate with your outer experience. Now, go forth and assimilate!

ABOUT THE AUTHOR

Steve Davis, MA, MS, is a former electrical engineer turned trainer, facilitator, business and life coach, and infopreneur. He coaches small business owners, people in transition, leaders, and cultural creatives over the phone and Internet. Steve helps people cut through the fog and chart a clear course to a purposeful and passionate life. Contact Steve for a free exploratory session at http://www.livingmastery.com. Subscribe to his free weekly e-zine for group leaders at http://www.MasterFacilitatorJournal.com, and check out his virtual university, packed with information for group leaders and participants, at http://www.FacilitatorU.com.

59

Finding True Love:
How "Not Looking" Is the Answer!

Deborah Leigh

Dianne, a long-term client of mine in her late 30s, recently celebrated her fifth anniversary: the fifth anniversary of her own personal quest to find the man of her dreams.

According to Dianne's personal calculations, she has thus far dated 12 military men, 9 police officers, 5 fireman, 3 pilots, and 2 lawyers over the course of those years. Yes, you could say Dianne has a thing for men in uniform. (The lawyers were just flukes, she insists, having succumbed to a momentary weakness for blonde, muscular, devilishly handsome men in three-piece suits while getting her will drawn up and the fine print of a real estate contract translated, respectively.)

Despite her best efforts to make these men fit her lifestyle and emotional nature like a glove, she has yet to find Him: her prince, her knight in shining armor, the man destined to be the One who will make her blissfully happy and emotionally complete, forever, who she believes will magically transform her life into a satisfying, deliriously happy existence.

No matter how I try to convince Dianne that what she seeks cannot be found, the more determined she is to prove me—and the card readings I give her—wrong. In frantic haste she scours nightclubs and the vastness of the Internet. She peruses personal ads and peers with anticipation into the face of every new male who saunters into the ad agency where she works.

She's convinced that he's out there. It's just a matter of *finding* him.

What Dianne fails to understand—along with a good three-quarters of the human race—is that this most lasting, pure, soul-deep kind of Love cannot be "found." True Love finds *us* . . . usually, when we least expect it! When we aren't wearing our best outfits, with our hair perfect and makeup on, when we aren't the least bit interested in loving or being loved, True Love simply *happens*—if we're willing to wait for it.

By waiting, I mean abandoning the urge to go out and purposefully hunt it down. I mean developing ourselves, emotionally and spiritually, to be the best we can be—living exclusively in the moment, the here and now, while concentrating on reaping deep maturity and wisdom from that moment, relying completely on our faith that when the time is right, True Love will indeed *find us*.

When it does, that love will naturally fit like a designer glove. It will seem so right from the instant it unfolds that it might very well scare the bejesus out of you. It's the kind of spiritual and emotional meshing depicted through the ages in movies, classic literature, paintings, and sculpture. It is so pure and complete in and of itself that it effortlessly transcends every difficulty, every hardship. It heals and restores. It brings joy and beauty to every aspect of our lives. It's the bonding of two souls that nothing—and no one—can ever divide or conquer.

We have to be willing to wait for True Love, having faith that it will arrive. If we aren't willing to wait or we lack the right amount of faith, of course, we can still find love: romantic love, sexual love, and platonic love.

Dianne found all three by dating 31 men in five years. Still, she was left wanting that "something more" and ended up getting hurt, despite how the readings she received urged her not to make emotional investments in these men, trying desperately as she was to somehow make what were essentially all the wrong relationships right.

How can you bring True Love into your life? The cards have told me for years that as soon as we stop trying to make True Love happen, it will. As soon as we sincerely abandon our search for that Mr. or Ms. Right, the man or woman we are destined to partner with and spend a lifetime with will quite naturally enter our lives.

The question is, can you wait and have faith that your mate will come for you?

Yes, of course you can. Focus on having enough faith to open yourself to the immense opportunity the Universe offers you. A scary proposition? Sure, it is. To say, "I'm going to let go, allowing Life to bring to me what it thinks I need, in its own time, in its own way, as I face my loneliness and pain, rather than dashing out to try to make Love happen on my own," is a scary proposition, indeed. By committing yourself to this statement, you are, in essence, allowing yourself to leap the great abyss of your own emotional insecurities. From that leap comes nothing but sheer spiritual strength.

Once you've achieved that strength, True Love can't help but find you!

ABOUT THE AUTHOR

Deborah Leigh has intuitively read ordinary playing cards for the past 25 years. She learned Personal Prophesy, a revolutionary method of achieving intuitive insight and wisdom from playing cards to achieve a more fulfilled life, from her own maternal grandmother. Over the years Deborah has offered intuitive advice to the public from AOL's Astronet, Women.com, iVillage.com, and VZ.com as the well-recognized Psychic Love Doctor. Author of *Personal Prophesy: Learn How to Create Your Own Destiny*, Deborah Leigh is also an award-winning newspaper columnist and certified therapist and interventionist. Contact Deborah for personal consultation and instruction in the Personal Prophesy method at http://www.psychiclovedoctor.com.

60

LOW SELF-ESTEEM ANALYSIS

Facing Ourselves with a Willingness to Change

Marilyn J. Sorensen

Katy nearly drags her husband, Jackson, to the therapist, though he readily admits that he has problems and frequently puts himself down. Married two years and with a baby on the way, the couple argue. At times, it gets nasty as Katy has a harsh tongue. She gets angry that Jackson won't talk more and won't open up to her. Jackson, a handsome young man with broad shoulders and a quick smile, doesn't understand her way of communicating and feels devastated when she raises her voice.

When he quite openly tells the therapist how he feels about himself, she leans forward with a concerned look and nods. "Jackson, I think you have low self-esteem." Jackson stares at her and then begins to cry. "It's okay, Jackson, you didn't cause this. It's not your fault that you have it, and best of all, you can recover from it," she says.

Wiping at his tears, Jackson rises from the couch. "I just have to leave now. I'll be back," he says, closing the door behind him.

A few minutes later, Jackson returns. He apologizes, and the therapist asks him if he is all right. He nods and says, "Low self-esteem. I just never considered it. It's so embarrassing."

Many obstacles stand in the way of peacefulness in our lives: stress at work, family issues, health problems, financial burdens, and relationship demands. The list seems never ending. How can we cope with these weighty concerns when we wake up each morning, let alone strive for contentment and a sense of well-being? The answer comes in being at peace with ourselves, something that can only be achieved if we feel good about who we are. The answer comes in believing that we are significant, of value, adequate to the challenges that face us, and worthy of choosing what's right for ourselves. The answer comes in possessing healthy self-esteem.

Low self-esteem (LSE), which affects millions of people, is a serious problem that destroys lives and relationships by sentencing those who suffer from it to years of entrapment from fear and anxiety, self-recrimination and misery, emotional turmoil, including depression, devastation, and despair, and endless periods of loneliness.

Men and women suffer from low self-esteem in equal numbers, and people of all ages and economic levels suffer from it. Yet, society and even the mental health community are oblivious to its severity and are often ignorant about what can be done to alleviate it.

It's important to recognize the symptoms of low self-esteem.

- Feelings of inadequacy, inferiority, or incompetence.
- Fear, anxiety, lack of confidence, and an unwillingness to try new things.
- Reluctance to share opinions, ideas, perceptions, or feelings.
- Fear of failure, rejection, criticism, or abandonment.
- Self-doubt about our abilities, worthiness, or lovability.
- Feelings of not fitting in, of being innately flawed.
- Inability to know who and when to trust.
- Frequent episodes of "self-esteem attacks" and depression.
- Underachieving or overachieving.
- Poor boundaries; controlling behavior, people-pleasing.

Once we become aware that we have low self-esteem, there is work to do because we can't recover from LSE without concerted effort over a period of time. There is no quick fix because once we've been conditioned to view

210

ourselves in a particularly negative way, this thinking is difficult to alter and permeates everything we choose to do or not do.

Many people think that a person can easily overcome low self-esteem if he wants to, but this is a sadly ridiculous notion because no one would continue to suffer from LSE if he could merely flip a switch and turn it off. Nearly as ludicrous is the idea that people can overcome their low self-esteem if they practice reading affirmations. Such ideas do more harm than good for those with low self-esteem. The first step in recovering is to recognize that low self-esteem develops in childhood as the result of negative experiences. Through these experiences the child develops a very negative view of himself. This might be due to excessive criticism, verbal or emotional abuse, neglect, abandonment, lack of support or affirmation, or negative feedback. In other words, people don't cause their own low self-esteem. However, once recognized, it then becomes the responsibility of the LSE sufferer to make a decision to recover from it. Otherwise, it will affect everything he does or says or avoids doing or saying for the remainder of his life.

The second step in recovering from LSE is to develop awareness, a skill that is necessary for making any constructive change. The LSE sufferer must become aware of the negative view he has of himself and recognize the numerous ways in which he tells himself stories about the behavior of others, stories that are made up and that distort the truth due to his insecurity. For example, a woman tells herself that her husband doesn't come straight home from work because he doesn't love her. A man who sees his wife losing weight and buying new clothes tells himself that she must be interested in someone else. Unless circumstances support these theories, they are just stories—they have no basis in fact, truth, or history—and do not represent reality.

Once a person recognizes how frequently he tells himself these inaccurate tales, he can then begin to evaluate these statements one at a time, asking himself if each one is based on fact, truth, or history. At first, this is very difficult to determine because the habit of distorting the truth due to self-doubt and insecurity is a pattern that accompanies low self-esteem. In time, however—and with help, if necessary—the LSE sufferer will eventually begin to see the extent to which he distorts the truth and thereby comes to inaccurate conclusions.

Developing this awareness is a critical step in understanding the self-defeating ways in which LSE sufferers regularly think and act because once we become aware, we can change the behavior, and because our feelings are the result of this distorted thinking, converting our inaccurate stories into truth will become the basis for altering the vicious cycle of emotional turmoil in LSE sufferers.

ABOUT THE AUTHOR

A licensed psychologist in Portland, Oregon, Marilyn J. Sorensen, PhD, has developed a program for recovery from low self-esteem and works with individuals, couples, and families in her Portland office and with people nationally and internationally by phone. Dr. Sorensen is also the author of five books on self-esteem, including the popular *Breaking the Chain of Low Self-Esteem*, and she is the founder and director of The Self-Esteem Institute. Take the interactive and *free* Self-Esteem Questionnaire at her Web site to assess your own self-esteem: visit http://www.TheSelfEsteemInstitute.com or http://www.GetEsteem.com. She answers one question per person if e-mailed at mjsorensen@GetEsteem.com.

61

MOTIVATION

The Most Important Meetings You'll Ever Attend Are the Meetings You Have with Yourself

Denis Waitley

You are your most important critic. There is no opinion so vitally important to your well-being as the opinion you have of yourself. As you read this, you're talking to yourself right now. "Let's see if I understand what he means by that . . . How does that compare with my experiences? I'll make note of that . . . try that tomorrow . . . I already knew that . . . I already do that." I believe this self-talk, this psycholinguistics or language of the mind, can be controlled to work for us, especially in the building of self-confidence and creativity. We're all talking to ourselves every moment of our lives, except during certain portions of our sleeping cycle. We're seldom even aware that we're doing it. We all have a running commentary in our heads on events and our reactions to them.

- Be aware of the silent conversation you have with yourself. Are you a nurturing coach or a critic? Do you reinforce your own success or negate it? Are you comfortable saying to yourself "That's more like it." "Now we're in the groove." "Things are working out well." "I am reaching my financial goals." "I'll do it better next time."
- When winners fail, they view it as a temporary inconvenience, a learning experience, an isolated event, and a stepping-stone instead of a stumbling block.
- When winners succeed, they reinforce that success by feeling rewarded rather than guilty about the achievement and the applause.
- When winners are paid a compliment, they simply respond, "Thank you." They accept value graciously when it is paid. They pay value in their conversations with themselves and with other people.

A mark of an individual with healthy self-esteem is the ability to spend time alone, without constantly needing other people around. Being comfortable and enjoying solitary time reveals inner peace and centering. People who constantly need stimulation or conversation with others are often a bit insecure and thus need to be propped up by the company of others.

Always greet the people you meet with a smile. When introducing yourself in any new association, take the initiative to volunteer your own name first, clearly, and always extend your hand first, looking the person in the eyes when you speak.

In your telephone communications at work or at home, answer the telephone pleasantly, immediately giving your own name to the caller before you ask who's calling. Whenever you initiate a call, always give your own name up front, before you ask for the party you want and before you state your business. Leading with your own name underscores that a person of value is making the call.

Don't brag. People who trumpet their exploits and shout for service are actually calling for help. The show-offs, braggarts, and blowhards are desperate for attention.

Don't tell your problems to people, unless they're directly involved with the solutions, and don't make excuses. Successful people seek those who look and sound like success. Always talk affirmatively about the progress you are trying to make.

As we said earlier, find successful role models after whom you can pattern yourself. When you meet a mastermind, become a master mime, and learn all you can about how he succeeded. This is especially true with things you fear. Find someone who has conquered what you fear and learn from him.

When you make a mistake in life, or get ridiculed or rejected, look at mistakes as detours on the road to success, and view ridicule as ignorance. After a rejection, take a look at your BAG. B is for Blessings, things you are endowed with that you often take for granted like life itself, health, living in an abundant country, family, friends, career. A is for accomplishments. Think of the many things you are proud of that you have done so far. And G is for Goals. Think of your big dreams and plans for the future that motivate you. If you took your BAG— blessings, accomplishments, and goals—to a party and spread them on the floor, in comparison to all your friends and the people you admire, you'd take your own bag home, realizing that you have as much going for yourself as anyone else. Always view rejection as part of one performance, not as a turndown of the performer.

And enjoy those special meetings with yourself. Spend this Saturday doing something you really want to do. I don't mean next month or someday. This Saturday, enjoy being alive and being able to do it. You deserve it. There will never be another you. This Saturday will be spent. Why not spend at least one day a week on You!

Action idea: Go for one entire day and night without saying anything negative to yourself or to others. Make a game of it. If a friend or colleague catches you saying something negative, you must put 50 cents in a drawer or container toward a dinner or evening out with that person. Do this for one month, and see who has had to pay the most money toward the evening.

ABOUT THE AUTHOR

Denis Waitley is more than a poet, lyricist, best-selling author, and speaker . . . Denis Waitley has studied and counseled leaders in every field—from Apollo astronauts to Fortune 500 top executives—and now comes to our living rooms. Denis Waitley has painted word pictures of optimism, core values, motivation, and resiliency that have become indelible and legendary in their positive impact on society. Denis has been described by his peers as "the poet laureate" of modern-day philosophers. For the past 40 years he has inspired, informed, and enlightened millions of individuals with his 15 nonfiction books, hundreds of audio programs, and entertaining, penetrating, live keynote lectures, seminars, and television appearances. To learn more, visit www.deniswaitley.com.

62

MUSIC CHANGES SUBCONSCIOUS BELIEFS

What's on Your iPod™?
The Power of Music to Transform Your Life

Marcia Breitenbach

Do you want a life of greater ease, balance, happiness, and prosperity? Of course you do! So why does it seem to take so long for our dreams and desires to manifest? The answer lies within.

Deep within us are subconscious beliefs that contribute to our actions, our responses, and thus to the actual conditions of our lives. If we believe at the subconscious level that we only deserve a certain amount of happiness, or that life is a struggle, or that we are unworthy, then we act accordingly.

To achieve our dreams and goals, it is imperative to change these limiting beliefs. Done consciously, with intention, the process of transforming your beliefs will be somewhat like making a path in fresh snow. The first time you walk across the snow, your boots leave indentations where there were none. Each time you walk the same path, the route becomes more defined, the snow shaped and deepened by the repeated trips.

It is the same in your brain. Your beliefs are like pathways, shaped by repetition from thoughts and responses and made stronger over time. In order to form new, healthier pathways that are solid and worthy of your footsteps and your dreams, you must define and use the paths. Repetition makes them stronger and gives them a fighting chance against the older, more established pathways.

There is a way to reach the subconscious easily, to replace limiting beliefs with positive, life-affirming ones. Music, especially songs with powerful lyrics, is an underutilized tool to heal your soul, change beliefs, and provide the fuel for igniting your dreams, passions, and goals.

Music Creates New Software in Your Brain

You are already on a path to manifesting your wholeness and your dreams. You read books, take classes, and make action plans, and you apply these principles to your life. Perhaps you wonder why you aren't progressing more quickly. Here's one reason: at the subconscious level you may not truly believe that you can do it and that you deserve it. These subconscious, limiting beliefs, and others like them, are sabotaging you.

Think of your thoughts, statements about yourself, and your beliefs about how the world works as the software that runs your life. Unfortunately, much of this software lies hidden within us, and we don't realize how we continually choose to keep running it, allowing it to interfere with all our hard work and the steps we have been taking toward our goals.

Music Bypasses Your "Keep Things the Way They Are" Radar

We have an internal radar that likes things status quo. It may also be the voice inside that wants you to play it safe and is nervous about change, and it may block some of the information that you have been gathering through your reading, classes, and discussions. This radar can suck your creative energy and inhibit your follow-through.

Music has the ability to bypass our intellectual radars, the ones that keep really good information from getting to our core, to that place that makes or breaks us. We all have beliefs and habitual patterns of response built up over the years, making it difficult to make lasting, positive changes. It isn't enough to read about these things and to listen to the experts give us tools to change our beliefs. We have to get past our cognitive "filters" because they are the gatekeepers to our subconscious. The actual vibrations of the music not only help you to slip past the status quo radar but also help to loosen the old limiting and negative beliefs and to put you in a more relaxed and receptive alpha mode for receiving the positive messages and lyrics.

You Must Be Your Authority

Another problem is that too often, we look to others to be our authorities, to help us find our way. It's okay to go outside ourselves to gather information, but then, it is up to each one of us to choose what information we will accept and to give ourselves the message that we are going to be changing, getting rid of what hasn't worked, and trying some new things. We must put ourselves back into the position of authority so that our subconscious will accept the new beliefs. Rather than listening to someone else tell you what to believe, activate your own passkey to your subconscious.

Choose Your Music Wisely

Music can be your passkey. It's important that you pay attention to the lyrics of songs that you play often. Are the words disempowering in any way or implanting negative thoughts or ideas? If so, you may want to consider letting go of that music and replacing it with positive, empowering lyrics.

Choose a few songs that have lyrics that support the changes you want to make, and put them on your iPod^{TM} or on a CD that goes with you in your car. Sing along, especially early in the morning or right before bed, when your subconscious mind is more receptive.

Music Gets "Stuck" in Your Head and Provides a Positive Focus

Music provides the focus that is often the missing ingredient in people's paths to their goals. It's easy to let everyday errands, unexpected events, and work and family priorities monopolize our focus. It's not that the intention is no longer there; it's that we allow other things to take over, and we can let days, weeks, and months slip by without completing the steps that lead us closer to our dreams.

Music provides the reminder, in a gentle and persuasive way, that our dreams matter and that we are worthy of having and pursuing them. We all have had the experience of singing a song over and over in our heads—whether we wanted to or not! This feature of music makes it a natural tool for creating new thought patterns that support our desires to change.

You Have the Choice to Change and Be the Best Possible

Now is the time to own, to really own, your personal power. Now is the time to discard feelings and deep-seated beliefs of unworthiness or of feeling that you can only have and do so much. You are only as limited as you believe you are. Give yourself the gift of choosing music that will support your magnificence and manifest the life you deserve. Your goals are only a song away!

ABOUT THE AUTHOR

Marcia Breitenbach, MA, LPC, is an author, speaker, musician, counselor, and loving mother. She has created a unique e-zine, a songletter, where you can get free, downloadable, empowering songs written by Marcia to assist you in changing your beliefs and your life. She also guides you in the process of identifying limiting beliefs and ones that will empower you. Go to http://www.thesongletter.com to sign up for your first songletter. Here's what some are saying about her music: "Standing ovation, Marcia! Beautiful message, music, and voices. Hope you're creating more." –Dr. Michael Norwood; "I have just been to a weekend workshop in Australia, and Sandy Forster shared your song, "The Magnificent You," with us. I wanted to say thank you—it's beautiful and inspirational. I know it will change my life." –Anne Dempster; "Total head-to-toes goose bumps! It is beautiful. You've created something extraordinary." –Peggy McColl.

63

NEGATIVITY

Poison: How to Avoid Negative People and Get Positive Results

Douglas Dane

If you don't want fleas, don't sleep with the dog! We've all been taught that if you want to reach your goals, you need to avoid negative people.

Unfortunately, it's not that simple. There is poison everywhere, like a fog permeating our lives. We live in a world where everyone has an abundant supply of criticism and loves to hand it out for free. Many people are quick to punish others with their criticism if someone is different from them.

How do you go about improving yourself, reaching your goals, and living your life big? It's about letting go of your ego and not taking things personally. Getting rid of your ego is the antidote to social poison.

Not a day goes by in my business career in which I don't witness gossip, criticisms, rumor, racism, and hate. It's so easy to become infected by the poison. Stand around in a group at a social or business function, and you'll be easily trapped in a discussion about something or someone. Rumors breed gossip. Gossip becomes fact.

As a young man, I left my job as a laborer in a car tire factory. I had hatched my escape plan over the three years that I worked the line: I had decided I was going to start my own business, and at 25, I went looking for the golden opportunity. The friends I left behind seemed resentful and couldn't see their way to supporting me, or maybe their teasing, cajoling, and criticism were the best they could muster. Maybe they couldn't relate to my desire to make something of my life and not continue the poisonous patterns in which I'd been raised.

The path to "success" was a long one. Along the way, people were always trying to drag me down, and others were hoping I would fail. All along the pathway to my future, the words and actions of those who wanted to me to fail burned into me, leaving scars to remind me of why I couldn't succeed, or wouldn't.

Getting through those times was not about a remedy or a cure; it was about immunizing myself against judgment and criticism. The poison invades your ego; we take what others say and do personally. If you care about what others think of you, then you can't help but let criticism hold you back.

It took me over 15 years of studying and practice to get it right. After failing at my second marriage I decided that I needed a different way. Everything I had learned and applied didn't seem to be enough. If I was succeeding in business, I was failing personally. I was at my wits end and frustrated. Everything that I read, I followed, but still, it wasn't enough. Success—financial, emotional, and spiritual—eluded me. They say that the definition of insanity is doing the same thing over and over again, expecting different results. I finally realized that I had to change my approach.

All the poison to which I had been exposed was embedded in me. Later, I realized that early abuse as a child was one of the key reasons I was so defenseless to all the criticisms both from my own second-guessing and from others. I was adopted into a violent, alcoholic home, where I was beaten and abused regularly. This led to two years of sexual abuse at the hands of four pedophiles and then ultimately to my own self-abuse through drugs and alcohol. Living this life, I was taught how to take things personally. Everything was my fault. My parents' alcoholism, my dad's beatings on my mom, and the sexual perversion all became part of my shame. Somehow I had caused them. No wonder I didn't succeed at first. I didn't think that I deserved to win.

No matter how you grow up, children are taught very early on to take things personally. It becomes automatic. Everything we are and everything in which we believe was handed to us by someone else. Think about it. The language you speak was chosen for you. The religion you practiced was chosen for you. Heck, even your name was given to you. Our parents, our teachers, our family, and our friends all taught us what was right and what was wrong. We were conditioned that if we did something right (according to other people), we were rewarded. If we did something wrong, we were punished. So, very early on in life, we trained ourselves to strive for approval and reward by doing things "right." We could avoid disappointment and pain by avoiding doing things wrong. No wonder we take things personally!

So away we went, along our paths without question, accepting what we were told was the truth about right and wrong. Do you remember when you were a teenager and you started to question your parents and challenge authority? Do you remember second-guessing yourself? So often, teens are convinced that they are confused and lost, and these questions begin to surface. I say it's "Truth" tapping you on the shoulder. It's Truth telling you that maybe everything you were told about right and wrong wasn't "right" for you. Most of us shrugged it off, but later in life, Truth comes calling again. For some of us it's a midlife crisis. Again, we shrug off the truth and listen to the criticisms.

It's time to stop taking things personally. What people say about you is based on their own truths. They see life through their own fog. If you realize that, then you don't need to care about what they think of you. You can let go of your ego and not worry about what others say and do.

Once I figured this out, it was like the miracle cure. The self-loathing and shame I had carried around for years dropped off my shoulders. My business took off, and my personal life was blessed with the woman of my dreams and a beautiful baby daughter. I reached and surpassed all my goals, and now anything I set out to do, I achieve. I'm not anybody special. We're all the same when we arrive in this world. The difference is our experiences, our beliefs, and our environment.

You can achieve *big* results. You just have to immunize yourself against social poison and stay out of the fog.

ABOUT THE AUTHOR

Douglas Dane is a motivational speaker and provides coaching for teens and adults. He has appeared on national television and in newspapers and is widely sought after as a guest speaker at high schools, corporations, and social organizations. Audiences have described him as someone who has a rare gift for reaching people of all ages with an inspiring and honest message, and he offers hope to those who feel victimized. His mission is to share his story and his secrets to living big and prove to people that they can do amazing things! Anything is possible! For more information about Douglas Dane, visit http://www.talkingworks.com.

64

NETWORKING

Network Your Way to a Better Life

Bob Burg

The word "networking" elicits a picture in the minds of most people as a business event filled with stereotypical salespeople all "working the room"; fast-walkin', slick-talkin', aggressively sticking their business cards into the face of everyone they meet and saying clever things like, "Hey, give me a call—I'll cut you a deal."

Even if we're speaking strictly in a business sense, the above certainly is *not* networking. Actually, it's . . . well, come to think of it, I'm not exactly sure *what* it is, but it's not networking.

Networking can be defined as "the cultivating of mutually beneficial, *give* and take, win/win relationships." A network itself is simply—at least according to *Webster's*—any arrangement of fabric or parallel wires, threads, etc., crossed at regular intervals by others fastened to them so as to leave open space.

Now, let's leave out the words and thoughts in both definitions (mine and *Webster's*) that don't apply to us and keep in those that do. Oh, and let's substitute the word "people" in the dictionary definition for the words "fabric," "parallel wires," and "threads":

> **Network**: An arrangement of people crossed at regular intervals by other people, all of whom are cultivating mutually beneficial, give-and-take, win-win relationships.

This definition of networking transcends business and applies to practically any aspect of our lives.

No matter the type of network in which you're involved, be it social, religious, charitable, or some other kind, you are at the center. Of course, everyone else is at the center of *his* network as well, and that's as it should be.

Each of the people in a network serves as a source of support (referrals, help, information, etc.) for everyone else in that network. Those who know how to utilize the tremendous strength of a network realize the following very important fact: "We are not dependent *on* each other, nor are we independent *of* each other; we are all interdependent *with* each other." The true strength really comes through when realizing that the people in your network are also part of other people's networks, and that, indirectly, makes each of those people part of *your* network too. (Since it's been documented that most people know about 250 other people, you can see how the numbers add up!)

However, here's the key ingredient—the *secret*, if you will—of those who derive the most benefit from their networks: they themselves are the biggest givers! Lots of people think that the way to derive the most from their network is to be a taker. In other words, the question they're continually asking themselves is, "What can I *get from* my network?" However, the biggest winners, and those who ultimately derive the greatest benefits, are the ones who, instead, ask, "What can I *give to* my network?"

This makes a huge difference. When it comes to networking in the sales vernacular, there's a saying I like to call the "Golden Rule":

> All things being equal, people will do business with,
> and refer business to, those people they know, like
> and trust.

Again, since networking is for more than simply business, we can even readjust the "Golden Rule" slightly and say that

> All things being equal, people will help and support,
> and go out of their way to find help and support for,
> those people they know, like, and trust.

In a sense, you could say that the goal of networking is to develop relationships with those you'd like to have in your network so that they know you, like you, and trust you, they want to see you succeed, and they will go out of their way to help you be successful. In fact, they will become your Personal Walking Ambassadors.

The question is, how do you cultivate those feelings of "know, like, and trust" in others? You become the type of person worthy of those feelings. One way of doing that is to be willing to freely give yourself to others in such a way that you continually "add increase" to their lives. How? Constantly ask yourself, "What does this person need, and how can I help her to get it?" Does she need information? A connection? What can you do to help that person attain what she needs?

Think of your network as an opportunity to provide as much value as you can to others. Your focus is on them, not on you, and this way, you're planting so many seeds of goodwill that you're developing that support system right before your eyes. Eventually, you'll have a powerful network of Personal Walking Ambassadors, just welcoming the opportunity to add positively to your life.

Is this "real-world" type of thinking? Yes, it is. Remember: "All things being equal, people will help and support, and go out of their way to find help and support for, those people they know, like, and trust." To develop these feelings toward you in others, you must first add to their lives in a significant way.

Yes, add to their lives *first*! If you want to make friends, you must first be a friend. If you want to make money, you must first invest some money. If you want to build a huge network, you must first *be* the networker, and that means to be a giver.

But here's the catch, the "Grand Paradox of Networking," and it's what the people I call "SuperStar Networkers" all know: while understanding that the more you give to others, in a genuine and caring way, the more abundance will eventually come back to you, you cannot be demanding, or *emotionally attached*, to the idea of having to receive directly from those to whom you gave. Doing that will position you negatively, not positively. People will forever be suspicious of your motives. Instead, just trust the many seeds of goodwill that you plant will come back to you. They will, many times over.

Understand, of course, there are people who will simply never buy into this concept and will think those of us who believe in it are naïve. All I can say is that the results have proved otherwise, and there's a good reason for that. Obviously, when you consistently give, in an intelligent way, to others and benefit them, they want to do for you; they want to tell others about you; they want to see you benefit as well. And the more you do this without the emotional attachment to receiving in-kind, the more powerfully you affect them and the more they feel as though they know you, like you, and trust you.

Here's one more secret: Superstar Networkers focus on connecting with other successful givers. They tend to refer each other to those in their networks. Before long, a huge web of Superstar Networkers is formed, each of whom is focusing on helping the others in his network. While helping the others takes very little in the way of resources (other than a bit of thought and time), the rewards are so lucrative that you'll be amazed and delighted.

In a sense, you could say that the ultimate goal of networking—regardless of the type of network it is—is the building, cultivating, and developing of a very large and diverse group of people, who will gladly and continually be there for you, while you are there for them.

Changing your attitude about networking is the first step. It's realizing that with a big enough network, there are a lot of people who you might one day have the chance to help.

ABOUT THE AUTHOR

A relationship leveraging pioneer, Bob Burg (http://www.burg.com) has shared the stage with such luminaries as Zig Ziglar, Tom Hopkins, Brian Tracy, and Harvey Mackay at public and corporate events on the topics, "How to Cultivate a Network of Endless Referrals," "Painless Prospecting," and "Winning Without Intimidation: The Art of Positive Persuasion." He is author of numerous best-selling books, including the underground business classic *ENDLESS REFERRALS: Network Your Everyday Contacts into Sales*, which has sold over 160,000 copies. You can download a *free* 22-page special report, "Referrals Fun & Simple," and subscribe to Bob's weekly "Endless Referrals Video Brief" by visiting http://www.EndlessReferrals.com.

65

PASSION

The Passion Principle:
How to Become an Expert Millionaire

Glenn Dietzel

Passion: A strong, barely controllable emotion, a strong enthusiasm.

Many things will help you on the road to success, but nothing will make you put one foot ahead of the other more than passion.

Information does not guarantee success. If it did, everyone that grew up with a set of encyclopedias or a local library would count themselves successful. In fact, everyone that has access to the Internet today would and should be a success if mere access to information was the key.

Upbringing, money, opportunity—they all mean nothing if you do not have the fire in your belly and lightning in your blood. That fire manifests itself in different ways. Some call it determination. Some call it belief. Still others call it persistence. However you label it, the symptoms are the same and are easily recognizable: you are not put off by setbacks; you are willing to pour yourself out to achieve your desire; you have already seen your success in your mind's eye.

President Calvin Coolidge was describing this very characteristic when he said,

> Nothing in the world can take the place of persistence. Talent will not; nothing is more common than unsuccessful men with talent. Genius will not; unrewarded genius is almost a proverb. Education will not; the world is full of educated derelicts.

Persistence and determination alone are omnipotent.
The slogan 'Press On', has solved, and always will
solve the problems of the human race.

Why do some press on while others falter? Why do some pick themselves up and continue while others lay down forever? Passion. Passion is the moving force of the universe. Greatness belongs to those with passion, as it should, and the passionate should enjoy the fruits of their labor as well. Throughout history, unfortunately, only a few have been able to parlay their passions to achieve the wealth and recognition that they deserved, for though passion is the key, ultimately, access to the masses and worldwide acceptance were also necessary to unlock the door to success. An artist, a sculptor, or an inventor would find himself severely limited to his small circle of influence when he attempted to live off of the fruit of his dreams. This is where the term "starving artist" originally came from.

Thankfully, the 21st century has brought us to a new era; an exciting time when, if he is willing, anyone can bring his passion to the fore and not have to starve to do it. Thanks in part to technology that is fairly evenly distributed throughout the world, we are now able to reach not just hundreds, but hundreds of millions, even billions of people. While these people may have different traditions and customs, we are all poured from the same mold. We have the same nature, the same tendencies, and, most importantly, many of the same passions.

What does all this mean for you? Let's look at the facts.

- Everyone has a passion. It's true. Sometimes, owing to our sedentary lifestyles, we forget what that passion is. We get ourselves so wrapped up in the claptrap of life—the hundreds of channels to surf, the banal programming, the endless sitcoms—that we forget about the fire inside.
- Through the Internet we can reach all corners of the globe. We have instant access to billions of other people with the same desires and needs as us.
- Many people out there, sometimes millions of them, will pay you cold, hard cash to share your passion with them. You and only you are the expert regarding all your life experiences, all the successes and all the pitfalls. Let me ask you this: looking back, what would you have paid someone to coach you on what things to focus on and what things to avoid? Hundreds of dollars? Thousands of dollars? Imagine the heartache and stress you could have avoided! Right now, there are people out there who are at the beginning

of the road you have already traveled. Like you, they are willing to invest in an experienced guide, who will walk with them and help them to avoid the potholes!

These facts mean that never before has it been easier to live off your passion. Never has it been easier to become a wealthy problem solver. As Russell Conwell illustrated in his allegory *Acres of Diamonds*, we all have the resources we need to be successful—and our passions are our greatest resource. All that we have to do is recognize them for what they are and utilize them.

That is why the concept of "entrepreneurial authoring" is gaining such widespread appeal. You do not have to travel the world for experience or enroll in a college course to get started in entrepreneurial authoring. All that is required to find your own diamonds is a little introspection and a computer. Put your passions to work for you. Finally, you can get fair market value for the diamonds that you have. These gems include what you know how to do (your skills), the body of knowledge you have gained through the university of hard knocks, and the attitudes you have instilled within yourself to succeed in the numerous areas that reflect your talents.

Remember, people come to the Internet because they have questions and they have problems; they are willing to invest in a solution if it answers those questions and solves those problems!

The process is ingenious in its simplicity.

> Step 1: Identify your passion.
> Step 2: Discover which part of the worldwide market will pay you to use your passion to solve their problems.
> Step 3: Provide that market with good value in products and services and pay yourself what you are *really* worth.

More than any other time in history, you have the opportunity to actually realize your dreams and build your life doing what you love to do. Your passion is calling. Use the fire inside to help the masses. They are looking for the answers that only you can provide!

ABOUT THE AUTHOR

What if you could author a best seller in less than 12 hours of actual writing and gain instant access to a New York publisher without an agent and a formal book proposal? And what if you had an entire team help you take your book and launch an information business using the power of the Internet? How? Follow Glenn Dietzel's simple, proven system for authoring success: http://www.AwakenTheAuthorWithin.com/passion.htm.

66

Six Characteristics for Achieving Peak Performance

Charles M. Marcus

We hear a lot today about being your best, taking care of business, achieving success, and performing at your peak. What we don't always hear is what it takes to sustain peak performance.

Peak performance is a commitment to your physical, mental, and spiritual being and to your personal growth and development. Peak performance, in my opinion, is not something you can switch on and off; it is what you commit to and strive for every day. It is not just about business and achieving goals. It is also about balance between work and family, friends and fitness. Finding the right combination for each of us is personal, but I will share with you six characteristics that have worked for me along the way.

Look after Your Health: Diet and Exercise

This is one so many of us take for granted. I know I did for many years. The sad but true reality is that if we don't have good health, the rest does not really matter because the other steps of peak performance will not fall into place, and we will not have an opportunity to enjoy the rewards.

- See your doctor on a regular basis. Don't be afraid or embarrassed to share personal details. I know that for some of us it is uncomfortable at times, but don't mess around if something is bothering you. For example, I went recently for a colon cancer examination, not the greatest test to have to go through, but the peace of mind afterward was worth a day of discomfort.

231

- Watch your diet. Educate yourself on eating right. There are lots of wonderful books out there on the subject, or go and see a qualified dietician if you like. Drink lots of water as well, six to eight glasses a day, at least. You will feel better and healthier for it, and for those of you watching your weight it will definitely take those hunger pains away in the afternoon and late at night.
- Exercise moderately. I have a treadmill in my basement; for years it just sat there and collected dust. Now, I use it three to four times a week for 30–40 minutes, which fits in with my lifestyle and schedule. Do what is right for you. Join a health club, walk, swim, play tennis, or golf. Exercising in moderation is wonderful, not only for the body but also for the mind.

Discipline Yourself to Get up One Hour Earlier

If you can't do that, strive to get up even 30 minutes earlier than you do now, and invest that time in yourself. I know that is not easy—we all lead such demanding lives and have family obligations. *Make* that time! Trust me, try it for 30 days, and you will be glad you did. I started this discipline in 1986 after a successful course I went on to overcome my stuttering disability. I had to find the time for doing my speech exercises to keep my fluency. Do I succeed every single day in doing this now, especially with a young family? Not always, but I do as often as I can. I always feel better for it.

Challenge Yourself to Learn

Peak performers constantly challenge themselves in many areas. They regularly read books and listen to motivational or business tapes to stay up to date. They are not afraid to be wrong. They are inquisitive and ask lots of questions. They spend less time watching television and more time educating themselves.

Plan for Peak Performance

Peak performers maximize their time. They prioritize, set goals for themselves, analyze their performance, and constantly ask for feedback. They go the extra mile and are single-minded in their pursuit of excellence and success. They work hard, but they also work smart, and they save and spend quality time with their family and loved ones. Life balance sometimes gets lost with people who are obsessive about success, but I believe it is essential for sustaining peak performance.

Take Quality Time Off

I know that it is not always possible for us to take regular vacations for one reason or another, but at the very least, take a mini-vacation, even a day off devoted solely to something other than work or business. Take a walk in the park or woods near you, and smell that fresh air. Take your children or nieces or nephews to the zoo. Treat yourself every now and then—it does not have to be grand and elaborate. Find what is right for you.

Be Comfortable with Yourself

Peak performers are comfortable with who they are. They know that things will not always go their way, that life is not always easy, and that there will be sacrifices to make. The bottom line is that people who succeed in the business of life know this. They surround themselves with a support system to help them, and they are comfortable enough with who they are to know that ultimately, they will get to where they want to be, and they know what it takes to stay there.

About the Author

Charles Marcus is a best-selling author, success strategist, and a highly sought after motivational keynote speaker. He specializes in helping organizations to consistently perform at their highest level and in challenging them to get out of their comfort zones. He works internationally with both corporations and associations. His high-energy, entertaining, and dynamic presentations delight audiences worldwide. For more information on how Charles can impact your organization and on his learning tools, please visit his Web site at http://www.cmarcus.com, or call toll-free at (800) 837–0629.

67

How to Live in the "Performance Zone": The Secret to Being and Feeling Your Best All the Time!

Michael L. Stahl

How do you get what you want, when you want it, from your life? The answer is shocking: force yourself to be uncomfortable.

Yes, that's right—only by pushing yourself outside of situations where you feel completely comfortable can you ever achieve your true potential. Try the following technique.

Stand in front of a person whom you know but don't know well. Each one of you put out your arms to judge an appropriate distance where you feel comfortable. Then, both people, take a half step forward. Make a judgment on how you feel at that moment. Then, both of you take another half step forward. Then, take another half step forward until you are nose to nose with each other, and then think about these things when you feel really uncomfortable:

1. Are you more or less aware of yourself?
2. Do you feel disengaged, or do you feel very "alive" at this moment?

You see, when you push yourself past the normal threshold of "comfort" to "discomfort," your focus improves, you become more aware of your performance, and you start to tap into your true potential. Few people achieve their ultimate potential because they simply are not willing to step outside their comfort zones. Yet, know this: outside your comfort zone lies the "performance zone." This is where you think more clearly, are able to use your talents to the best of your ability, and achieve your dreams.

This involves every area of your life, both personal and professional. I have met many people who say things like, "Well, I have a great career, but I guess I was never meant to be happy with a good relationship," or, "I really love my family and hate what I do for a living, but oh well, it pays the bills and I could never afford to do anything else." These statements, and others like them, are limiting, self-sabotaging beliefs. They are self-fulfilling prophecies. Sure, people have challenges in different areas of their lives, and yet, the bottom line is that people who make statements like those above just want to be comfortable. Ironically, they have become secure in their unhappiness and even more secure in their acceptance of it. It has become comfortable to accept the status quo, to complain, and to live without true satisfaction and contentment.

Your comfort zone is defined by boundaries in your mind as to what you have accepted you could or should do, think, and become. Your personal growth is determined by the size of your world, and the size of your world is directly defined by how you choose to look at it. If you allow fear of the unknown to keep you trapped in your comfort zone, you will never live life with the success, satisfaction, or contentment that you deserve. If you choose to have the courage to step outside your comfort zone of self-limiting beliefs and into your performance zone, it's possible to find a life that you may have never thought was in your reach—simply because you allowed yourself to believe it wasn't.

Achieving your dreams and living the life you always imagined takes a willingness to do the things that make you feel uncomfortable—on a daily basis. Define the actions you need to take to get what you want, and discipline yourself to do the things it takes to achieve your goals. There isn't any magic to it, and it certainly isn't easy. I mean, let's be serious, nobody likes to feel uncomfortable, and yet, when you push yourself outside of your comfort zone and into your personal performance zone, you will love the results you get.

However, results will never come if your attitude is not right. It is your attitude about yourself, your surroundings, your potential, and your life that provides one of the cornerstones to your growth and the ability to push outside your comfort zone. Attitude literally defines who you are as a person. Attitude creates belief systems, and beliefs create who you become. Remember that you don't become what you *want* in life. You become what you *believe!*

As we all know, life does have obstacles that must be overcome in order to live in your performance zone. Everyone has his own view of success, and it is inevitable that all of us will, at some point in our lives, encounter some kind of challenge or roadblock. Life itself is an adventure. Yet, potential problems are not something that we need to dwell on, and in many cases we actually create obstacles for ourselves that are only real because we give them power over our lives.

Even the simplest of things in life illustrate the intense human desire to follow what someone else tells us is the right direction or what we *think* someone tells us is the right direction. How many times do you see a long line at a toll booth or at a bank drive-through when there are three or four lanes open with shorter lines or not one car in them? People just assume that they have to wait a long time, so they choose the line that is already long. They literally create an obstacle for themselves.

People tend to assume the worst, accept the obstacle, and quietly stay inside their comfort zones while they go through life unsatisfied. Step outside your comfort zone, and start taking the path that you know is right for you, not what someone else tells you is right or wants you to believe is right. Engage the attitude of expecting the best and looking at life through positive filters. Don't let anybody else tell you what line to take or in which direction to go. Define the way that is right for you, and believe that you can get to your destination with enthusiasm!

Action creates momentum. It takes discipline to do the things that push you out of your comfort zone. Yet, it is always when you are the least comfortable that you are learning and growing the most. The person who can ultimately exercise the most discipline over your life is you. Define what you want, and then go get it. Will it be easy? *No.* Will consistently stepping outside your comfort zone and into your performance zone give you great satisfaction and well-rounded success? *Yes.*

ABOUT THE AUTHOR

Michael L. Stahl is a professional speaker, corporate trainer, and motivational performance coach. He has traveled to 18 countries around the world and focuses on teaching individuals and organizations how to achieve peak productivity and success. He has appeared on "CNN Financial News," discussing success strategies, and is the President and Founding Partner of Motivational Concepts in Orlando, Florida. To join his "Motivational Moment Club," go to http://www.michaelstahl.com.

68

Leading a Life of Personal Ownership

Richard Gorham

> It's not only what we do, but also what we do not do,
> for which we are accountable.
>
> –Moliere

Ownership.

Too often, people strive to own *things* in a misguided effort to achieve inner peace and happiness. They believe that having a new wardrobe, a new car, a bigger home, or other such material possessions will make them happy or successful. What so many fail to understand is that happiness truly comes from within; it comes from a strong sense of self, not from the acquisition of external things.

Taking personal ownership of your current state of affairs is the first step to achieving a happier and more fulfilling life. When you accept that your current situation is the result of all the choices you've made in your life right up to the present moment, you then realize that you are also in direct control of your future. No one else is pulling the strings of your life, unless you are allowing them to. Only *you* have the authority to steer your own ship.

Beginning today, you can make a choice to change and take complete ownership of your life. In one single moment in time you can decide to take a new path and free yourself from the crippling mind-set that has been holding you back. Never again will you allow yourself the luxury of making excuses for why you cannot make progress. No longer will you indulge yourself with self-pity and the endless "poor me–isms." Blaming other people or outside events for your own misfortune are exercises not worthy of your consideration—your integrity is diminished, and your self-esteem will only suffer from these unproductive, time-wasting habits.

Tragedy is prevalent throughout our society. It's a sad fact of life that too many children grow up in abusive environments. Too often, otherwise perfectly normal people battle drug and gambling addictions or alcoholism. Poverty, hunger, and disease continue to be real challenges for millions of innocent people. In most cases, however, isn't it true that whatever your personal situation, there is someone else who is worse off than you? If the answer is yes, then doesn't it make sense to replace the thoughts of "woe is me" with thoughts of gratitude for the many blessings you do enjoy?

Rather than giving up, *become determined* to make your life better! You can, if you decide that you can.

In general, people who are chronically unhappy suffer from low self-esteem and have a strong sense of personal insecurity. Surprisingly, many of these same people are seen by others as appearing to have everything in the world going for them. They appear to be in-control, goal-oriented high achievers. It's common for these individuals to be strong type-A personalities; they tend to be overachievers and even admit to being somewhat of a perfectionist. Yet, in the back of their minds these very same people suffer from feelings of anxiety and even depression. Despite their obvious strengths in the eyes of their peers, they continue to feel as if they just don't measure up. As a direct result of their ongoing negative self-talk, the physical body finally responds with ailments such as sleep disorders, anxiety, and panic attacks. In the worst cases, depression can overtake the individual, and it can even lead to suicide.

Whether you are simply unhappy with your current situation or you suffer from more serious obstacles, your decision to take personal ownership of your past and present will determine your future.

As a first step, you must begin to take note of the things you are constantly telling yourself. Your self-talk is a primary factor in your ability to overcome any major challenge. If you are constantly telling yourself that you aren't good enough or that you aren't smart enough or attractive enough, it should not surprise you when you continually sabotage yourself in business and relationships.

Taking ownership is more than simply accepting your situation or taking responsibility for the decisions that have brought you to this place in your life. Taking ownership also means that you are committed to taking action toward resolving the challenges that you've identified as barriers to your personal success. Taking action may involve getting help from a doctor, a pastor, a friend, or from anyone who has the knowledge and skills to guide you toward a path of self-reliance, self-acceptance, and an improved sense of self-worth.

If more people would put the same level of energy and enthusiasm into taking personal ownership of their lives as they do in blaming, complaining, and finding fault in others or in "the system," just imagine how much more meaningful their lives would be. Imagine the sense of fulfillment they would enjoy.

Unhappy/low-ownership individuals focus on

- making excuses
- getting even
- having others help them out
- asking, "What for?" or, "What's the use?"

Happy/high-ownership individuals focus on

- making progress
- getting going
- finding answers to help themselves
- asking, "Why not?" or, "What do I need to do next?"

Now, imagine yourself being that happy, successful individual who has taken ownership of his life. You've overcome your personal challenges by stepping out of your comfort zone and by taking action. You've educated yourself to the point that you are now an expert on the very issue that was once holding you back.

Personal growth and development is not always easy. Nothing worth having in this life is easy. However, going through life assuming that the best is yet to come versus believing that the worst is here to stay is simply a more thoughtful and productive choice.

My wish for you is that you decide today to take personal ownership of your life. Take credit for all the good things you've done, and take ownership of any bad choices you've made. Accept the blame or the glory for your personal circumstances. Learn from the mistakes that you've made in order to avoid repeating them. Read, learn, grow, and live a happier life—for you and for the benefit of all of those who love you.

What's the alternative now that you know what it takes to improve your life? Isn't it true that a person who chooses not to read is no better off than a person who can't read? The bigger failure would be the person who has the tools to succeed but, because he lacks the self-discipline or the work ethic, simply chooses not to make the effort. Understand that in the past, fear has paralyzed you from taking action. Fear of failure, fear of the unknown, all of the obstacles and barriers that seem to be adding weight onto your shoulders today can soon become sources of motivation that prepare you for a brighter tomorrow.

Begin now; decide today.

> I will find a way, or make one.
>
> – Orison Marden

ABOUT THE AUTHOR

Richard Gorham is President of Leadership-Tools.com, which is dedicated to providing free tools and resources for today's aspiring leaders, offering high-quality, results-focused tools in the areas of business planning, leadership development, customer service, sales management, and team building. Download your free gift and subscribe to the monthly newsletter today.

69

PERSONAL RESPONSIBILITY/SUPPORT

Take Charge of Your Life: Align with and Strengthen Your Internal Support System

W. Jane Robinson

Understanding self-direction and taking responsibility for your life is vital to your personal success. How you handle adversity, face challenges, and make everyday decisions will shape the course of your future. In the absence of self-direction you may one day discover that you are on a different life path than the one you want to follow. You can change that path by redirecting your life and taking charge of your life decisions, thus reclaiming your personal power.

Two primary pillars of your internal support system are key in attaining self-direction and personal power: a healthy internal locus of control and emotional resilience. Your internal locus of control governs how you handle the situations that impact your life and, ultimately, how you support yourself and direct your life; it is how you use your inner determination, self-direction, and self-motivation. Resilience is how you rebound from adversity and return to your place of inner power and support. Resilient individuals do not just simply cope; they are able to flourish after enduring tremendous life challenges. Your internal locus of control is significant in developing resilience, and both are protective emotional factors. This combination of internal locus of control and resilience enables you to play out the hand you are dealt rather than folding. Taking charge of your life is a skill, and just like with any other skill, you can practice personal responsibility through developing your internal locus of control and resilience until you are confident and are able to play your cards and win the hand of success.

Individual resilience grows through the support of others during childhood and continues into adulthood. This support can be found in parents, mentors, siblings, teachers, peers, and inspirational books. If you didn't receive this support as a child, you can work to develop it in adulthood. You may choose to work with a counselor who can support you and help you to gain a greater understanding of what you have endured emotionally; a counselor can also help you to work through emotional issues and move into your power. We all know how great it feels to have someone support us emotionally when we pursue our dreams, are excited about a new adventure, are worried about work issues, are physically ill, or feel disappointed or sad. Think of how you feel when someone you love congratulates you on a job well done or how you felt as a child when someone stepped in to help with your homework or a difficult project you needed to tackle. Perhaps someone listened with a compassionate ear when an important romantic relationship ended. Self-motivation and determination coupled with an external support system are a powerful team.

You might ask what causes one individual to choose a productive life and another to lead a less desirable life when both have faced similar adversity or lived in the same environment. You might wonder about the determinant that causes some people to achieve great success and rise out of poverty, in comparison to others, who may have had privileged childhoods and yet live lives of mediocrity and quiet desperation. This determinant is your internal locus of control. With a strong internal locus of control you are self-directed and motivated. You look to others for support, but you assume responsibility for your choices.

Resilient people with a strong internal locus of control

- are able to give of the self in order to help others or support a cause;
- use healthy life skills, such as responsible decision-making;
- are assertive or confident in interactions with others;
- use impulse control and are able to delay gratification;
- are problem solvers and critical thinkers;
- are able to be a friend and form positive relationships;
- have a healthy sense of humor;
- are perceptive to the signals of others;
- are autonomous and independent;
- have a positive view of their personal futures;
- are flexible regarding change;
- have a capacity for and interest in learning;
- have the ability to follow through;

- are self-motivated and develop talent and personal competence;
- have a feeling of self-worth and self-confidence;
- value integrity;
- have faith in something greater than the physical or believe in God or a divine source.

Review these characteristics, and take positive action in the areas you need to develop. Having a sense of your inner power, working for what you want in life, taking steps toward your goals, persisting with discipline, and holding on to your dreams are the internal characteristics that will drive you to rise from the ashes. Surround yourself with supportive people who can help you to achieve your dreams and live a more fulfilled life. Sometimes, our emotional wounds are deep and inaccessible without closer examination. We may need someone, a professional counselor, who can offer guidance in healing. While your internal support is perhaps the most critical component in determining your happiness and success, it is also beneficial to have a reflection of that strength and vision from those who support you on your path.

Begin to take charge of your decisions today. Free yourself of those who sap your energy, and keep company with those who see your light and support you on your life path. Use the following affirmation as a tool to help you connect with your personal power, take responsibility for your life, and strengthen your internal locus of control. Your success awaits you!

> I take charge of my life today. I take steps to move forward in the direction of my dreams. I surround myself with people who support me and release anyone who is hindering my growth and personal development. I let go of the naysayers and bless them out of my life. My life is on track with my highest good, and I fill my life with people who support my highest good. I also support them on their life journeys. We share a mutual trust and encourage happiness, health, and abundance. I find greater support as I connect with my personal power and take responsibility for my life decisions. This connection provides me with great strength and determination as I take charge of my life and create success today.

About the Author

W. Jane Robinson is the author of *The Divine Declaration—Awaken to Your Divine Inner Power, Your Life Depends On It*. Having grown up in the state foster care system, she learned about self-reliance and personal power at an early age. She holds a BA in Psychology, and human behavior, motivation, and spirituality have been the central focus of her education and life experience for 20 years. She has studied both areas academically and experientially. You may contact her at Infinite Endeavors Publishing Company, P.O. Box 1236, Oxford, GA 30054, e-mail her at wjr@ieservicegroup.com, or visit her at http://www.ieservicegroup.com.

70

PERSPECTIVES

Don't Take It Personally!

Eva Gregory

Do you sometimes feel like there is a conspiracy and that the whole world is picking on you—your friends, family, colleagues, and even strangers? You know that they are really talking about you, even though they are making general statements. Who do they think they're kidding? Strangers even seem to be going out of their way to make your day difficult—you've been bumped with shopping carts *and* cut off on the road by inconsiderate people. Sound a little familiar? Here's the question: is everyone *really* out to get you, or is it your own baggage that makes you perceive that everyone has an agenda with your name on it?

Is it possible that people are just carrying on with their lives and that the things that are happening are just . . . happening? Perhaps people really *are* speaking in generalities, but you are taking it personally? Here's a scenario: Glen is driving home from work in his sleek, low-to-the-ground sports car. He's had an incredibly bad day and cannot wait to get home and relax. He is almost near his exit and needs to merge from the middle lane to get to the off-ramp. He puts on his signal, sees an opening, and starts to go for it when the person behind him jumps right in. Glen is livid! He calls the person a few well-chosen names and stews about it the rest of the way home. Glen knows that the person behind him did it on purpose.

In reality the person behind Glen had not noticed Glen's signal. He had not been sure how to reach his destination and had asked his wife for directions. At the last minute she had realized that their exit was fast approaching and had told him to get over right away. He had not been out to get Glen. He never even saw him. Boy, talk about two different perceptions of the same situation.

Ironically, this week has not been a good one for Glen. Earlier, a deer had darted out from the woods as he had been driving along, bounced off the top of his car, spun around, and returned to the woods from where it had come. Just yesterday, as he was pulling into his driveway after a long day, he heard that all too familiar sound of pavement scraping the bottom of his beautiful car. Glen was not having a wonderful week. Funny, though, in these instances Glen had not been pleased at what had occurred, but he had not blamed the deer or the pavement or swear that they had been out to get him. If someone had even suggested such an idea to Glen, he might have even considered them a little silly. It never occurred to him to take these situations personally, yet he was completely convinced that the other driver was purposefully provoking him. Is the answer because it had been a person and not a thing? Probably. If so, Glen could work on changing his perspective.

What might a change in perspective accomplish for Glen? For starters he would not be in a bad mood about being cut off. It might also help him to lighten up and relax—it takes a great deal of emotional energy to be angry and defensive. Glen would probably also laugh a little more. When you stop taking things personally, you can see the humor in situations. Wow, a change in perspective could make a dramatic difference in his life. What about in yours?

So, what is the right perspective to have toward people who mean no more harm to you than the deer or the pavement did to Glen? It can be different for each person. Is it tolerance, or acceptance, or perhaps even ignorance? If you find yourself reacting like Glen, try exploring a few different perspectives as an exercise to find the one that works best for you, the one that will help you to shrug it off and *not* take it personally. You'll be amazed at how you can change the quality of your life, simply by changing perspectives!

ABOUT THE AUTHOR

Eva Gregory is a master coach, speaker, and the author of *The Feel Good Guide to Prosperity*. Her internationally acclaimed Leading Edge Living One Year Success Program™ (http://www.leadingedgecoaching.com) is based on her unwavering belief that we all have the power to change anything in our lives and design it purposefully. Eva is currently working on her next book, *Chicken Soup for the Prosperous Soul*, with Jack Canfield of Chicken Soup® fame. She is regularly featured on radio and in the media and is a recognized authority on the Laws of Attraction. Her radio show, "The Thrive Factor" (http://www.ThriveFactor.com), can be heard globally on VoiceAmerica Radio.

71

PLANNING

======

Rise Early and Catch the Golden Worm

Michael Masterson

> Early morning hath gold in its mouth.
> —Benjamin Franklin

Every successful businessman that I know (or about whom I have read) gets up and gets to work early. It's such a universal trait of accomplished individuals that I'm tempted to say it is a secret for success. "Early to bed and early to rise," Ben Franklin said, "makes a man healthy, wealthy, and wise."

Healthy, wealthy, and wise. Let's talk about how getting up and getting to work early helps you to achieve those goals.

In my experience, there is no better time to collect your thoughts and plan your day than early in the morning when the office is quiet. Not only are you undisturbed by phone calls and interruptions, but ahead of you is the potential of an unopened day. The solitude promotes a kind of relaxed, contemplative mood. You feel free to think in an expansive way. Later on, when the place is noisy and the pressure is on, it's difficult to pay attention to what's important. You feel your attention drawn in several directions at once. You feel the pressure of deadlines, and you may be hit with bad news, which could put you in a bad, unproductive mood.

A Near-Perfect Morning Routine

Over the years I've studied hundreds and experimented with dozens of time-saving techniques and organizational systems. The simple, three-step routine that follows is the best of the best.

249

Step One: Getting Healthy (6:30–7:00)

The first thing I do every day is run sprints. After a four- or five-minute warm-up, I run eight 50-yard dashes, with 30 seconds of rest in between. Then, I do a serious 10-minute stretching routine (yoga moves, mostly). Finally, a cold shower and a fresh set of clothes complete the process.

This workout is a condensed version of everything I've learned about health and fitness for the past 45 years, and it has dramatically improved my health. For example, I no longer have the back, shoulder, and neck pain that troubled me for so many years. I am as strong as I was when I was playing football in college, and I rarely get sick.

Step Two: Planning the Day (7:00–7:30)

I begin each day with a list of "to dos" that I've usually created the night before. I add to that list by going through my inbox and selecting any items that are important enough to make it to my daily list.

I used to scan my e-mail for things to do but found that I couldn't resist the lure of trying to knock off a bunch of little things that wasted my time and drained my energy. Now, I scrupulously avoid e-mail in the morning. In fact, I don't even open it up. I check phone messages and faxes and add any important items to my daily task list. Again, I don't respond to anything at this point. My job is simply to organize it all—to figure out what I will do today and what I can delegate or do later.

Now comes the fun part. I get out a clean sheet of paper and write the date on top. Referencing all the inputs I have just gathered, I select 15 to 20 that I intend to accomplish before the end of the day. (You have to be realistic when you do this. There is no way you can do more than 15 or 20 significant things in a day.) Of the 15 or 20 items, I highlight four or five of them. These are all important-but-not-urgent tasks. (The urgent tasks you have to do. The important-but-not-urgent tasks are the ones that will advance your long-term goals. They are critical to your success, but you will almost certainly fail to do them unless you make them a priority.)

As a general rule, it's a good idea to structure all your tasks so that none lasts more than an hour. Tasks lasting 15 and 30 minutes are the best. If you have something that takes several hours to do, break it up into pieces, and do it over a few days. It will be better for the extra time you give it, and you won't get crushed on any one day.

If you adopt this simple system, you will see how well it works. Before your colleagues, competitors, and coworkers are even sipping their first cups of coffee you will know what your priorities are, and you will already be thinking about some of them. You will not have to worry about forgetting something important, and you will have a strong sense of energy and excitement, knowing that your day is going to be a productive one.

Step Three: Give Your Day a Boost. (7:30–8:30)

Here's the best step. Select the single most important task of the day—the one highlighted task that will best help you accomplish your most cherished goal—and get to work on that. Don't worry if something else is more pressing. Don't pay any attention to what someone else wants you to do. Heck, it's not even nine o'clock yet. It's your time, so spend it on yourself!

If you are having trouble figuring out what is the most important task, ask yourself this question: "If I knew I was going to die in a week, which task would be most important to me now?"

If you spend the first working hour of every day on something about which you deeply care, it will give you more energy than you can possibly imagine. (I know this is true because it happens to me every morning.)

Success Is What Happens When You Do a Little Bit Extra Each Day

I suppose it's possible for success to come in a single windfall, but most often, it arrives bit by bit. Here's what I want you to do: I want you to figure out, on the average, what time you have been getting to work each day, and I want you to promise yourself that you'll get there at least 15 minutes earlier from now on.

Don't fool yourself. If you've been trying to get to work by eight but get there at that time only two days a week, admit that your starting time is 8:15 or 8:30, then fix your new objective.

Fifteen minutes a day multiplied by 50 weeks is 62.5 hours of extra work. That gives you more than a full week's advantage over those against whom you are competing. You can accomplish a lot in a week, so don't underestimate what this will do for you.

It's not just about doing extra stuff. It's about getting a jump on things. Getting in early makes you better prepared, more thoughtful, better organized, and more effective in every area of your life.

Early to bed, early to rise. It will make you healthier . . . and wealthier and wiser, too.

ABOUT THE AUTHOR

Michael Masterson, author and businessman, has developed a loyal following through his writings in "Early to Rise," an e-newsletter that mentors more than 400,000 success-oriented individuals to achieve their life goals. Over the course of his remarkably successful business career Michael has been involved in the development of dozens of successful businesses, including two that grew beyond $100 million. At one time or another he's owned and run companies that were public/private, onshore/overseas, local/international, service/product-oriented, retail/wholesale/direct mail, and even profit/nonprofit. What do you want to do this year? Become wealthier? Get healthier? Read more books, travel the world, and become wiser? Sign up for ETR at http://www.earlytorise.com, and we'll show you how to do all of that and more . . . in just five minutes a day.

72

POSITIVE SELF-TALK

A Matter of Chatter

John Harricharan

I first met Cindy during my second year of college, in the cafeteria where she bumped into me. Yes, she literally bumped into me, and the food on her tray went flying all over the place. I heard her mutter under her breath, "What an idiot!"

"Pardon me," I replied, not knowing what else to say but definitely feeling that it was not my fault.

"Oh, no," she said, "it's always my fault. I'm really so clumsy. I'm very sorry."

Then, I realized that she had been referring to herself. Over the months I got to know her a little better. Sometimes, we'd sit at the same table in the cafeteria, and other times, I'd sit next to her in class.

It never ceased to amaze me how often she would call herself an idiot at the smallest thing that happened. It was as if she had been programmed to respond to the slightest misfortune with self-blame. One day, I finally asked her why. Her eyes opened wide as she said that she was not aware that she did. She confessed that it was probably a habit and that she always felt that when anything bad happened, it was her fault. She told me that the voice in her head always told her that she was an idiot and pointed out that she was not as good as others. The constant, negative chatter in her mind was preventing her from achieving her greater potential.

Cindy managed to graduate, and we eventually lost touch with each other, but I always wondered how she was doing. I always hoped that she was able to still the chatter in her mind and to change the programmed voice to a more positive one. The matter of chatter is a very serious one. If we were to listen carefully to what we are saying to ourselves, we would find very interesting conversations going on. If we are happy and fulfilled, these internal conversations are positive, but if we are constantly worried and depressed, we probably have sad and confusing conversations.

We can literally change the outside world by first changing our inner world. Generally, it's our inner conversations that determine what our outer world looks like. If we constantly think sad thoughts, then our self-talk will focus on sad things, and the entire world will appear depressing. If we always think angry thoughts, the world will appear angry—even a beautiful sunset will appear to be filled with angry shades of red. However, if we think peaceful and positive thoughts, the world will seem peaceful and positive to us.

How do we silence the endless chatter in our heads?

- Try to find some quiet time each day and listen to what you are saying to yourself. Don't be like Cindy, who kept calling herself an idiot. Once in a while, we all say terrible things about ourselves, but if we do it too often, it becomes a habit, and we start believing those things.
- As you listen to the conversation in your head, do not follow it. Just observe it, and let it go. If you start to focus on the thoughts, you get caught up in them and then carried away by them.
- After observing your thoughts for a while, you'll find that they move on and that you are not trapped by them. Remember that your thoughts are not you. You only have them. Don't even worry about replacing them with positive thoughts—that will come later.

Simple as the above exercise may seem, it will have the most profound effect on your life. Gradually at first, and then more quickly, you'll find that a greater calm comes over you. Because you've let go of the chatter, the noise diminishes, and you become able to hear the voice of intuition, the voice of the universe seeking to guide and to help you.

Yes, it's a matter of chatter, clatter, and clutter, and if we turn the volume down, we will be able to hear the beautiful symphonies of life.

ABOUT THE AUTHOR

John Harricharan is the award-winning author of the best seller *When You Can Walk on Water, Take the Boat* as well as the ground-breaking *PowerPause* and other books. John, a unique blend of East and West, well-educated and professional in demeanor, brings a welcome, practical approach to life. Named "Businessman of the Week" and "Outstanding Young Man of America," among many other honors, John is a magnetic speaker, who shares his insights and pragmatism in a very direct manner. Visit his Web site at http://www.Insight2000.com.

73

Two Negatives Must Always Make a Positive!

Lester J. Robinson III

Learned life experiences move us forward rather than back. As you grow forward, you become a more rounded individual, and even with ups and downs, good events begin to happen. It's the things you learn as you move forward that help to shape your future for good. Since I've experienced the move from negative to positive, I can share some tips that can help make the change possible.

- Recognize that you are not moving forward. If you've found your goals unattainable and you've given in to accepting that as your life situation, you need to think again. You may have to reposition your goals for a time or make new goals, but change is a positive move.
- Identify the problem. This may take some honest digging. Where has the hope been lost? What caused the derailment?
- Come to terms with the problem. Identifying the steps needed to make the necessary changes again calls for an honest assessment.
- Realize that you have learned something in the process that will not only help you now but will be a constant asset to you in handling your future. You have given yourself a life skill in self-management.
- Accept this growth, and move through the door you have opened into a new life. This is where you realize that you have taken the stress and tension out of past problems, and you can enjoy life in a new way.

Despite following these tips, you might find yourself asking an interesting question: what if the negative events hadn't happened? What if I'd married the girl? What if I had gotten the sale? What if I had gotten that house? What if I'd shot the moon and bought that car? Thinking through my life, I have come to see that things happen for a reason. These small negatives turn into a positive—a positive that you would not have experienced if the negatives had not been part of your life. If they had come true, you might have experienced a still bigger negative in expense and concern. It may be a good thing that you did not marry that person, get that sale, or buy that car or house.

One cannot escape everything. If you experience a truly negative circumstance, find a way to release it to the universe. When something affects you personally or wrecks your day or your week, why would you want to hold on to it? So many things can affect you negatively: not getting the date, not getting the sale, not getting the house you want, not getting the job you want, problems at work, waiting for ages in line in a store, or losing the big game. When things of this nature struck me, I would carry the negativity around inside me for days and sometimes weeks. I wasn't enjoying life at all. I was halfway through my Complementary Health TV Series when I figured out how to release these tensions. It took me a long time to learn to come to terms with the negative, to do my best to consider how to manage the negative, and then to say good-bye to it. I'm a happier person for developing this process. Reducing my stress and tension have led to a more balanced and fulfilling life.

I want to give you one last tip: it is to enjoy your new life and the opportunities it presents. Experiencing your new life to the fullest means being in the moment. Our days bring us these special moments, and we must not let others keep us from experiencing them fully. Enjoying your good moments is essential to keeping the positive in your life.

Planning your day and your work are necessary to be successful, but your planning should not exclude the special moments along the way. Recognize them, and hang on to them. Being in the moment means that you are not missing out on life—and that's a very positive thing.

ABOUT THE AUTHOR

Lester J. Robinson is a successful insurance professional, a public access TV host, and a lifelong learner. As an enthusiastic master of ceremonies for western New York's Complementary Health TV Series™, Les further shares his vast knowledge with viewers via his very popular Web site, http://www.chswlr.com. He also helps consumers locate practitioners through an online directory at http://www.healthlistingscenters.com. His speeches, guiding audiences to discovery, are acclaimed for their style, information, and uplifting messages. Write Les at P.O. Box 346, Lockport, NY 14095. E-mail him at HealthListings@aol.com or phone him at (716) 634–5656, ext. 3014.

74

THE PRESENT

Power of Now

Karim Hajee

Do you ever catch yourself thinking about something that happened some time ago, or even something that may or may not happen in the future? Chances are that you're like most people, and you regularly think about something from the past, or you're focused on something that could happen in the future. You're not here—you're not living in the now, and you fail to utilize what I call the "power of now," which can dramatically improve your life in ways you never thought possible.

If you want to achieve success and happiness, start living in the now. Be here now by experiencing the present moment for the gift that it is. We all live in the present moment, but very few of us utilize the power of now.

The only thing that exists is what is happening right now. The past doesn't exist; it's over with and should be nothing but a fading memory. The future doesn't exist; it hasn't happened yet. The past and the future are only a part of your thoughts and memories. They only exist in your mind and not in reality.

The only thing that exists right now is the present moment, and from this present moment you can draw tremendous power, the kind of power that can change your life and allow you to achieve your goals. You may not like the present moment, but that's only because you think that the present should be different. You're comparing the present moment to something else and not appreciating what is happening right now. You're either focusing on mistakes of the past, or you're consumed with the future. You're probably thinking about what the now should be instead of dealing with what is going on.

If you don't have a job, then it's time to look for one. I know you're probably looking for work, but don't focus on the fact that you don't have a job, and don't focus on how difficult it may seem to get a job. Simply concentrate on going out and getting that job. At the end of the day, see where you are, and focus on what needs to be done next. If your children need attention right now, then give them attention. If you need to go out and look for work right now, then do it. Don't compare your present situation to anything; accept what it is and make the most of it with the intention of making the present better.

I'm not saying that you should accept your present situation and do nothing to improve it. Instead, deal with your present situation, and do everything you can to improve your life. When you begin living in the present moment with the intent of improving your life, you begin to utilize the power of now; you leave the past in the past, you don't concentrate on the future, and you start doing everything that you can to improve your life in the present. You send a powerful message to your subconscious mind. You tell your subconscious that you're here now and ready to get to work to improve your life. It then begins working for you because your subconscious only understands the present moment. Your subconscious does not understand the future or the past.

While many of you will be able to understand the concept of living in the now and working with the power of the present moment, practicing it is another thing. To work with the power of now, you have to get your mind to work differently. You have to get your mind to simply focus on what is happening and what needs to be done right now. No more comparing, and no more hoping for things to get better. Just deal with what is and what has to be done. You then start moving forward, and you allow your subconscious mind to help you achieve your goals because you are here now, working with your subconscious to create the situation that you want.

The only thing that is taking place right now is the present moment. As you read this article, that's all that you are doing. When you are done, the moment that you are currently experiencing will never happen again! The only reason that people are unhappy is because they fail to live in the present moment, and they fail to embrace the now. If you're at work, focus on work. If you're at home, focus on the home. If you're with friends, focus on your friends. You'll then release your subconscious mind, and it will help you to improve your life.

How to Live in the Now

If you're ready to start living in the now and to begin creating the life that you want, then take a look at your present situation, and ask yourself what's wrong with the moment you are in. Don't think about what happened yesterday or sometime in the past. Don't focus on what might or might not happen tomorrow. Take a look at the moment you are in, and see if there is anything wrong. I want you to focus your mind on what is happening, then see what is wrong with that picture.

You should find nothing wrong with the present moment—it is what it is, and once you accept it, you can start living again.

Let's face it: you can't turn off your mind, but you can get it to work differently, and that's what you should start doing. If you don't take control of your mind, your mind will control you—and that's not going to help you to improve your life.

Ask yourself some questions.

- Do you find yourself waiting for something to happen?
- Are you waiting for more time?
- Are you waiting to make more money?
- Are you waiting to meet the right person?
- Are you waiting for the right opportunity?

Waiting is another game the mind plays because it doesn't want to live in the present moment. If you answered yes to any of the above questions, then you're not living in the now.

I know that you can't live in the now 24 hours a day, but start by using these techniques for a few minutes each day, and then continue expanding the exercise. Track your progress. See how you feel when you only focus on what is happening right now, and you'll begin to enjoy the process.

Here's a suggestion: the next time you're driving or walking, pay attention only to what is happening around you. Listen to the sounds, and observe the people. Don't think about what you have to do or what happened yesterday or what might happen in the future. Focus only on what is happening at that moment.

261

You'll then start living in the present moment, and before you know it you'll be able to focus your mind and utilize the power of now.

Be here now, and you'll start changing your life instantly.

ABOUT THE AUTHOR

Karim Hajee has been a teacher for the past 20 years. He is an award-winning television reporter in Canada and the United States, where he now makes his home in New York City. His unique Creating Power System is proven effective and helps you to live the kind of life you want and to achieve your full potential. For more information, visit his Web site at http://www.creatingpower.com.

75

PROBLEM SOLVING

Sleep On It

Holleay Parcker

Old enough to have my own problems, yet young enough to believe my father's word without question, as a child, I spent countless evenings seeking his advice. At 6 P.M., I'd sit at the kitchen table, facing the back door. I wanted to be first to present my concerns to him. It was always a short wait. Like clockwork, my father walked through the door at 6:15.

He sat beside me, patiently listening and sometimes asking questions. A man of few words, Dad's answer to all of my dilemmas was simply, "I think you should sleep on it." For many years it was a familiar routine. I talked. Dad listened. Then came his advice: "Sleep on it."

One day, my teenage frustration got the better of me, and I could stand it no longer. "How will sleeping on it help, Dad? What does that solve, anyway? Don't you understand? I have this problem, and I need an answer, *now.*"

My father was silent. He looked at me, and in that moment I could see that he was making a decision. I grew quiet, realizing that something important was about to happen.

Then, Dad said, "I think you're old enough now to understand this concept. Let me give you an example. Last night, I was working on my model ship. Often, the kits come incomplete. Parts are missing, the instructions are in disarray or, even worse, inaccurate. Assembling the model itself is challenging enough, but when you run into problems of this nature . . . well, I find that I end up having to improvise quite a bit.

"There's a certain point in building the model where you have to proceed very carefully. A wrong move can mean lots of wasted time and energy. I could try to explain what the problem was, but since you're unfamiliar with model ships . . . the point is, I was perplexed. I just couldn't figure out the next step, no matter how hard I tried.

"When I went to bed last night, I thought again about the situation. And then I asked for the solution to the problem to come to me while I was sleeping."

"Who did you ask, Dad? Who were you talking to?" I interrupted.

"Well, I believe that we all have the answers *within* us. When we listen, we can hear the answers. And you know what? I woke up about two in the morning with the solution! I don't know why I hadn't seen it before. It may seem really simple, but it works. I've found answers to all kinds of problems this way. I could tell you about times when your mother and I have had difficult decisions to make, or I've been worried over something at work.

"When you're faced with a problem and need a solution, sleep on it. Ask for the solution to come to you. It can't hurt, and it just might help. It sure works for me."

"I think you need to sleep on it" has proven to be among the best advice Dad's ever given me. Over the years I've used this simple technique in a variety of ways.

Early on, I found great benefit simply by distancing myself from the problem. By allowing it to marinate overnight, meat is tenderized. By allowing a problem to marinate for a few hours, often, its "toughness" is reduced as well, and sometimes, the problem even resolves itself completely! Other times, I wake up with an "ah-ha" experience, where the solution is laid out before me. Just like my father, I wonder why I hadn't seen it before. It seems so simple when you know how.

Recently, I've discovered a brand new use for this technique: inspiration! I don't always have to have a problem that needs solving; it's okay to ask for *inspiration* as well! I stumbled onto this discovery through a real estate deal. I'd purchased a fixer-upper, and boy, did it need fixing up, from new siding and windows to all new flooring and furniture and everything in between. It took several months to renovate. When it was finished, I looked around and said to myself, "You know, this is good. Really good."

Then, I went outside and under the house to the pool area. (I live in a coastal community, and the houses here are built on pilings.) I saw that it was bad. Beyond bad. Awful, really. All the magic was inside the house! I needed magic *under* the house, too, but the months of renovations had exhausted me. I was worn out and weary, clueless as to what the right touch was or even how to approach it.

It had been a difficult day, and a long one. I flung myself onto the bed that night, too tired to undress. Frustrated, I called out, "I want a fabulous tiki bar. I don't know how to begin. I cannot see what to do. I need inspiration. Show it to me, show it to me, *please*."

Then, I fell into a deep sleep.

I awoke at 3:30 A.M. I had had the most wonderful dream! I'd seen how to do it; I saw the tiki bar built and painted. The underpinning was alive, the colors of a tropical sky in Caribbean blues and blue-greens. The pilings around the pool had been transformed into palm trees, the tops of the trees painted on the underpinning as though they were swaying in the gentle midsummer's breeze. Toucans, parrots, macaws, and cockatoos sat perched on the branches in the trees or peeking through the colorful foliage near the bottom.

The outdoor shower nearly glowed in lime green, pink, and purple hues. Inside the shower a mermaid beckoned, an octopus guarded a treasure chest, a seahorse swam lazily by, and a dolphin leapt. Deeper blues and greens striped the outside of the bar, and inside, splashes of bold green and orange, red and yellow.

There was more. Much more.

I hardly slept the rest of the night. At the paint store early the next morning I had a list of colors to mix. The trunk of my car loaded down with paint, I went to work. After the background colors were finished I hired a local artist to paint what I had seen. Each day, a new idea would come. The more I turned my thoughts to it and reflected on the tiki bar, the more I was deluged with even *better* ideas!

When it was completed, I looked around, amazed at the result—it really was fabulous! I'm filled with wonder at the inspiration and creativity that was just *waiting* to be tapped into . . . when I chose to "sleep on it."

ABOUT THE AUTHOR

Holleay T. Parcker is a realtor whose many successes are attributed to listening to the "still, small voice" within. It is her firm belief that great success in the real estate world is directly proportional to using the power of intuition. She shares her wisdom with other realtors and anyone else who is interested in the "intuition–real estate" connection through her book, *The Enlightened Realtor*. Holleay invites you to learn how to use your intuitive guidance radar system for success, not only as a real estate agent or broker, but in any field you choose. For more information, or to see a picture of the tiki bar described above, visit http://www.RealEstateIntuition.com.

76

PROCRASTINATION

Does Procrastination Sabotage Your Success?

Rita Emmett

Even if you consider yourself to be a hopeless procrastinator, you can get help. How can I be so sure? Because I was born the world's greatest procrastinator. (My mother claims that her pregnancy with me lasted 10 months—that I actually put off being born for a month.) As an adult, I converted. Now, I'm a "recovering procrastinator." If I can change, you can, too.

The STING Strategy

Here are five steps to take the STING out of being overwhelmed. Doing any one of these steps will help you to stop putting things off, but when you put all five together, they form a powerful strategy that will help you to accomplish your top priority, no matter how many other priorities are nipping at you.

Where to start? You know that old expression "a journey of 10,000 miles begins with but a single step"? Your first step is the "S" of STING: **select** one task you've been putting off. You're right, you can't do everything, so do just one thing. If it has many components to it, keep narrowing it down. Break it into smaller tasks. Select just one task to do.

Now, the first thought that many really good procrastinators will have is, "Well, I've selected my task. Now I have to wait until I have a whole day free to work on it." However, we all know that you'll never, ever have a whole day free. You probably find it almost impossible to carve out a whole morning or afternoon as free time, but you can always find one free hour, right? Maybe not every day, but at least one hour a week.

Next, the "T" of STING is to **time** yourself. Buy an ordinary kitchen timer, and set it for one hour. Sometimes, people say that they can mentally time themselves, but the ticking of a timer adds a wonderful sense of urgency to the project.

Two Simple Rules

Even if you have attention problems or a difficult time focusing, you can stick to something for one hour, can't you? During that time you can follow two simple rules to help you get the job done. The first one is to **ignore** everything else. Focus on doing just this one task.

This is the downfall of most procrastinators. They decide that today, they will accomplish this one task, but then they think that maybe they'll first check their e-mail, then perhaps make one quick phone call, and next, it's time to organize all the paper clutter in the area, and then one—just one—computer game. In the blink of an eye, 15 things are started, none are completed, and the procrastinator says, "Well, I was multitasking." However, it's not productive if nothing is completed.

Then, all of a sudden, time's up. The procrastinator looks at the clock and says, "It's too late to start this today. I better leave it 'til tomorrow." It's a terrible rut to be in, but this rule will help you to stay out of that rut. For only one hour, ignore everything else.

Here's the second rule to the STING strategy: **no** breaks allowed while the timer is ticking. To be honest, back in my procrastinating days, this is where I excelled . . . or, I should say, this is where I sabotaged myself. I could take a one-hour job and make it last 14 months because I was *so* terrific at taking breaks.

When I first incorporated these two rules into my strategy, I realized it was the very first time in my life that I did one hour of pure work, with no breaks and no goofing around starting a million other projects. These two rules will help you to accomplish an incredible amount of work.

The Power of Rewards

So, what do you do when the timer dings and your time is up? Your last step in this journey is the "G" of STING: **give** yourself a reward when the job is done.

This is an important part of the strategy, but it also can be the hardest. You can probably identify rewards for your family, your customers, your boss and coworkers, and your friends, but many people never give any thought to what would make *them* happy.

As you start your journey to become a "recovering procrastinator," list several rewards for you that would get you going on this project. Don't cop out and say, "The satisfaction of completing the job is enough reward for me" because if it truly was, then why in heaven's name were you putting it off in the first place?

Plan big rewards for big accomplishments, and little rewards for little ones. Of course, a trip to Hawaii for making a call to a customer would be terrific, but that's not going to happen. We're talking about things you can give yourself today, or at least this week, as a reward for one hour of work.

For example, don't allow yourself a favorite beverage or the chance to check your e-mail until the hour is up. Or think of all those things you love to do but never have time to do—read a novel, spend time with your spouse or children, walk out in nature, go to a movie or a museum, or take a nap. Then, when your hour of "pure" work is complete, you can enjoy your reward *guilt-free*.

There you have it—five steps that together form a surefire strategy that will take the STING out of feeling overwhelmed:

- **Select** one task you've been putting off.
- **Time** yourself. Give the task one full hour.
- **Ignore** everything else. Focus on doing just this one task.
- **No** breaks allowed while the timer is ticking.
- **Give** yourself a reward when the job is done.

Every step you take in conquering procrastination leads you to a greater sense of freedom. Now, go ahead and set that timer. Build the success of which you dream. The world will be a better place when you do. Start becoming the effective, productive, goal-achieving person you want to be, and you're likely to notice that each step becomes lighter as you travel your journey of 10,000 miles—your journey to becoming the leader you are meant to be.

ABOUT THE AUTHOR

Rita Emmett is a professional speaker and the author of *The Procrastinator's Handbook* and *The Clutter-Busting Handbook* as well as a free monthly e-zine, "The Anticrastination Tip Sheet." You can reach her or sign up for the Tip Sheet through her Web site, http://www.RitaEmmett.com, or call (847) 699–9950. If you'd like a free visual reminder of the STING strategy, go to Rita's Web site and click the "Looking for STING?" link.

77

PRODUCTIVITY

How to Get More Work Done in a Day

Zig Ziglar

How do you achieve employment security in a world where there is no employment security? I start with a question: do you consider yourself to be honest and at least reasonably intelligent? Okay. As an honest, intelligent person, do you, as a general rule, get about twice as much work done on the day before you go on vacation as you normally get done? Now, I am going to ask you a long question, so stay with me all the way through. If we can figure out why and learn how and repeat it every day without working any longer or any harder, does it make sense that we will be more valuable to ourselves, our company, our family, and our community? The answer is yes.

I want to make it crystal clear that I am communicating with you about you—I'm not referring to anybody else, but to you about you. You have undoubtedly already confessed that you are honest and intelligent.

Now, on the night before the day before vacation, do you get your laptop or a sheet of paper out and plan, "Now, tomorrow I've got to do this and this . . . ." We've coined a very clever name for that—we call that goal setting. So, you set your goals. Then, you get them organized in the order of their importance.

Let me encourage you to make one slight change there. Get the disagreeable and difficult things out of the way first. Free your mind so you can concentrate on what else you have got to do. You get it organized. You accept responsibility. You make the commitments. You know that some people are about as committed as a Kamikaze pilot on his 39th mission—they just aren't serious about it.

Now, commitment is important whether it is to get your education, make one more call, keep the marriage together, or whatever. Commitment is important because when you hit the wall—not *if*, but *when* you hit the wall—if you have made a commitment, your first thought is "How do I solve the problem?" If you haven't made the commitment, your first thought is "How do I get out of this deal?" And we find literally what we are looking for. When you make that commitment, things happen. It shows that you really care about the other people on the job. It demonstrates that you are dependable. Even though you're leaving town, you're not going to leave an unfinished task for others to do. Your integrity comes through.

Have you ever participated in organized team sports? Did you ever go home one night and say to your parents something like, "Mom, Dad, you won't believe the game plan the coach has worked out. Man alive, it is incredible. We're going to kill those suckers tomorrow. You can count on it." You were optimistic simply because you had a plan of action, and likewise, you are optimistic that tomorrow you are going to be able to get all of the things done that need to be done before you can go on that vacation.

Now, some of us are born optimistic, and some are born pessimistic. For your information, the 1828 Noah Webster Dictionary does not have the word pessimist in it. It has the word optimist. Now, I am a natural-born optimist. I really am. I would take my last two dollars and buy a money belt with it. That's the way I'm put together. But the good news is if you are a natural-born pessimist, you definitely, emphatically, positively can change. You are a pessimist by choice because you are what you are and where you are because of what's gone into your mind. You can change what you are; you can change where you are by changing what goes into your mind.

Anyway, on the day before you go on vacation you not only get to work on time, you are a little early, and you immediately get started. You don't stand around and say, "Well, I wonder what I ought to do now." You can't wait to get after it. You want to do the right thing, so you get started in a big hurry. You are enthusiastic about it. You are highly motivated. You decisively move from one task to another.

Now, I am going to camp on this one for just a moment. Have you noticed that as a general rule, people who have nothing to do want to do it with you? It's true, isn't it? Now, on this day before vacation, when you finish one task, you move with purpose to another one. And people just will not block you for that two-minute gossip session or four-minute or five-minute or six-minute chat. I am absolutely convinced and have no doubt about it that the listener has more to do with gossiping than the speaker does because if you don't listen, nobody is going to gossip to you. They just won't.

When you move with purpose, people will step aside and let you go. I will absolutely guarantee that you will save a minimum of an hour a day in two-, three-, five-minute spurts of time. An hour a day is five hours per week is 250 hours per year. That is six weeks of your life that you've wasted and six weeks of combined time that you have wasted with people who have been gossiping with you. What could you do with six extra weeks every year?

Focus on the issue at hand. Discipline yourself to stay with it until you finish. Cybil Stanton gave me the best definition of discipline I have ever read in her book *The Twenty Five Hour Woman*: "Discipline isn't on your back needling you with imperatives. It is at your side encouraging you with incentives."

Treat every day like it's the day before vacation, and you will get more work done!

ABOUT THE AUTHOR

Zig Ziglar has been featured in *The New York Times*, *The Washington Post*, and *The Dallas Morning News* as well as in *Fortune*, *Success*, and *Esquire* magazines and has appeared on "The Today Show," "20/20," "60 Minutes," and "The Phil Donahue Show." He has that rare ability to make audiences comfortable and relaxed, yet completely attentive. As an author, he has written 24 books on personal growth, leadership, sales, faith, family, and success. Nine titles have become best sellers, including *Over the Top* and *See You at the Top*. Subscribe to the free, weekly "Zig Ziglar Newsletter" at http://www.zigziglar.com.

78

Three Simple Mind Tricks for Attracting Wealth

Andreas Ohrt

Do you ever wonder why you don't have enough money in your life? I can guarantee that your problem stems from your thoughts about money: somewhere within your mind are specific beliefs that are blocking its flow. In this short article I cannot begin to delve into the many subconscious reasons for this truth, but I would like to share some simple ways you can begin, right now, to change this.

Using the power of your mind to attract wealth is like a magic trick. You simply trick your mind into believing that you have what you want, and then your life begins to change to reflect your new belief. Just like a magic trick, it seems impossible until you learn the trick, and then you realize that it is actually very simple.

Mind trick #1: Show gratitude for any money that enters your life. In order to attract money into your life, you must show gratitude for the money that is already in your life. Instead of whining about how little money you have, bask in gratitude at the many ways in which you are already wealthy. For example, if you earn over $2,182 in a year, you have more wealth than 85 percent of the people on earth. When you focus on what you have rather than on what you want, you realize that you are already rich. Give thanks often for all the riches in your life.

Action step: The next time money enters your life, instead of barely noticing what has happened and mentally beginning to spend it, use a few moments of time to give thanks to the universe for bringing this money into your life. Every time you receive a paycheck, every time someone gives you money for any reason, every time you get a great deal or save money in some way, appreciate the fact that money is flowing into your life. Doing this every time money comes to you will attract more money into your life.

Mind trick #2: Act as if you are rich. This is the fundamental truth of all mind power work—you must act as if what you want is already yours. Act as if you already have the money you wish to have. Ask yourself if you were already rich what you would do, how you would act, and how you would feel, and then do, act, and feel in those ways.

Of course, you shouldn't quit your job and move to the South Pacific, but start small, and with each success, build your way to greater wealth. Eat a little better, dress a little nicer, take that class you think you can't afford, or do anything at all that you wish to do but believe you can't because of a lack of money.

When you do these things, bask in joy at your inner state of wealth, and know that this state will be reflected in your outer world. You'll be amazed at how life provides for the things that bring you joy.

Action step: The next time you are about to buy something, anything at all, purchase an item that is of slightly higher quality and price than you would usually buy. Even if something only costs a few pennies more than what is usual for you to spend, buy that item, and thank the universe for providing for your new, expanding lifestyle. Even though it is a tiny step, you are beginning to teach your mind that you are expanding your limitations, and as you practice this, you will begin to purchase more of the things you want in your life, and the money will come to you to pay for them.

Mind trick #3: Open up to money-making opportunities. One thing that all self-made millionaires agree on is that there are opportunities everywhere if we are open to seeing them. You can prove this for yourself by looking at your own life. There are probably many times in your past that you think back to and wonder what might have happened if you had taken an opportunity at just the right time.

If you are like most people, when you think of your past opportunities, you believe that you once had a chance but that now it is gone. The difference between rich and poor people is that rich people realize that new opportunities are always all around us, all the time. You simply need to keep a lookout for the opportunities, keep an open mind, and be prepared to take advantage of them when the opportunities arise.

Action step: Today, get a notebook, and write down all the money-making ideas you can think of. It doesn't matter how stupid or outrageous the ideas might seem—write them down anyway. This does two things. First, you realize that there are plenty of money-making opportunities around you right now, as there always have been and always will be. Second, this exercise will stimulate your mind to see money-making opportunities where it might have ignored them in the past and will help you practice to see opportunities in the future. If you keep adding ideas to your notebook consistently, one day, you will see an incredible opportunity on your list that is perfect for you. Then, go for it!

That should get you started: three simple actions you can take to begin to expand the prosperity in your life. But don't stop there. Never let fear or doubt enter your mind. There is nothing you need in order to succeed, except the power of your own mind. If you worry that you are not smart enough, not connected enough, not talented enough, not young enough, or not old enough, you are simply creating limiting beliefs that will manifest in the outside world. All you really need to know is that the outside world is a reflection of the state of your inner mind. Know that you can make every day from this day forward a little more joyful and a little more abundant, and then, watch your life begin to change.

ABOUT THE AUTHOR

Andreas Ohrt is the editor of "Mind Power News," a weekly newsletter dedicated to news headlines, scientific research, and the most powerful resources available to help you unleash the power of your mind. Get your free subscription and three free gifts to help you get started at http://www.MindPowerNews.com.

79

PURPOSE

A Reason for Living in a Nutshell

Laurent Grenier

Perhaps there is no greater means of improving one's life than striving to answer in the most enlightened way this single question: Why live? I started to ask myself that question about 30 years ago after my diving accident, which left the husky and lusty teenage athlete that I was a near-quadriplegic. What had given meaning to my life until then had become largely impossible. As a result, my life seemed absurd.

"Seemed" is the operative word here. Many years of reflection and study have taught me that the lack of meaning is always a lack of wisdom. Everything I have learned and that has turned the bitter and suicidal young man that I was into a mature and serene life-lover is what I impart to my reader.

Listed below are some cardinal points that may serve as guidance toward greater wisdom.

1. There can be no contentment without acceptance of the limits of reality, within which excellence and joy are possible, but not perfection and infinite happiness. Furthermore, there can be no contentment without the courage to pursue excellence and joy persistently, against failures and misfortunes. Above all, our minds are at our command and determine our moods. Independently of circumstances and results, contentment follows from positive thinking and positive action—though admittedly, it is not possible without circumstances and results being at least favorable enough to permit thinking and action.

2. In the pursuit of excellence and joy the awareness of our adaptability is paramount. Change, and sometimes extensive and traumatic change, is part and parcel of life. Fortunately, we are able to adapt to this change; that is, the favorable habits we develop within relatively stable circumstances—for example, eating, working, or dating habits that are conducive to our happiness—do not truly define who we are. What does truly define who we are is our innate ability to acquire favorable habits, whatever the circumstances (if the latter are not so bad that they cannot be turned to good account). In a word, we are by nature adaptable, just as the world is by nature changeable.

3. The one fact that differentiates life from infinite bliss is the struggle that is required of the living to achieve satisfaction, which is never complete and permanent. We can either sorrow over this fact or rejoice in it. Why rejoice? Because with the struggle comes merit, and merit is a joyful emotion that any valiant soul knows intimately and values immensely.

4. Just as we cannot build a house without first securing a solid foundation, we cannot reach fulfillment without first ensuring that our bodies are sound, thanks to a healthy diet and lifestyle.

5. To be free to do what we please is a precious right that we have as members of a liberal society. This right comes with a corresponding duty: to respect that right in others. Indeed, we are free to do what we please if what we please is not to make our fellow creatures suffer. Mutual respect is the *sine qua non* of collective harmony. It is the chief principle behind human justice.

   The right to freedom, within the liberal society, also means that we are free to believe what we please. No institutionalized ideology is imposed on us besides the basic moral principle dictating that we respect one another so that society, however liberal, remains sufficiently ordered to be operational. The reverse of order is chaos, which only knows the law of the jungle: dog eat dog.

   Now, the right to believe what we please comes with a corresponding duty: to think carefully to define our own ideologies, according to which we see and do things in different ways. Again, the only imposition is the basic moral principle dictating that we respect one another.

6. Within the context of my own ideology, which I cannot impose but only propose, love is the essence of life, its essential purpose. It includes the love of ourselves, which consists in promoting our own lives. This love is instinctive and foundational; it is instrumental in the love of others as we feel solidarity with them.

7. At a deeper level, love extends to that of everything. It proceeds from the divine principle behind the universe, thanks to which everything is the way it is, capable of being and better still, within certain limits, capable of flourishing. Like this principle, these limits can be ascertained through their obvious manifestations but never explained. Ultimately, the universe and our relative knowledge of it are founded on a fathomless mystery.

In summary,

- the lack of meaning is always a lack of wisdom;
- there can be no contentment without acceptance of the limits of reality;
- there can be no contentment without the courage to pursue excellence and joy persistently;
- our minds are at our command and determine our moods;
- we are by nature adaptable, just as the world is by nature changeable;
- with the struggle comes merit;
- we cannot reach fulfillment without first ensuring that our bodies are sound, thanks to a healthy diet and lifestyle;
- mutual respect is the *sine qua non* of collective harmony;
- we must think carefully to define our own ideologies;
- love is the essence of life, its essential purpose;
- the universe and our relative knowledge of it are founded on a fathomless mystery.

Thank you for your attention. I wish you every happiness!

ABOUT THE AUTHOR

Laurent Grenier's career as a full-time writer and philosopher spans over 20 years. He has released various articles in art and philosophical magazines. He has also written some philosophical essays, a collection of memories and thoughts, and a compendium of physiology and nutrition, still unpublished. His part autobiographical, part philosophical book, *A Reason for Living*, published in December 2004, under the NardisPress imprint (ISBN: 1589611659), constitutes his best work to date. Visit his official Web site at http://laurentgrenier.com/ARFL.html.

80

10 Lies We Think Are Love

Carol Tuttle

Real love is an energy that supports us in feeling good. When we feel genuine self-love and self-worth, we experience ourselves as good and capable. A reverence and humility accompanies this deep knowing that we are valuable just for being ourselves. Our worth is not dependent on our doings or our belongings. When genuine self-love and self-worth is present, we attract love and respect from others.

We come into this world with the need to be validated as loveable. We are looking for someone, primarily our parents, to tell us that we are important, that we are loved and cherished, and that we count unconditionally. Even though our spirit knows that we are loveable, our cognitive selves need to hear it. We are looking to be validated all through our infancy, childhood, and teenage years as we move through developmental stages. If we were not given that message and our environment caused us to feel threatened, we may still be looking to have the message that we are loveable given to us as adults. We are stuck in patterns of codependency, looking for love and validation outside of ourselves.

When we were little and love was not as available or predictable, we learned to live without it. We subconsciously created ways of thinking and behaving that helped us feel safer in what seemed like a random world. You may have tried different things to get more love and to support you in feeling more loveable. Some of those ways worked, and to this day, you may subconsciously still believe that you need these patterns in order to be loveable.

The 10 Lies We Think Are Love

- **Food is love.** Our bodies require love through appropriate touch. When that need has not been met, we often turn to food. The root cause of all addictions is the body's need for attention. Food feels good to the body. The body will begin to believe that food is love and will continually seek it out.

- **Sex is love.** This belief supports people in fearing, hating, and despising sex or becoming addicted to it. If you were sexually abused or prematurely affected by sexual experiences, it is common to have the deeper belief that you can only be loved for sex. Sexual addictions are supported by the body's need for affection, and it has come through sexual encounters. Again, the body needs touch and support. If you were sexually abused as a child, your body may go through a cycle of feeling starved for love, getting a quick fix with sex, and then feeling bad for satisfying its need for love with sex.

- **Money is love.** This pattern can get set up in families with money. When emotional love is not flowing freely, money is often used as a substitute. Mom and Dad's money and possessions represent the energy of the real love that children of these families never had. As adults, money represents security. The more money you have, the more safe you feel, and the more loved you feel.

- **I have to be ill to be loved.** If you were given more attention when you were ill as a child, you may still believe that you need this pattern to get noticed. Your sickness may be a way to keep you from living your life fully or from taking responsibility for your life because you feel incapable and afraid. It is something to fall back on when you need to escape and want to hide.

- **I have to suffer to get love.** People in abusive relationships are not familiar with healthy love and how it operates in a relationship. If you were physically punished in your childhood, you may believe that love is being hurt. You will even sabotage healthy relationships to create this so that you can feel your familiar experience again.

- **I have to fix people to be loved.** Many people have a deeper belief that if they are not helping people to get better, then they have no value. If they have no value, they cannot be lovable. The problem with this pattern is that if you need to fix sick and dysfunctional people in order to feel loveable, you will continually attract these people into your life, and they will not get well. You need them to be "unfixable" so that you can stay "loveable."

- **I have to control you to make it safe to let you love me.** Control is one of the biggest patterns in relationships. The deeper belief is that you want to control others before they can control you. It is common for two controllers to be together in a relationship, both only seeing the other in the controlling pattern. At a deeper level, if you still believe that you are a victim, you may use control to create a feeling of safety to prevent yourself from ever being a victim again.

- **I have to please others to be loved.** This pattern is the opposite of a controller pattern. It is more common for women to play this role in a relationship with a controlling man. In this pattern the person is always thinking of other people before she thinks of herself. Everything she thinks or says is processed with the underlying thought of what others will think and what others want. Chronic Fatigue and other energy depletion disorders are common with this pattern.
- **If I let you love me, you will leave me.** Abandonment is at the core of this pattern. If you were abandoned as a child, you may fear that the people you love get hurt, die, or go away. In order to prevent this from happening, you will not let a relationship go very far, or you will sabotage it first. That way, it doesn't hurt as much, and it is more predictable.
- **Love hurts; relationships are painful.** This belief will only support you in creating unhealthy, painful relationships. You will continue to attract people with whom you create a lot of pain. You will support your relationships in being painful in the way you perceive them, think about them, and the choices you make in them. You will go from one relationship to another feeling victimized and hurt, wondering when real love will come your way.

The first step is to understand that your beliefs create your experience. Whatever you believe, either subconsciously or consciously, is what you will get in life. If you don't like what you are getting, change your beliefs. Many of these beliefs are at a subconscious level and are generational beliefs. Limiting beliefs are also rooted in our childhood experiences. You have the opportunity to take control of the phenomenal power of your mind to release these old beliefs and create new ones.

Be willing to end any relationships that cannot be healthy. Hold the following as your motto.

> I am worthy of real love. I deserve to be loved and admired by a healthy, loving person. I am attracting people that can and want to create healthy, loving relationships with me. I am ending relationships that cannot be healthy. God loves me, and I love myself.

ABOUT THE AUTHOR

Carol Tuttle is a master emotional release therapist and the author of the best-selling book *Remembering Wholeness: A Personal Handbook for Thriving* in the 21st Century. Learn powerful language techniques to assist you in creating the life you want on Carol's best-selling audio CD *The Art of Manifesting*. Just click on the title to review this product and all of Carol's life-changing books, CDs, and DVDs, which are highly recommended by SelfGrowth.com. Visit Carol's Web site at http://www.caroltuttle.com.

81

REALITY CHANGE

Mental Alchemy

Edwin Harkness Spina

Back in the Middle Ages, alchemists sought to transform base metal into gold. They searched for an elusive substance, the philosopher's stone, which would bring about this conversion, known as alchemy. However, to initiates of the ancient mystery schools, alchemy was primarily an allegory for the real work of spiritual and mental alchemy.

Spiritual alchemy is the process of transforming a less evolved soul personality into a more refined one. The founders of all major religions have attempted to expedite this transformation by providing rules to help people achieve this goal and also lead happier and more productive lives. Enlightenment, illumination, and the perfection of the soul all point to this ultimate goal. Mystics from all religions have studied the universal laws to speed up this process, which they believe occurs over many lifetimes.

Mental alchemy is the process of transmuting your thoughts to improve your life and expand your mind. The good news is that this discipline can produce immediate, beneficial results in your current life, in some cases instantly. Mental alchemy involves the replacement of beliefs that are hindering your development with positive ones that will help you. You might say that this sounds straightforward—why would this be so difficult?

It turns out that it's extremely difficult to change beliefs. There are three reasons for this.

1. **Most people mistake their beliefs for the truth.** Even if it's not in their best interest, some people resign themselves to their fate because they mistakenly accept a belief as true.

2. **Beliefs operate at the subconscious level.** Most people are unaware of their subconscious beliefs, which are often in conflict with their conscious thoughts. For example, a woman may consciously be seeking love, but subconsciously, she may feel that she's unworthy. Unless her belief is made conscious and transmuted, it will continue to sabotage her efforts.

3. **You see what you believe.** Less than 100 years ago, physicists were trying to determine whether light was a wave or a particle. The answer depended on what you believed you would find. If you believed light was made of particles, then you could design an experiment that proved it. Conversely, if you believed light consisted of waves, then you could design a different experiment to prove that.

   The placebo effect provides another example. In drug trials required to gain FDA approval, 40 percent of patients, on average, will obtain relief from placebos. They get better simply because they believe that they will get better. Placebos have actually helped people with Parkinson's disease.

The mystic principle behind these results is called the Law of Attraction, or "like attracts like." In the mystic world, and now in the world of quantum physics, we know that everything is energy. Everything has its own vibration, including a belief. People attract to themselves those experiences that match their existing belief systems. They get to see what they believe.

How Does Mental Alchemy Work?

Neurologists tell us that the brain doesn't know the difference between what's actually experienced and what's imagined to be experienced. The same electrical patterns are fired between the neurons in the brain. The electrical patterns in the brain reflect how we store and process information, including beliefs.

The ramifications of this are profound: you can change your beliefs using your imagination. It doesn't matter whether the belief is true or not.

Let's take an example of a basketball player who misses the final shot of the state

286

championship game, and his team ends up losing by one point. This is a traumatic experience that would reinforce negative beliefs in the player that he's a choker or a loser. Had he made the shot, he would be a hero and filled with the confidence of a winner.

Let's say that you are the basketball player. What should you do?

1. Go to a quiet place where you won't be disturbed for 10–15 minutes. Make sure that none of your objective senses (sight, hearing, smell, touch, taste) is being stimulated. Take a few deep breaths. Your goal is to relax and get into an alpha state. Scientists have shown that you can learn new skills much more readily while in this state. Meditation is ideal for this.

2. Replay the end of the game in your mind, only this time, when you take the final shot, do it with confidence and watch it go in. Visualize all the fans going wild as the buzzer sounds and your teammates carry you off the court. Involve all your senses, and imagine how it feels to be the hero!

Michael Jordan is arguably the greatest basketball player of all time, but he probably missed just as many shots at the end of the game as he made. You can be quite certain that he didn't dwell on the missed shots but simply remembered the game-winning shots. You can do the same. Use the technique of mental alchemy to change your life.

ABOUT THE AUTHOR

Edwin Harkness Spina is the author of the award-winning spiritual thriller *Mystic Warrior: A Novel Beyond Time and Space*. Ed earned an MBA from the University of Chicago, a BSE from Tufts University, and has been studying and practicing mysticism for many years. Receive a free copy of *Mystic Secrets Revealed* when you sign up for the "Mystic Warrior Newsletter," with more mystic techniques to improve your life and expand your mind. Please visit http://www.MysticWarrior.us.

82

Do You Remember How to Play?

Rhoberta Shaler

Do you still "go out to play"? Do your friends still knock on your door and invite you out to play? I hope so, and I hope you go.

This world seems to send strong messages that play is frivolous, time-wasting, and useful only to procrastinators and slackers—unless, of course, you can find a suitable way to include it in your business life, like golfing. Now, I'm not talking about exercise as play, although I hope you do find some redeeming features in exercising. I'm talking about doing things strictly for the joy of it, the fun in it.

When is the last time you lay out on the grass on a summer evening and looked at the stars? When did you last watch clouds and look for pictures? When did you last have a wonderful, tear-producing belly laugh? When did you last make music or dance? When did you last build a sand castle? When did you last play hooky from life?

Adults *need* to play. If we don't, we can lose our perspective. We think that everything we are doing is important, necessary, and critical to financial success. Surely, some things are. Some folks even think that they are indispensable. Do you? If your answer is yes, then I suggest you try this: put your finger into a glass of water. Take it out. Observe the hole your finger left. You get the picture. There are other kinds of success beyond those that society measures in dollars, homes, and positions. Which ones do you want to achieve?

Some folks pay lip service to the need for balance in their lives. It makes a good story. It makes others think that they actually have it. Isn't that true? Most of us can speak with eloquence and authority on what we need to do in order to be truly healthy. There is no shortage of information, simply a shortage of action. I was giving an optimal living seminar once on Vancouver Island in Canada. As I was introduced, I came up the aisle from the back of the room, asking folks, "Who wants to be healthy?" Most hands shot up. Next question: "Who knows what it takes to be healthy?" Most hands shot up. "Tell me what it takes." I wrote their shouted suggestions on a flip chart:

- Enough sleep.
- Eat nutritiously.
- Give up junk food.
- Relax.
- Have goals.
- Drink lots of water.
- Have good relationships.
- Spend time alone.
- Reduce stress.
- Have regular medical checkups.
- Exercise.
- Love someone and be loved.
- Laugh.
- Play.

A bright crowd. They had the main bases covered. My next question: "So, why are you here if you know all this?" Silence. Then, the million-dollar question: "So, how many of you are doing this?" Very few hands.

Isn't it true? *You know what to do.* You could give your best friend excellent suggestions, but do you take your own advice?

My greatest challenge is exercise. I'll do almost anything to avoid it. I have to trick myself into it some days. Here's one of my tricks: I can watch one of my favorite daytime TV shows as long as I am exercising through it. Okay, okay. You're right. It's simpler to give up watching the show than it is to exercise. It's easy to justify sabotage! But most days, I do at least get more exercise than I would if I didn't make that deal with myself. I've made it into a game with benefits.

Recently, my husband and I took our fold-up chairs out to the darkest, highest spot we could find, far away from city lights. We lay back and scouted the skies for the Perceids meteor showers. Each time a shooting star made its way unexpectedly across the sky, we were delighted, just as we had been as children. It was play.

How are you playing? Who are your playmates? What time do you set aside just for restorative play? Explore this idea: by any chance, do you and your friends have an unwritten contract to avoid playing? Have you convinced yourselves that you are only "doing the right thing" when you are seriously exhausted and morbidly overworked? Do you only laugh when you've had a drink or two with colleagues while discussing business after a tough day at work?

If you have children, they need you to play with them as much as you need to play. You are teaching them to live balanced lives while showing them that you care about them. You all benefit.

Some folks simply exchange one form of competition for another and think that they are playing. I knew a man who was highly competitive at work, and his supposed relaxation was playing competitive tennis. Oh, really? This may get his body moving and his heart beating, but is it play? At the end of the game, when he has lost, he is not a happy man. This is not play. It is an exchange of venues for his competitive spirit masquerading as play.

Be good to yourself. Take care of yourself. There is a part of you that remembers the joy of skipping stones across the water and singing songs around a campfire just because it felt so good. Go do it again.

Get out there. Play. Have fun. Laugh. Skip. Wrestle. Go to the zoo. Rent funny old movies. Be silly. It's good for you. Enjoy!

ABOUT THE AUTHOR

Rhoberta Shaler, PhD, is a "people skills" expert. Dr. Shaler, a noted international speaker, author, and executive coach, is founder of both the Optimize! Institute in Escondido, California, and an online Center for Spiritual

Living. Dr. Shaler has taught thousands of people communication, negotiation, conflict, and anger management skills to strengthen all relationships calmly and effectively. She works with organizations that know their people are their top resource and with leaders who know that building relationships is a top priority. Her latest book, *Wrestling Rhinos: Conquering Conflict in the Wilds of Work*, is receiving rave reviews worldwide. Visit her Web site at http://www.RhobertaShaler.com.

83

RIGHT LIVELIHOOD

"Follow Your Bliss" Myths

Stacey Mayo

The saying "follow your bliss" was made famous by a book of the same name. People have generalized that statement to mean many things, some of which are inaccurate, so I thought I would give you the real skinny on this topic and dismantle some old myths.

Let me start by saying that I think it is very important that you get in touch with and follow your passions. Life is too short to spend your time doing something that is not fulfilling, especially if you work 20–60 hours a week, year after year. When you do what feels good, things flow more easily. All of this is true; I am a living example of it. When I coach people and they have breakthroughs and begin to create a life that they truly love, I get all warm and fuzzy inside. Even after 10 years, it can bring tears to my eyes. Okay, so I am a little sappy. That's okay—my life is very rewarding.

On that note, here are some myths that I would like to dispel.

Myth #1: You cannot do what you love and make good money, too. If that's true, then how come I am doing it? What about Oprah? What about Elton? Why not you? There are people in nearly every profession who are barely scraping by, others who are doing okay, and others who are highly successful and prosperous. You get to choose where you want to be on that scale, and the best way to get to the high end of the scale is to learn from people who have done it.

Take a moment to think about who is already doing what you want to do and doing it successfully. How can you learn from them? Perhaps they teach a course or have written a book, or you could do an informational interview to learn more about how they did it. Maybe you could even hire them as your mentor coach. There are many ways. Choose the way that works best for you, but do it.

Myth #2: To follow your bliss or purpose, you have to be saintly like Mother Teresa. Following your bliss means doing whatever you are passionate about. For some that is service, for others it is using their creative talents, for others it is pursuing adventures. It is different for everyone, and there is not any one way it should look. What is important is that it lights *you* up.

Stacy Allison, the first American woman to climb Mount Everest, followed her bliss. There was nothing saintly about it, but there was plenty of passion. She said, "Climbing is where my spirit soars. When I am climbing, whether it's a sheer rock cliff or a mountain, I belong in no other place. I am absolutely where I should be. It's where I feel the most connected to this Earth and the most at peace, even if I'm in an absolutely dangerous challenging situation."

Myth #3: If you follow your bliss, the money will follow. As stated in myth #1 above, you can create money in alignment with your passion, but it just isn't as simple as the statement above. You also have to know what your natural talents are and combine those with something you are passionate about, and do it in a setting that is conducive to your personality. (If you don't know what your natural talents are, you can take the free self-assessment at http://www. igetpaidtodothis.com/bookresources2.htm.) Additionally, you have to take inspired action and implement strategies in alignment with your dream, and you need to be visible.

Using the example of Stacy Allison again, she became very visible as a result of her feat. She was offered book deals and speaking engagements, and over time she honed her writing and speaking skills, which enabled her to make a living in alignment with something she was passionate about—climbing.

Myth #4: If you follow your bliss, everything will be easy and just flow. This definitely has some truth to it, but again, it is oversimplified. If you are doing what feels good to you, you do not have any doubts about your ability

293

to succeed, you are not worried about whether it will work or not, and you don't stress out when things don't go perfectly according to your plan and timeline, *then* things will flow. You have to learn how to focus on what you want and not on what you don't want and to manage stress differently so that you can relax. When you do this, things happen with more ease and less effort. Learning how to do this is a journey, not a quick fix—trust me on that—but it is worth it.

What is the bottom line of this message? Definitely follow your bliss, but understand that it is step one in a multistep journey toward making your dreams come true.

ABOUT THE AUTHOR

Stacey Mayo, the "Dream Queen," founded the Center for Balanced Living (http://www.balancedliving.com) in 1995 to empower people to live out their dreams with ease and abundance. She is author of the award-winning book *I Can't Believe I Get Paid to Do This! Remarkable People Reveal 26 Proven Strategies for Making Your Dreams Come True.* It includes the in-depth story of Stacy Allison's journey along with stories of many other remarkable people. It also includes proven strategies and action steps to support you in making your dreams a reality.

84

SANCTUARIES

A Sense of Place:
Taking Time to Rest Your Ambition

LuAn Mitchell-Halter

I think everyone should have a sanctuary. It might be a special corner of your garden, a special chair in a quiet corner, or a home office. My sanctuary is a bathroom. It has more art on the walls than did my entire first home. It's decorated lovingly with my favorite colors and fabrics. There are gold butterflies on the ceiling and candles everywhere. A custom-ordered tub has lots of jets, providing me with wonderful back and foot massages. Perhaps the best design feature of my special sanctuary is a lock on the door that ensures my privacy. Almost every day, I soak in a bubble bath in my tub and enjoy solitary thinking time with a fragrant bath bomb.

If you think this sounds selfish, you're missing the point. This 10 or 15 minutes to myself is an investment that pays off handsomely. I tell my family that it's my time-out, and they're happy to respect that. I'm a better parent, a more thoughtful manager, and a more effective leader as a result of time in my sanctuary. I have instincts that I trust implicitly. They tell me to take a little time away now and then, and I listen.

One of things that I contemplate in my sanctuary is balance and what it means to me. A balanced lifestyle means different things to different people. We all need to devise our own definition of balance: that point where we're comfortable and productive. A few minutes spent in your personal sanctuary will remind you that 10 years from now, you'll remember your child's school play more than those extra hours spent straining away at your desk, probably slouched in all the wrong postures, plagued with guilt because you are missing an important time in one of your children's lives. One of the points in my new book is to remember that sometimes, there just aren't enough hours in the day. A few minutes in your sanctuary is the right time to realize that it's important to remain flexible. Things will always come up, and if you have to shift a few things, do it, and let go. It can really take the wind out of your sail if you have an overloaded to-do list and you don't accomplish a bunch of things on that list. It's much more rewarding and effective to focus on the important priorities than to be worrying about an unrealistic, long list that drains your energy and brings you down.

My sanctuary is a place that helps to keep me balanced, to remind me of the importance of my personal life. Work is important, but it's not everything. Some things have to give, or you risk some very precious commodities, and we all know that you can't turn the clock back. There's no place like a personal sanctuary to remember that.

I can't count how many times people ask how I've been able to continually overcome adversity. I was called a "survivor" long before the hit TV show was ever invented. In fact, my winning formula is very simple: whatever the situation (and you must stay focused on the situation, not the players)—whether I'm dealing with the death of someone I love, considering a strategic alliance or public offering for my company, or making an important decision about my family or my lifestyle—I always follow my three easy steps.

- Make a realistic plan that will get you closer to your dream.
- Follow your God-given instincts.
- Find the seed for good.

These strategies have never failed me. In the good times and the bad I keep following these steps religiously. This is my game plan for overcoming obstacles, doing good in the world, and leading a happy, fulfilling life. I know that these steps can work for you, too. Let me take you by the hand—and remember, I've been there.

Some people may look at me and think, "It was easy for her; she married the successful CEO of a large company." But that's the fairy tale, not the real story. These people didn't see me having my heart torn out repeatedly looking after a chronically ill spouse. They didn't see me striding the halls of the Stanford Medical Center, my baby in a backpack, pacing as my husband rebounded from a risky and miraculous transplant. They didn't see us when I was about to hock my precious wedding ring, when we were fighting to save the company and its special people. And they didn't see me put my fist through a bathroom wall after my husband drew his last breath. No, it hasn't been easy, and it hasn't been simple for me. But believe me, if I can do it, you can, too.

I have been fortunate in my life to be able to cut through the public's image of me as just a "paper doll," a piece of fluff, a headliner, and get to the core of my being, where the seeds are contained—seeds for good—where there is a person who is multidimensional and a person who is fully exposed on life's journey based in the undying wisdom of life eternal and believing in miracles.

ABOUT THE AUTHOR

LuAn Mitchell-Halter knows business. With long experience as one of the most accomplished women in the world, she has an intimate understanding of today's competitiveness and global pressure. As a highly sought after motivational speaker, with extensive training from the "masters," she is known as an international best-selling author and a first-class personality, and her inspiring message of perseverance and triumph is known around the planet. LuAn works hard with like-minded individuals to plant "seeds of good" around our beautiful world. She has helped others reach their true potential, and she can help you!

85

SELF-AWARENESS

Become the Creator of Your Own Reality

Bill Harris

There is a Zen story of a great enlightened master, who, upon hearing of his own master's death, began to cry uncontrollably. His followers were shocked to see him cry. They asked him, "Why are you crying? You're enlightened. You're supposed to be beyond suffering. What will people think?"

He composed himself as best he could, and turning to them, he said, "What can I do? My eyes are crying. They are so sad that they will never again see this teacher I loved so much."

As this story so poignantly points out, sorrow upon experiencing loss is a normal part of being human. The Four Noble Truths of Buddhism point out that all life involves suffering, that suffering is caused by desire or attachment, and that suffering can be ended by giving up attachment (the fourth Noble Truth is the method of doing so).

The Four Noble Truths are based on an obvious, often overlooked, but fundamental reality of human existence: all things exist "in time" and eventually pass away. Not getting what you want involves suffering, but it's equally true that getting what you want also involves suffering because the thing you wanted is, like everything else, transitory.

I vividly remember the first time I experienced this truth. I was four years old, and my mother had bought me an ice cream cone. As I began licking the sweet and creamy ice cream off the top of the cone, I was in heaven, but when I'd eaten about half the ice cream, the realization hit me that this wonderful experience was going to end. While I certainly enjoyed the rest, the experience was definitely tainted by the fact that I knew the experience would soon be over. Even in the midst of my pleasure, I suffered.

The fact is that being overly attached to particular outcomes causes pain and suffering. Yet, we are trained to believe that happiness is tied to specific events or, especially in our culture, to specific things. All around us are messages that connect positive emotions to the things we do and own.

Because we live in a mass culture where meaning is centralized, we are used to having others interpret our lives for us. We have become passive observers of our own experience, waiting for other people to tell us what it means. Outside influences so often direct our attention to what we should care about and what we should strive for that the truth of our own power escapes us.

I want to suggest another idea basic to transformational mystical teachings like Buddhism. Instead of believing that there is an absolute value and meaning to reality, a "reality code" that young people learn to decipher, I want you to consider an alternative view: as a conscious human being, you give your world, and each event that happens, any and all the meaning it has. There is no intrinsic meaning to anything. In most cases we did not consciously choose the meanings we give to things. Rather, they were taught to us, according to the conventions of our culture and our family, when we were too small to know any better. The great news is that we could have consciously chosen our own meanings if we had wanted to, and that, in fact, is just what people who are continually happy and peaceful have learned to do.

This means, of course, that you are the creator of your own reality, and this principle has a corollary: you will be able to make wise and resourceful choices to the extent that you live consciously rather than unconsciously. If you have become an automatic response mechanism, unthinkingly adopting those responses chosen for you by your culture and society, then your inner journey will be stalled. Your individuality and creativity will remain stillborn. What is more, you will spend a lot of time suffering.

If, on the other hand, you are able to wake up and become more aware of what moves and motivates you, you will see that you have picked up the paintbrush; you are painting the shapes of your feelings on that blank canvas. Because you are the artist, you can paint anything you like. What you are painting is as ephemeral as anything else in life, but the lines you draw, the shapes you form, and the colors you choose are what give your life meaning.

The implications of living this way, as a conscious being, are staggering. Here is one of them: since you create the world you inhabit, pain and suffering are optional. Only when you acknowledge your role in your life—and understand your own power—is there the possibility of improving your situation or creating a different story. If you see yourself as a passive character who is acted upon by (and then reacts to) external forces that you can neither understand nor control, then you become a helpless victim.

Along with this idea of self-agency comes another one: what is, is. You have some ability to change what is, but there are real limits to what you can do. Your power instead comes from how you respond to what is, not from misguided attempts to control what is. How things are for you is, to a great extent, the product of how you feel about what is happening—and how you feel is the result of the meaning you have placed on what is happening.

It is a very interesting exercise to stop whenever you feel other than happy and peaceful and ask yourself what meaning you have placed on the people or events that seem to be causing your suffering, and then to consider what meaning you could give things that would allow you to be happy. Are you so attached to a meaning that causes suffering that you are unwilling to let it go and change it to one that creates happiness and peace? If so, that is your choice, but do realize that it is a choice, not something thrust upon you.

This new meaning (the one leading to happiness) is no more real or intrinsic to the situation than the first meaning (the one leading to suffering). This is, again, because nothing has any intrinsic meaning. However, if you're going to place a meaning on what is happening, which would you want, the happiness meaning or the unhappiness meaning? Again, it's your choice.

The idea that you could really choose to be happy and peaceful may sound very utopian and unrealistic. Becoming conscious enough to notice when you are suffering, to notice what meaning you have placed on a situation, and to consciously change that meaning does not come easily. Those who can do this have generally spent years meditating or pursuing some other arduous spiritual practice to gain this degree of conscious awareness. One of the incredible benefits to the Centerpointe program is that it creates this kind of awareness in those who use it, and it does so in a relatively short period of time. Using

Holosync offers you a view from a higher spot on the mountain, one allowing you to consciously make new and more resourceful choices.

ABOUT THE AUTHOR

Bill is frequently invited to speak at scientific and transformational forums and conferences across the United States, and over the years he has taught a wide range of workshops and seminars. In the past he has conducted his own private therapy practice, utilizing cognitive psychology and neurolinguistic programming. Bill is currently President and Director of Centerpointe Research Institute, started in 1989, and creator of The Holosync Solution™ program and The Life Principles Integration Process™. As of 2004, over 200,000 people in 172 countries have used Centerpointe programs to improve their lives.

86

How to Build Your Self-Confidence and Live a Better Life!

Bob Griswold & Jeff Griswold

It's no secret that self-confidence is very important to achieving success in any area of life. The thing about self-confidence is that it's *very* sensitive to our personal experience and is inherently unstable, which means that low self-confidence tends to get lower and high self-confidence tends to improve. In other words, your self-confidence experiences a "snowball effect."

How the "Negative Snowball" Works

1. If you start out with low self-confidence, you're less likely to take on challenges or try new things.
2. On the rare occasion that you try to accomplish something your low self-confidence can sabotage your efforts, and you're much less likely to succeed.
3. Your lack of success reinforces your low self-confidence.
4. Then, it's back to step 1, and the cycle repeats, limiting your ability to live a better life.

How the "Positive Snowball" Works

1. If you have self-confidence, you're more likely to try new things.
2. When you attempt something with confidence in your abilities, you're very likely to succeed.
3. As a result, your success increases your self-confidence.
4. Return to step 1, and repeat until you reach your full potential!

Wearing a Groove into Your Brain

At the risk of oversimplifying a phenomenally complex process, what's happening in your brain is that these snowball cycles "wear a groove" through the vast array of neurons and synapses. Neurologically, you are physically carving a path of least resistance through your brain. With enough reinforcement you develop a reflex to certain kinds of stimuli.

For example, if a smoker tries to quit smoking and fails—and he allows a negative snowball cycle to take place—he'll lose confidence in his ability to quit, and he'll eventually develop a *negative reflex* to the idea of quitting. Once that happens, if anyone suggests that he quit or someone offers a new way to try to quit, his brain will automatically reject the possibility. In his brain the mere suggestion of quitting will trigger an impulse that will follow that well-worn path of least resistance, the path that equates "trying to quit" with "failure."

This works the other way, too. A positive snowball cycle will wear a groove that creates a *positive reflex*. We've all known people who exhibit this—they're the ones who are eager to try anything and seem to succeed at everything. On the rare occasion that they fail they are undeterred. The positive reflexes they've created in their brains allow them to learn from their mistakes and equate failure with "I'll do even better next time!"

How Does the Low Self-Confidence Cycle Start?

Unfortunately, virtually everyone has been programmed from childhood with negatives that make him believe that he can't do things that he's innately capable of doing. A lot of it is self-imposed programming. If we fail to do something perfectly the first time we try, it's only human nature to begin to believe that we can't do it.

Fortunately, when some people are told that they can't do something, they refuse to accept that programming and go on to prove that they indeed can. For example,

- Beethoven's teacher said that he was hopeless as a composer.
- Thomas Edison's teachers said that he was too stupid to learn anything.
- Leo Tolstoy, the author of *War and Peace*, was told that he couldn't learn.

303

- Albert Einstein didn't speak until he was four and didn't read until he was seven. His teacher called him mentally slow.

Each and every one of us has given up on at least one thing because we lacked the confidence to try! The world has undoubtedly been robbed of the great contributions of countless gifted people because of such negativity.

The good news is that a negative self-confidence cycle is completely reversible! You can learn how to eliminate existing negative thought reflexes and replace them with positive thought reflexes. There are several effective techniques for building self-confidence. Among them, *positive affirmations* are possibly the most powerful and easiest to use.

Using Positive Affirmations to Build Self-Confidence

Positive affirmations are carefully worded positive statements that are designed to establish new thinking patterns in your mind. Using affirmations is a *very* effective way to build self-confidence. It seems simple, and initially, it can actually be a little uncomfortable, but remember that what you're trying to do is to wear a new groove into your brain. You're trying to create a new path of least resistance and establish a *positive reflex* in your mind.

The way to use affirmations is to repeat the statements to yourself (out loud or silently). When you repeat an affirmation, feel it, believe it, and *know* it! Put some positive emotion into it. Emotion-backed programming is the most powerful and long lasting. Allow yourself to experience feelings of joy, satisfaction, power, and self-confidence as you recite each affirmation. Make each one a true part of your reality.

Use your favorite affirmations routinely throughout the day, and *really feel* them. You will eventually make a quantum leap. You will suddenly be far beyond the doubts that accompany wishing, hoping, daydreaming, and even believing. You will enter the zone of *knowing*.

When you enter the zone of knowing, supreme self-confidence is automatically there. All doubt is gone. You *know* you can do it. When you enter the zone of knowing, your self-confidence is unshakable, and your untapped potential is released. You feel invincible!

Another great way to use affirmations is to say them while looking in a mirror. Say them with feeling, and soon, you'll become aware of how powerful your eyes are. We send messages with our eyes that show how we think of ourselves and how self-confident we are, and that influences how others respond to us. The more our eyes bespeak self-confidence and self-esteem, the more other people are likely to hold us in high esteem. As you practice your affirmations in the mirror, you'll see this in your own eyes, and soon, others will feel the confidence that you project.

Start Today

You can use many other powerful techniques to improve your self-confidence and build your self-esteem, but this will get you started in the right direction. Remember that repetition and positive emotions are critical to changing the way you think.

Employ whatever resources you need to commit to improving your self-confidence. Whether it's an audio program or help from your friends, family, or therapist, your self-confidence is too important to allow it to wither away. Be *confident* that you can improve your confidence, and it will change your life.

ABOUT THE AUTHORS

Bob and Jeff Griswold are the Founder and President, respectively, of Effective Learning Systems, Inc., the leading creator of audio CDs and tapes for personal development and self-improvement. With over 100 titles available their programs are among the best-selling self-improvement audio programs in national bookstores, including Barnes & Noble and Borders. Bob's book, *How to Attract Money*, has been printed in seven languages, and he's personally taught over 50,000 people techniques for relaxation, memory, stress management, goal achievement, and self-esteem through seminars for corporations, government agencies, and the general public. You can find Effective Learning Systems online at http://www.efflearn.com/101 or by phone at (800) 966–5683.

87

SELF-LOVE

Dr. Len's Advanced Self-Improvement Method

Joe Vitale

Two years ago, I heard about a therapist in Hawaii who cured a complete ward of criminally insane patients—without ever seeing any of them. The psychologist would study an inmate's chart and then look within himself to see how *he* created that person's illness. As he improved himself, the patient improved.

When I first heard this story, I thought it was an urban legend. How could anyone heal anyone else by healing *himself*? How could even the best self-improvement master cure the *criminally insane*? It didn't make any sense. It wasn't logical, so I dismissed the story.

However, I heard it again a year later. I heard that the therapist had used a Hawaiian healing process called *ho'oponopono*. I had never heard of it, yet I couldn't let it leave my mind. If the story was at all true, I had to know more.

I had always understood "total responsibility" to mean that I am responsible for what *I* think and do. Beyond that, it's out of my hands. I think that most people think of total responsibility that way. We're responsible for what *we* do, not what anyone else does—but that's wrong. The Hawaiian therapist who healed those mentally ill people would teach me an advanced new perspective about total responsibility.

His name is Dr. Ihaleakala Hew Len. We probably spent an hour talking on our first phone call. I asked him to tell me the complete story of his work as a therapist. He explained that he worked at Hawaii State Hospital for four years. The ward where they kept the criminally insane was dangerous. Psychologists quit on a monthly basis. The staff called in sick a lot or simply quit. People would walk through that ward with their backs against the wall, afraid of being attacked by patients. It was not a pleasant place to live, work, or visit.

Dr. Len told me that he never saw patients. He agreed to have an office and to review their files. While he looked at those files, he would work on himself. As he worked on himself, patients began to heal.

"After a few months, patients that had to be shackled were being allowed to walk freely," he told me. "Others who had to be heavily medicated were getting off their medications. And those who had no chance of ever being released were being freed."

I was in awe.

"Not only that," he went on, "but the staff began to enjoy coming to work. Absenteeism and turnover disappeared. We ended up with more staff than we needed because patients were being released, and all the staff was showing up to work. Today, that ward is closed."

This is where I had to ask the million dollar question: "What were you doing within yourself that caused those people to change?"

"I was simply healing the part of me that created them," he said.

I didn't understand.

Dr. Len explained that total responsibility for your life means that *everything* in your life—simply because it is *in your life*—is your responsibility. In a literal sense the entire world is your creation.

Whew. This is tough to swallow. Being responsible for what I say or do is one thing. Being responsible for what *everyone* in my life says or does is quite another. Yet, the truth is this: if you take complete responsibility for your life, then everything you see, hear, taste, touch, or in any way experience *is* your responsibility because *it is in your life*. This means that terrorist activity, the president, the economy—anything you experience and don't like—is up for you to heal. They don't exist, in a manner of speaking, except as projections from inside you. The problem isn't with them, it's with you, and to change them, you have to change you.

I know this is tough to grasp, let alone accept or actually live. Blame is far easier than total responsibility, but as I spoke with Dr. Len, I began to realize that healing for him and in *ho'oponopono* means loving yourself. If you want to improve your life, you have to heal your life. If you want to cure anyone—even a mentally ill criminal—you do it by healing you.

I asked Dr. Len how he went about healing himself. What was he doing, exactly, when he looked at those patients' files?

"I just kept saying 'I'm sorry' and 'I love you' over and over again," he explained.

That's it?

That's it.

Turns out that loving yourself is the greatest way to improve yourself, and as you improve yourself, you improve your world. Let me give you a quick example of how this works: one day, someone sent me an e-mail that upset me. In the past I would have handled it by working on my emotional hot buttons or by trying to reason with the person who sent the nasty message. This time, I decided to try Dr. Len's method. I kept silently saying "I'm sorry" and "I love you." I didn't say it to anyone in particular. I was simply evoking the spirit of love to heal within me what was creating the outer circumstance.

Within an hour I got an e-mail from the same person. He apologized for his previous message. Keep in mind that I didn't take any outward action to get that apology. I didn't even write him back. Yet, by saying "I love you," I somehow healed within me what was creating him.

I later attended a *ho'oponopono* workshop run by Dr. Len. He's now 70 years old, considered a grandfatherly shaman, and is somewhat reclusive. He praised my book, *The Attractor Factor*. He told me that as I improve myself, my book's vibration will raise, and everyone will feel it when they read it. In short, as I improve, my readers will improve.

"What about the books that are already sold and out there?" I asked.

"They aren't out there," he explained, once again blowing my mind with his mystic wisdom. "They are still in you."

In short, there is no "out there."
It would take a whole book to explain this advanced technique with the depth it deserves. Suffice it to say that whenever you want to improve anything in your life, there's only one place to look: inside *you*.

When you look, do it with love.

ABOUT THE AUTHOR

Dr. Joe Vitale is the author of way too many books to list here, including the #1 best-seller *The Attractor Factor: 5 Easy Steps for Creating Wealth (or Anything Else) from the Inside Out*. His next book is *Life's Missing Instruction Manual: The Guidebook You Should Have Been Given at Birth*. Browse a catalog of his products, read dozens of articles, sign up for his free e-zine, or see a picture of Dr. Len at http://www.MrFire.com.

88

Life Is a Trip, But Where Are You Going?: The Art of Choosing "Who to Be" Rather Than "What to Do"

Yanni Maniates

Whenever I mention to people that I teach stress management, meditation, and life mastery skills, they almost always say to me, "Boy, do I need that!" We live in a very fast-paced world. Information, opportunities, and challenges are expanding exponentially every day. Life is full, to say the least!

Too often, our experience of life is like a series of breathless, unconscious, one-after-the-other chase scenes in a fast-paced movie. Rather, I believe life is meant to be a series of vibrant still shots or landscapes, to savor and enter into with just a sprinkling of the right amount of madcap scenarios to add some spice.

Often, as soon as we wake up in the morning, we are immediately mentally inundated with an infinitely long "to do" list. Instead, I would propose that we start off our day by focusing on creating an exquisite, rich, high-quality "to be" list.

As I see it, it's not about what you want to do today that is most important, but rather, what you want to be, or feel, or experience. What qualities of life do you want to primarily participate in today: peace, balance, love, courage, happiness, joy, humor, harmony, confidence? Or do you really want to go into a lowest-common-denominator default mode and experience their opposites?

Why not begin your day by jotting down the quality that you would like to experience and embody that day? Then, as the day progresses, create various practices that will help you to remember and reinforce that quality so that your day is filled with what is *really* most important to you and with that which will bring you the greatest lasting value. For instance, you could choose feeling "peaceful" as the most important "to be" quality for a particular day. Therefore it would be with peacefulness that you would want to begin, follow through with, and end every activity and interaction in your day.

In other words, let the quality you want to experience be more important than the list of goals you want to accomplish. Wherever you are, whatever you are doing, and with whomever you are doing it, always ask yourself, "How can this interaction be permeated with the quality I have chosen today?"

Here is a technique, one of many I have developed and taught over the years, that can help you to refocus on your quality again if you realize that you have lost it.

First, slow yourself down; next, take seven deep breaths. As you breathe in, imagine that you are breathing in the quality that you have chosen for that day; see and feel it permeating your whole body-mind, and then, on the exhalation, see and feel its opposite being expelled. Really feel it and see it as you breathe in deeply and gently. At the end of these seven breaths you will feel refreshed and on target again.

Just trust that as you learn to be consistent with focusing on your quality, you will be surprised that you not only have had the pleasure of experiencing the positive quality you have chosen, but as an added bonus, you also find that what was most important on your "to do" list has been accomplished easily and effectively.

Note that what I am suggesting you begin practicing here is an "art," and sometimes, when you first sit down to create a work of art, things can get quite messy. Don't be discouraged if at times you lose your vision and just can't seem to be able to keep your chosen quality in focus. In time you *will* get better at it. In time, as well, you will learn that if you do lose your focus, it doesn't really matter! When you do lose it, first, just notice that you have lost it, and then, with a sense of humor, have a good laugh at yourself, give yourself a break, and when you have calmed down, gently come back to practicing the quality you have chosen.

So, when you wake up in the morning, why not begin with your "to be" list, and then, let the quality that you have chosen permeate your whole day. To help you stay focused, do the breathing exercise described above as often as you can remember; do it while you are driving your car, standing in line, waiting for someone, etc. Also, some folks find it helpful to put Post-it® notes up everywhere, with the quality written on them as reminders. You can even write your quality on the palm of your hand or automate a message on your computer.

Just imagine, after a year of practicing this, how rich and full a tapestry of qualities and experiences you will have woven into the fabric of your life and into the lives of your loved ones as well as many others. I know many people who have turned their lives around practicing this simple approach!

It *is* possible! Give yourself a chance; you deserve it. You won't always do it perfectly, but it's never about being perfect, is it? It *is* all about the journey and not the destination. Remember, you can always, every day, in every moment choose "to be" filled with a wondrous joy, peace, and love. It is a choice, and it's *yours*. You are a human being, not a human "doing"! Begin your day by putting first things first: claim your mastery and step into and experience who you want "to be" today!

About the Author

Yanni Maniates, MS, CMI, is the founder of The Life Mastery Institute. He has been teaching meditation, intuitive development, healing, and metaphysical subjects for the past 20 years. He is certified in mediumship and numerous holistic and esoteric healing modalities. Yanni has published articles, book reviews, three meditation CDs, and a number of certification programs. He is also publishing a book on self-mastery to be released in 2006. The primary focus of all his work is to help people experience the "Embrace." Yanni offers individual intuitive consultations, the Mentor with the Masters® Program, Spiritual Renewal Retreats, and much more. Visit his Web site at http://www.LifeMasteryblog.com.

89

SIMPLICITY

Simplify to Simplicity

Donna Karlin

In a world where shoulds, coulds, and expectations have become the norm, life can become a complicated juggling game. "Simplify your life" is a catch phrase many coaches use with clients who are wound too tight—they have tremendous personal and professional responsibilities and stressors (some self-imposed), and the only way that they can slow down to the speed of life is to cut knots or, as I often say, to let go of the rope in a tug-of-war. Even though life is becoming increasingly complex, that doesn't mean that it has to be overly complicated—an important distinction.

Take the time to define what it is you want in your life. It may otherwise be defined by someone or something else, such as your job, your culture, your past, the media, or parental programming. As long as this is happening, you aren't free to enjoy life completely. Choices based on external influences box you in. Given the number of those influences and their powerful nature, it's paramount that you decide what is important to you. Simplify your life, and choose your personal priorities to release you from what is no longer meaningful or relevant. It's a matter of choosing whether you want to build a life or a lifestyle—another key distinction.

Reduce Self-Expectations

Breathe . . . relax . . . let go of the clutter. Clutter can take on many forms: thoughts, toxic relationships, piles of paper, and juggling all those balls in the air. Learn how to say no to things that drain you of energy and yes to those that energize you. This will start clearing the way toward a simpler life.

Stop Trying to Fix Others

If you're in a relationship with someone you're continually trying to "fix," then it's time to revisit why you're in that relationship in the first place. We all have a limited amount of free time, which seems to be continually diminishing. Why not spend it with those who energize and inspire you?

Choices Eliminate Clutter

Everything you create is because of the choices you make, and through choice comes freedom. You can make choices right now that will create a life you love. Many are angry at the rat race, not so much because of what the world has become but because they have not done something about their place in it. We want a better life for future generations, but if all we show them is an absence of the work-life balance, how are they supposed to know better?

Live in the Present

By living in the present, what we do, want, and how we think about life becomes simpler. Use the past as a compass to guide you to where you want to go instead of falling backward into an abyss. Get rid of the clutter so that you can define your priorities and make clear decisions. One by one, reduce your number of commitments, goals, and obligations. This will reduce stress in many forms. Once you've simplified what you already have, you will have the mental and physical space to truly enjoy life, people, and experiences. You will get to know yourself better.

Reorient around What Makes You the Happiest

Complexity leaves you with a great deal to manage and juggle, and with that a lot can go wrong. A simple life is rich in its subtleties. Strengthen your strengths, and let go of the notion that you have to be great at everything. Hone your skills so that you're masterful at them, and leave the rest to others.

Truth itself is always simple. If what you're creating is complicated, either simplify it, or make sure that every aspect of it is directly connected to your needs in a clear and truthful way. Once you see and act with clarity, you will be sensitized to all that emerges in life with few distractions. Distractions create mind clutter.

Life has gotten extremely complex, rich with opportunities, external stimuli, and limitless possibilities. Juggling your lifestyle, managing your finances, developing your career, and striving to get ahead takes its toll on you. Even wonderful opportunities create pressure at a great cost. Success is seductive and often elusive when we chase after it instead of attracting it to us.

This doesn't mean that you should walk away from life. Rather, it means that you should let things go until there is very little energy expended to manage your life. It simply flows.

The first step is to get rid of possessions, goals, and behaviors that have complicated your life. Second, redesign your day so that you have at least two hours of free time with nothing planned or scheduled. Get rid of whatever it is that is holding you back. Prune your life of toxic relationships, and let go of situations that are draining you. Remove self-doubt and uncertainty and whatever else is distracting you.

Enjoy Silence

Eliminate a life of expectation. Expect less from people, and disentangle yourself from obligations. Learn to say no so that you have more time and space to say yes to what you want in life.

At home:

- Get rid of stuff you're always moving from place to place. If you don't love everything around you, then toss it.
- Do your shopping once a week. Those quick pit stops to the grocery store a few times a week take time away from something else.
- Do laundry less often. Simplify your wardrobe, and you'll have more pieces to mix and match.

For life:

- Downsize. Now that you have less stuff, do you really need all that extra space?
- Stop the junk mail. Take your name off lists.
- Get out of debt. Live off what you earn. Even better, live off less than what you earn, and invest the rest.

315

- Eliminate binge shopping. If you buy for need, great. If you buy for the adrenaline rush, then it's something to seriously look at.
- Automate everything that's automatable. Don't you have something better to do with that time?

For your health:

- Laugh more, stress out less.
- Simplify your meals. Eat healthy. They don't have to be five-course meals.
- Drink more water.
- Get off the treadmill, and go for a walk instead.
- Stop running in all directions. Slow down to the speed of life.

Finally, for you:

- Be yourself. If you're always trying to please others and be like everyone else, who will be you?
- Trust your intuition. It will never let you down.
- Set your personal boundaries. Trying to place what isn't acceptable into that gray zone of "almost acceptable" will wear you down. There is no halfway between the two.
- Do nothing once in a while. Let the world in.

Simplicity creates more time and space. Then, it's your choice as to how you fill both.

ABOUT THE AUTHOR

Donna is an executive coach, author, lectures internationally, and is founder of Mindsful™, an international research and development team. In response to widely expressed interest in her highly successful and innovative approach to coaching, she established the School of Shadow Coaching™ to enable others to learn the practice. To learn more, visit http://www.abetterperspective.com.

90

Double Your Reading Speed in 10 Minutes: Save an Hour a Day for the Rest of Your Life

Paul R. Scheele

One simple question: would you be willing to invest a few minutes right now to save an hour a day for the rest of your life? To read a book twice as fast as you can now? To get through the morning paper in minutes? To absorb those reports, Web pages, e-mails, journals, and magazines with less stress and more enjoyment?

You can, and it is actually easy. All you need is a timepiece (a kitchen timer that counts down to a beep works best) and a willingness to explore a new way to use your brain.

To begin, pick another chapter in this book, and read for 20 seconds. When you are finished, count the number of lines you read, and write down that number in a convenient location. This will give you an idea of your present reading speed. Now, let's learn a little about the reading process.

Three-Step Process

Three aspects of the way you read determine your speed: physical posture, mental posture, and reading technique. While the magnificently powerful human brain instantly recognizes words at speeds hardly imaginable, in school we were programmed, like a sports car that only shifts into first gear, to go slowly, be careful, back up, sound it out, and comprehend every single word. This snail-in-the-mud programming undermines your potential and wastes a lot of precious time. Get ready to shift into fifth gear and enjoy a lifetime of fast, effortless reading.

Step 1: Get Physical

Studies show that the following specific physical posture helps you to read more quickly and to comprehend more: place your feet comfortably on the floor, sit up straight, and fully relax your shoulders as you exhale. Do it now. Then, relax your face and gently smile—can you feel a difference?

Prop up or hold up the book about 45 to 60 degrees, and slightly tilt your head downward. You're now in the ideal posture for reading.

Step 2: Expectancy and the Tangerine

Next, create an ideal state of mind using the "tangerine technique." It's an odd technique, but it gets your brain working in such a way that you can read swiftly through anything. Play along to see how it works for you.

- Expect success. Tell yourself what you want to get from your reading. Never blindly read. Always have a purpose.
- Use your hand to reach out in front of you and pick up an imaginary tangerine—do it right now, as you are reading this. Imagine its color, skin texture, and maybe even its sweet, tangy smell. Then, lob it from hand to hand to sense its weight.
- With your dominant hand, position the imaginary tangerine on the upper-rear portion of your head. Touch that area gently with your hand and imagine the tangerine floating a couple inches above your head. Bring your hand down and relax your shoulders completely. Pretend that this magical tangerine always stays there, no matter how your head moves.
- Close your eyes, and let the tangerine float above and behind your head a few inches. Notice how much more relaxed and alert you feel. Imagine your field of vision opening up.
- Maintain this feeling, and gently open your eyes. Make sure your book is properly propped up, and read for another 20 seconds.
- Again, write down the number of lines you read.

How was that? Is it now easier to read? Did the words flow more effortlessly? In most classes I teach, students notice a 50 percent increase in reading speed using these two techniques alone. To review: in step 1, set posture, relax, gently smile, tilt your head, and prop your book; in step 2, expect success, and use the tangerine technique.

Step 3: Upper-Half Reading

Now, glide your vision across the upper half of the words you read. In other words, don't focus on the full word, just on the upper portion. Play with this technique using this paragraph. Do you notice a difference? Most people find that it is easier to get the meaning of a sentence by gliding across the top portion of the words. It's a novel idea based on scientific research that actually works! Another tip: when you finish one line, quickly zip your eyes back to the beginning of the next line. You should now find it easier to comprehend whole words and phrases at much higher speeds, while eliminating bad habits such as rereading and focusing on individual words to sound them out.

Let's read for another 20 seconds. Set posture, relax, gently smile, tilt your head, and prop your book. Close your eyes and expect success for your session. Put your tangerine in place, touching the back of your head to get the feeling while imagining your visual field opening up. Now, gently open your eyes, and again, begin reading for 20 seconds, gliding your eyes across the top of the words and zipping to the next line.

Count the lines again. What differences did you notice? How many more lines did you get through? Isn't it amazing that you improved that much in less than 10 minutes?

Try it again for another 20 seconds. Use everything you just learned. This time, push yourself a little. Challenge yourself to read faster still.

You Are Brighter Than You Think

In the *Genius Code* home-study course that I coauthored with mind development pioneer Win Wenger, we say, "You are brighter than you think." You have great resources of mind, which you accessed today with these remarkable three steps to double your reading speed.

Commit to using these reading techniques on everything you read. You may find it helpful to put a note in your calendar to remind yourself every day for the next couple weeks to use these techniques. Review this article at least a couple more times. Feel free to make a personal copy of these pages to keep on your desk or in your briefcase.

Enjoy the benefits of increased speed and comprehension. You'll see the ease of reading continuing to grow as you strengthen your new skills as an efficient, effective reader.

ABOUT THE AUTHOR

In 1981, Paul founded Learning Strategies Corporation, a respected private school and publisher in Minnesota. He has authored numerous books and audio programs to help you maximize your potential, including the popular PhotoReading program. With PhotoReading you activate your mind to get through reading material as quickly as you can turn the pages. Can you imagine that? For a free CD that includes two videos, a 30-minute audio session, and a sample chapter from Paul's book on PhotoReading, visit http://www.LearningStrategies.com/PhotoReading. When checking out, use Customer Code TRSG106 to be automatically entered into a quarterly contest to in $250.

91

SPIRITUAL CONSCIOUSNESS

Wholeness

Rebbie Straubing

> Spiritual consciousness means that when the intellect
> affirms the Divine Presence the whole consciousness
> feels the meaning of what the intellect has affirmed.
> –Ernest Holmes

Spiritual consciousness often sits on the sidelines of our lives, waiting for us to come to it in our moments of spiritual practice. It need not be relegated to such a narrow piece of the pie. At its core, spiritual consciousness means wholeness, so why not apply it to the whole of life? It brings joy, love, and serendipitous revelations wherever it is invited.

Challenges

If there is something that you want, but you cannot seem to bring it into reality, consider cultivating wholeness. Not just wholeness in general—I'm talking about wholeness in relation to manifesting the life your heart desires.

As you become whole on any subject, you bring yourself into powerful alignment with the Divine Presence. Wholeness, in this context, means that you are quiet within on a subject that shows much activity without. Wholeness, regarding manifestation, means that you have no conflict in your vibration. You are a united being, an uninterrupted flow, a single voice. You are clear and strong on the subject, whatever it may be. Once these attributes are yours, your manifestation is assured.

Whether the topic on your mind involves relationships, finances, career, body, mind, or emotions, becoming whole on the subject offers you a total transformation of your current circumstances.

321

Try This

How do you become whole on a subject that is troubling you? First, pick your topic. Anything will do. You may want to focus on a general issue such as your career or your marriage. You may be distracted by a very specific challenge such as a computer malfunction or a health setback. Whatever is calling to you in the moment presents the perfect doorway into this process.

This is also a good exercise to do in the morning before getting out of bed. Your theme does not have to reflect a challenge. This exercise can simply focus your energy for the day. Keep this page on your night table. See what's on your mind when you wake up, and choose that as your topic.

1. Sit quietly, and turn your attention inward. Invite the Divine Presence into your awareness. Open your mind to an expanded perspective. Consider the possibility that a beneficent force of immense proportion has partnered with you on this journey.

2. Now, turn your attention to your topic. Get a little distance from your swirling emotions. Do this by sensing the shape created in your energy field by all the mental and emotional activity on your chosen topic. Although you may perceive a distinct shape, you will more likely encounter a general feeling or an abstract sense of its pattern of movement. You can't do this incorrectly. Just get a sense of the issue as it sits in your energy field.

3. Once you have a sense of this cloud of activity and its shape, maybe even its color and texture, realize that you are bigger than it. You can tell you are bigger than it because you must be outside of it in order to sense its shape.

4. Once you have a sense of yourself as larger than the calamity of energy crosscurrents, look within your true heart for your singular desire on this subject. Look for the desire that harmonizes with every part of you—one that is undeniable, incontestable. It is rooted in your essence. It will probably be related to a desire for unconditional love, inner peace, or personal freedom as it relates to your chosen topic. For example, your desire for money may be rooted in a desire for freedom; your desire for a romantic partner may have its roots in a desire for unconditional love.

5. Once you discover the desired root feeling, find it within yourself (even though circumstances may not yet match the feeling). Seat yourself in the center of that feeling of unconditional love, personal freedom, or whatever you found to be at the center of your desire. Become soaked in the feeling of that essence. It does not need a name, a form, or any other distinctions. It may simply be a feeling, but you recognize it as your own, just as clearly as you recognize your face in a mirror. As you bathe your awareness in this feeling, you can tell that this desire is the natural extension of your spirit, and it feels good when you fill your world with its essence.

6. Imagine that the air is filled with this feeling. Imagine that your world is made of this tone.

7. Become whole on this feeling. Sense that it is who you are. It is all that is.

This process should feel soft and incomparably soothing. If it doesn't, go back and do some tweaking. The purer you get in recognizing your heart's desire, the better this process will feel, and the more miraculous will be your manifestation.

Achieving wholeness on a topic invokes the Divine Presence. It is a purification practice, and it promotes inner alignment. It also unfurls, in colorful and satisfying ways, the life your heart desires.

A version of this article was first published in *phenomeNEWS*, 18444 West 10 Mile Road, Suite 105, Southfield, MI 48075, http://www.phenomeNEWS.com.

ABOUT THE AUTHOR

Dr. Rebbie Straubing is a workshop leader, Abraham Coach, and spiritual writer. Rebbie evolved The Yoga of Alignment (YOFA™) from a mystical awareness of the relationship between consciousness and the three dimensions in which we live. She teaches a natural and simple approach to daily life that you can use to cultivate your own direct access to the Infinite. Rebbie is a teacher of teachers. Her approach cuts through appearances, clarifies the mind, frees the heart, and nurtures the soul. You can receive Dr. Rebbie Straubing's free e-course, "7 Secrets for Manifesting Your Heart's Desire," at http://www.YOFA.net.

92

<hr>

Everyday Spirituality

Ariel Kane & Shya Kane

In this world, where technology has eclipsed our humanity, many of us are looking for a way to operate in our lives that fulfills our spiritual nature. People have tried different religions or disciplines with varying degrees of success or failure. They have taken motivational workshops to try to discover some meaning to apply to their lives, and many have come away wondering, "Is this all there is?" This vague sense of emptiness or dissatisfaction can permeate our lives, even when we accomplish the goals we set for ourselves.

People listen to a private, internal radio station that plays oldies-but-not-so-goodies. This station plays tracks that are repetitive and self-defeating. Have you ever listened to the recording that says something like, "I am in my mid-thirties, and I don't have a relationship. All of the relationships I have ever had haven't worked. I'll never have one. Why bother trying?" Another similar track asks, "What is the use? No matter how hard I try, I will just be disappointed again anyway."

The way we humans function is very similar to modern-day computers, which can only operate through the applications that are installed in them. For instance, a computer that has a word processing program but does not have a spreadsheet program installed will never be able to do spreadsheet-type activities. This is not a fault of the computer because if the computer did have a spreadsheet program installed, it would handle this task quite easily.

You, too, are not at fault if your internal voice repeats self-defeating messages. If you have never had a relationship that worked, the prospect of one working in the future is very dim. In other words, if it hasn't already happened, you cannot conceive of it happening. Minds function like a closed system. They extrapolate from what is known. Einstein said, "No problem can be solved from the same consciousness that created it. We must learn to see the world anew."

How can we learn to see the world anew? What can we do to create a future that isn't either a repeat of the past or simply an incremental improvement on what we have had before? How do we have quantum leaps in the quality of our lives?

The answer is surprisingly simple. In order to jump spontaneously into your potential rather than reinforcing your self-imposed limitations, you need to discover how you actually are rather than how you think are. This is accomplished through honest self-observation, without self-reproach. You don't have to worry about or focus on how you have been in the past in order to build a new future. This is because you will continue to behave in this present moment as you have in the past until you bring awareness to unwanted and unneeded patterns of behavior. Awareness is a nonjudgmental seeing of what is. In other words, it is about noticing your behavior without judging yourself for what you discover. This will empower you to naturally stop doing those things that you have done automatically. Then, life becomes vital and filled with meaning.

Spirituality exists in all aspects of our lives when we experience life directly, not through the filter of our judgments, agendas, or thought processes. You can only do one thing at a time. You can either think about what is happening in your life, or you can be in the experience of what is happening in your life, moment-to-moment. This does not mean that one stops thinking. It does, however, mean that the conversation that judges, evaluates, and rates how you are doing fades into the background and no longer dominates your life.

One of the side benefits of living life in the moment is that relatively mundane acts take on a sense of fullness, and your actions become appropriate, not based on past decisions or agendas. Agendas are those ideas we have of what will fulfill us or produce satisfaction in the future. These agendas all come from the known. They come from what society holds to be true (or the resistance to society) rather than from your experience of what is actually fulfilling for you. Therefore fulfillment or satisfaction can never be achieved by completing these agendas unless you are already satisfied. True satisfaction comes from living your life directly, not from judging yourself for how you are doing.

Living life directly includes your agendas and goals but is not merely driving forward to achieve them. For example, you may have the goal to be physically fit and have planned a regimen at the gym to support this desire. However, the people who exercise with the intention of experiencing purity of motion and having optimum form while performing each move will come away enlivened from the experience. They will also be simultaneously moving toward being physically fit. In contrast, people who look in the mirror and complain about what they see, those that exercise in order to be all right someday, inadvertently reinforce the inner story that something is wrong with them, and even when the goal is achieved, the sense of being not all right lingers.

How does one live life directly? How does one become satisfied? Here is a hint: engaging in any activity as fully as you know how is the beginning. If you are washing the dishes and find that you are talking to yourself about whether or not you want to be doing what you are doing, this is a clue that you are not fully engaged.

Here is the tricky part. If you are preoccupied or complaining, that is all you can be doing in that moment. That *is* your moment. However, with awareness (a nonjudgmental seeing of what is) the conversation to which you are listening will complete itself, or you will be able to intentionally disengage from it and redirect your energy.

About the Authors

Ariel and Shya Kane are internationally acclaimed authors, seminar leaders, and business consultants whose revolutionary technology, Instantaneous Transformation, has helped thousands of individuals and companies worldwide. The Kanes lead workshops dedicated to supporting people in living in the moment and having extraordinary, fulfilling lives. For more information, including dates and locations for upcoming courses, call (908) 479–6034, or visit their Web site at http://www.ask-inc.com.

93

Eight Out of Ten Fast Ways to Rapidly Reduce Your Stress

Frank Barnhill

In today's fast-paced society, more than just professionals and those of us with management jobs fall victim to the pain and suffering of life's stresses. Today's never-ending rat race can cause us to develop such fast-moving, impulsive, stress-filled lives that we often fail to achieve the success that would normally be ours under different circumstances.

It's really hard to focus on reaching your greatest potential in life when you're constantly stressed from putting out little fires. Over the past 30 years we've all become hyper-focused on success at any cost, which greatly increases our stress levels. Fortunately, learning a few life skills management tools can significantly reduce your stress and make you much more likely to reach satisfaction and success in life.

1. Get control of your future. Most of us avoid planning for the future, whether it's just a week ahead or 20 years in advance. For some reason, admitting that we need to plan ahead can be stressful and anxiety provoking—it's almost as if we think that if we have to plan, we're not in control of our lives.

When we fail to plan, we essentially plan to fail. Then, when things start to fall apart in our lives, we feel overwhelmed, threatened, get anxious, and struggle to do things to decrease our mounting anxiety and stress. Unfortunately, we're often not mentally and emotionally prepared to handle both the everyday facets of living and all the unexpected, unprepared, unplanned things that fall apart. When we panic, our adrenaline systems go into full throttle and cause even more stress and anxiety.

A wise man once said, "If you don't know where you're headed, then it really doesn't matter how you get there!" Just having a road map by which to chart your course will decrease your daily stress tremendously.

2. Learn to say "no" gracefully. This is really a toughie as saying "no" tends to make you feel guilty (it's almost as if you'll cause disappointment or even personal harm if you don't say "yes"), but if you learn to say "no" gracefully, then you won't feel guilty, and less guilt means less stress. Next time, try this: "Sorry, but I had better decline your offer." "I really won't have the time to dedicate the effort you need to make your (event) a success."

3. Set aside time every day to think about and solve your problems. It may only be 30 minutes at the end of the day, but quiet thinking is essential to problem solving and to your ability to cope with stress. Quiet surroundings allow you to get in touch with your higher executive brain functions, consider your life, and analyze problems. Find a sanctuary to ponder and explore your "self." Each of us needs a place where we feel safe and secure enough to be by ourselves and think through all the things in life that are really important to us. You'll be surprised how easily solutions pop into your head when you're able to dedicate all your mental abilities to the task.

4. Control technological demands on your life, and don't let technology dictate your time schedule. Do you feel compelled to answer e-mail as soon as possible? You're not alone—most of us get anxious or feel guilty if we don't answer those e-mails right away. You must be the master of any technology, or you become its slave. Would you visit the post office ten times a day to get your mail? No? So, what is the worst that could happen if you don't check your e-mail five times tomorrow?

5. Learn to accept mistakes. Some of us live in fear of making a mistake, whether big or little. It's not just the fear of failure that ties up our brainpower and concentration abilities; it's also knowing that we will mentally punish ourselves if we do make a mistake. Once you learn that it's okay to make little mistakes, you'll learn to deal with big mistakes without beating yourself to death. After all, if you never fall down while learning to walk, you'll never learn how to pick yourself up. We all learn from our mistakes and would fail to mature as adults if we were never allowed to make them. Some behavioral scientists think that we should be teaching our kids to make mistakes at an early age so that they can learn what we have missed. A mistake is an opportunity to do better.

6. Be positive with yourself. Accept praise gracefully and honestly, and deal with criticism the same way. Most of us tend to downplay our strengths and overexaggerate our weaknesses. Doing so causes a mental conflict with our self-esteem and decreases our ability to concentrate on what is really important in life. How often do you reject or downplay a genuine compliment given to you by a friend, only to later beat yourself to death over a small, insignificant failure? You, too, can be a success in life, no matter who you are, but if you think you're not worthy of success, then you're probably right.

7. Ask for help when you need it. You are not admitting defeat or inadequate if you ask others for help. Asking for help is truly just as human and natural as any other basic survival trait. How often have you offered to help someone that you know needs help? How good did it make you feel when you were able to help? Does that mean you don't want someone else to feel good when they help you? When you wait until you're overwhelmed and struggling to keep your head above water, asking for help can be very damaging to your ego and self-esteem. It's far better to ask for help earlier rather than later.

8. Learn to have fun. Most of us are under the erroneous belief that we are obligated to make sure others have fun before we're allowed to enjoy ourselves. That's emotional garbage! If you want to be successful in life, you have to experience emotional, mental, and physical recreation on a regular basis. You can't do a good job for yourself or for others if you can't learn to have fun without all the guilt of not including everybody else. Recreation is a condensed "Old World" word meaning to "re-create"—go out and "re-create" yourself. Watch your stress levels drop and your focus toward success become clearer.

ABOUT THE AUTHOR

Frank Barnhill, MD is a board-certified family physician in South Carolina with a fantastic medical practice dedicated to improving the lives of the world's best patients. Dr. Frank is affectionately known as Dr. Huggie Bear because he hugs hundreds of patients a week in his quest for the most feel-good medical practice in the United States. He writes and lectures extensively on life success traits, child and adolescent medicine, ADHD, and similar topics that impact our daily lives and our efforts to live successfully. Dr. Frank publishes an award-winning content information–based medical Web site, http://www.drhuggiebear.com, that offers articles to help you and your family reach your maximum potential in life.

94

STRESS RELIEF

Getting Off the Treadmill
and Getting On with Life

Jacquie Hale

I've been wondering why so many of us are so busy; after all, we're not being forced to labor against our will. What gives?

I hate to put the blame directly on the busy person, but I believe that we are too busy because we choose to be. We like to think that it's the boss who is piling on all the work or some looming project that fills our hours, but is it really some elusive bad guy, or are we willing participants?

One night, while working alone in a hospital blood bank, I was overwhelmed by horrendous accidents coming into the Emergency Room at the same time that a hemophiliac was having a bleeding crisis and an emergency C-section began in Labor and Delivery. While I chose to work in an intense environment, I didn't choose to be overwhelmed. If such events happened every night and if I continued to work that shift alone, I was the one choosing a chaotic, crisis-driven world. Eventually, I said, "No more!" and chose a less stressful career. When the unusual becomes usual, the responsibility for being overcommitted falls on the person who chooses to be part of the process.

How Do You Know When You Are Too Busy?

If you can't tell from the feelings of stress (anxiety, sleeplessness, a nagging sense of never being able to do it all), you might get signals from your family and colleagues. Are you constantly late? Do you miss your kids' activities so often that they don't even ask you anymore? Does your spouse complain? Are your coworkers or your boss irritable with you? Has your blood pressure crept up? Do you sleep badly and awaken still tired? Are you on the treadmill because you choose to be there?

Why Do People Choose to Be Too Busy?

It may be because they don't set good boundaries—people keep giving them stuff to do, *and they keep doing it*. In that case they are choosing not to say no. Being busy is a choice.

Another reason people get overly busy is because they need approval. They are hoping that just one more perfect report or fabulous design will get them the recognition that they long for. Again, this is a condition that they choose to be in, even if it is an unconscious choice.

What's a Busy Person to Do?

Sometimes, people can change their lives when they notice that they are too busy; however, often the epiphany involves some personal tipping point, where they realize that their busy-ness is keeping them from enjoying life. A relationship suffers, a career explodes, or health issues crop up. Whether the messenger is gentle or brutal, the first step to stop being too busy is to decide not to be busy.

For some people, that's all that's required—just deciding. For them, setting boundaries is easy once the decision is made. For others the process may need to go deeper. If the reason someone is too busy is because he or she is desperately seeking acknowledgement, the road to complete success will involve soul searching to discover the source of that feeling. This can be a long and sometimes painful journey, or it can be one filled with delightful discoveries involving courage and honesty. Again, it's a choice of how to view one's life.

What Simple Activities Reduce Stress and Allow You to Discover the Best Course of Action?

The short answer is breathing. Simple. Easy to do. Taking conscious breaths can calm you so that you have more clarity and are in better touch with what has heart and meaning for you.

331

How about doing that right now? Take a deep breath, and when you let it out, relax your shoulders and let go of thinking about what you were doing. Now that you have the idea, do it again. And now, one more time.

"Take three deep breaths" is something I often suggest to my coaching clients, friends, family—even to my dogs. Breathing is a common starting point for exercises in workshops and trainings about personal growth and development. Taking three breaths frequently can change your day; it can even change the way your life goes. A deep breath, taken consciously, can be the best stress reliever you own.

Set Aside Some Time for Yourself

This is best done first thing in the morning.

- Begin your time for yourself by thinking of three things from the previous day that you appreciate. These might include that you found a great parking space during a downpour or that you just landed a publisher for your book. Some days, it's a struggle to think of anything. When that happens to me, I use a fallback option like "birds at the feeder" or "dogs at my side." Don't skip this step! It's very important.
- Once you've noted what you appreciate, allot time to sit quietly. I suggest beginning with three minutes and increasing it later to 15 or 20. Don't hum or plan or knit, just sit quietly—breathing. Be aware of your breath going in and out. During this time you might encounter two things: mind chatter and the fidgets. Just notice whatever is going on and go back to being aware of your breathing. Ultimately, sitting quietly allows you to hear your inner wisdom.
  - o Set a timer so that you are not constantly looking at the clock.
  - o Sit in any position you want—no need for special pillows or postures. No need for incense, sacred music, finger positions, or special breathing techniques. Sit any way you feel comfortable.
  - o Just sit and listen.

A colleague was doing this program, and his first awareness was that he had been so busy, he hadn't realized how dissatisfied he was with his life—he was having trouble thinking of anything he could appreciate. Within a few weeks of starting this reflective routine he decided to act on something he had been intending to do for years: he signed up to teach reading to illiterate adults. This became such a satisfying endeavor that now he is thinking of leaving his mind-numbing office job and becoming a teacher.

That's the secret for getting off the treadmill: appreciate what's in your life and breathe. Decide not to be busy, and then give yourself the time and space to hear your heart's desire. That will give you the reason to make the changes you need to make. There's far more to discover than you might imagine!

About the Author

Jacquie Hale has tapped 30 years of health care experience, an advanced degree in Natural Health, and her expertise as a life coach to create programs and materials that bring calmness and purpose to people who are committed to having a better life. You can buy her book, *Serenity Is an Inside Job: How to Relieve Stress and Reclaim Your Life*, on which this article is based, and review her services on her Web site, http://www.serenitycoach.com. Send e-mail to jacquie@vibrancecoach.com, or call her for a sample coaching session at (510) 548–2585 (Pacific time).

Copyright © 2006, Jacqueline Hale.

95

THE SUBCONSCIOUS MIND

What's the Matter with Mind over Matter?

Evelyn Cole

I truly believe that your thoughts create your life, but I don't think that your thoughts are easy to change, at least, not by your own will. What you truly think about yourself, you perceive nonverbally before you are three years old. Trying, as an adult, to think positively when your gut feels negative never works. In fact, trying to do or be anything requires lying to yourself.

Here's one example.

Josh had everything going for him. He greeted his mother every morning with a big smile. He arranged it at the bathroom mirror first. He was convinced that his success in school and in sports resulted from his positive attitude. He maintained a body builder's physique and dressed in all cotton clothes that enhanced his looks without showing off. Also, he was the star of the high school basketball team.

"It's all in your mind," his parents used to say to him whenever he ran home in pain, crying. Gradually, he developed mind control over his body. By age 14, he had memorized *The Power of Positive Thinking*.

After earning an MBA degree he went to law school. This was part of his game plan. Every day, he checked off at least three actions he had made toward achieving his goal for the month.

When he finished law school, he married a beautiful young lawyer and accepted a position with a Fortune 400 corporation. Floor-to-ceiling windows in his private office on the 24th floor gave him a panoramic view of San Francisco Bay.

On his 28th birthday he picked up a small replica of Michelangelo's *David* that decorated his teak desk and threw it at the window. The window broke. He kicked it open and jumped to his death. No one knew why.

Have you heard similar stories?

Josh's positive thinking took place in his left frontal lobe. His subconscious mind drowned in unshed tears. Denying feelings can be dangerous. Expressing feelings can be dangerous, too.

Children need to learn how to control themselves, but how they do it has long-lasting effects. If you are content with yourself in all areas of your current life, then you found the right balance between emotional expression and self-control. You don't need to *try* to be somebody or *lie* to yourself. If, however, there are any areas in which you are not satisfied with yourself, you can be sure that your subconscious mind is out of synch with your conscious one.

I tell you this story of Josh because I, too, wanted to commit suicide when I was 28. I, too, had everything going for me, on the surface. I had no right to be unhappy, I thought. Luckily, I found help.

Long after my mother died, I started writing to her one day. My letter started out resentful, grew angry, then became understanding and sad—very sad—and finally, forgiving. It took a few pages. I didn't realize that I had an understanding of her and forgiveness in me. The process mellowed me.

There are many ways to discover what's on your mind. Writing is mine. It has always worked for me. Hypnosis works, too. Explore. Your subconscious mind won't lie to you. Just *accept* whatever comes up, then, if it's a hot potato, drop it. You can make the conscious choice when to let a feeling go. Feelings are just energy in motion.

Have you stopped trying lately?

Here's to you.

ABOUT THE AUTHOR

Evelyn Cole, MA, MFA, known as the Whole-Mind Writer, publishes a weekly e-zine, "Mind Nudges," and offers an e-course called Brainsweep at http://www.write-for-wealth.com. She writes, "My chief aim in life is to convince everyone to capture the power of the subconscious mind and synchronize it with the conscious mind. That takes knowing how your own subconscious mind operates." She has published three novels and poetry that dramatize that passion.

96

SUBLIMINAL CDS AND TAPES

Subliminal Audios:
Taking the Struggle Out of Personal Change

Susannah Lippman

- Anne had grown up believing in the virtuous poor and the evil rich. Now, she feels guilty about charging her clients what her services are worth. How can she stop unwittingly sabotaging her own success?
- Bob had battled procrastination all his life. It had been difficult even with a supervisor breathing down his neck, but now that he's on his own, he wonders if he can give himself that extra push.
- Janice needs strong motivation and support for her weight loss program to keep her from sliding back into her old eating patterns.

What these people have in common is their desire to free themselves from deep-seated habits of thought, habits that go back to childhood and often lurk unnoticed beneath the surface for decades. Yet, these hidden inner mind-sets can severely limit our success in reaching personal goals.

The conscious mind is only the tip of the iceberg. Most of the mind's power is lodged in the subconscious, a vast memory bank that stores everything we have ever experienced. It is this subconscious mind that truly rules our lives. That's why the same people seem blessed with success again and again, while others, despite all the seminars and wise books they experience, don't move forward toward their dreams.

Most self-help methods engage only your conscious mind. If you're lucky, a little bit filters down to your subconscious. A decision to change does not go deep enough. We make promises to ourselves, only to keep slipping back into well-worn patterns. If you've smoked for years, your mind is programmed as a smoker. All the horror stories about how black your lungs are and how soon you will die may convince you to quit, but they won't make it happen. In fact, until you change your subconscious programming, quitting is impossible.

The same is true not only for habits like smoking, drugs, and alcohol, but for habits of thought, which are possibly the most difficult of all to change because they are so subtle that you may not know they are there. There are habits like putting yourself down, not believing in your own abilities, thinking that you will always be overweight or in poor health, that you are unattractive or stupid, or that you will never find a fulfilling, loving relationship—all habits of thought that can keep you stuck where you are for the rest of your life.

Yet, it's highly likely that your habits of thought are all that's holding you back and all that's preventing you from having everything you've ever wanted in life—health, wealth, love, career, happiness—everything.

Finding a Way to Access Your Subconscious Mind

You need to change the programming! That's what subliminal tapes and CDs are designed to do. Yet, we've all heard the debate about whether subliminals work. Many of us experience profound benefits, while others do not. Let's look at the confusion surrounding subliminal audios.

What Is a Subliminal Program?

It is a sound recording of a series of positive affirmations. On a conscious level you hear only music or nature sounds. Since the messages are "drowned out" by this louder, "masking" sound, they bypass your conscious mind and go directly into your subconscious. Thus they also bypass your resistance to change. That is why a high-quality subliminal can affect you much more powerfully than words you hear consciously.

Does It Really Work?

This is no longer a matter of speculation. Scientific studies have proved beyond doubt the effectiveness of subliminals, but psychologists have drawn this conclusion: all subliminals are not alike. Here's an excerpt from our "Tape Shoppers' Checklist" that tells what to look for in a subliminal.

1. Are Alpha and Theta brain waves increased? In the Alpha state you are calm and relaxed, yet alert and clear-headed. This is the best state for listening to most subliminals. In the Theta state you are even more receptive, but not alert enough to go about your usual activities, so it is used only for audios promoting deep rest, sleep, or meditation. You are more receptive when you are relaxed and open. Many subliminal brands do not address this goal, which helps to explain why some don't work. An introduction that increases your Alpha and Theta brain waves promotes receptivity. Without this the affirmations may have little effect.

2. Are the messages in stereo? Most audios use stereo only for the covering music or nature sounds, while the messages themselves are on a single track. An effective sound track needs separate channels scripted differently for right and left brain hemispheres.

3. Are the scripts entirely positive? Hardly anyone would write a negative script intentionally, but well-meaning amateurs write sentences like, "sugar is poison," planting negative seeds in the mind and creating new problems for the user. There is enough negativity coming into our minds daily, without adding more!

4. Are the scripts written in the language of the subconscious? The subconscious is very childlike. It takes everything literally. Sentences must be short and simple and avoid complicated "if" and "when" clauses. "If I eat too much, I will get fat" could be heard by the subconscious as, "I eat too much. I will get fat." Could this ever backfire! Long, involved sentences are a sure sign that the writers lack expertise.

5. Are the affirmations in present tense? The subconscious knows only the present, so a good script avoids the future tense. After all, the future is always ahead of us. "I will succeed" tells the mind that you are not succeeding now.

6. Is there a money-back guarantee on results? This is essential!

The "Tape Shoppers' Checklist" contains a total of 14 items.

Popular Myths

Myth #1: Some fear that subliminal audios might make them do something they don't want to do. The truth is that they cannot. They can help you reach your goals, but they must be *your* goals. You are still very much in charge.
Some part of you must want the change. For example, in a struggle to lose weight, there is usually a battle between the part of you that wants a slender body and the part of you that wants the piece of fudge cake. Subliminals can strengthen your motivation for change and help you toward your goals. They cannot make you do something you have no desire to do and certainly not anything against your ethics.

Myth #2: Some think that if they have never used subliminal audios, their minds have not been subliminally programmed. Untrue! We are all subliminally programmed every second of our lives. Why? Because all the sounds in our environment that are a little bit out of the range of conscious hearing are heard by the subconscious. All sounds that are "drowned out" by something louder are also heard by the subconscious.

This means that when you passed that construction site this morning that remark on your anatomy, buried beneath the jackhammer's roar, was heard by you subliminally. The same is true of conversations at other tables in restaurants and all those TV commercials you don't listen to. The same is true for all the sights and sounds (and smells and tastes and touches) around you from the very beginning of your life to the present!

The problem is that much of this input is negative. We're bombarded from all sides with blaring radios, angry words, harsh criticisms, distorted advertising slogans, and lies and manipulations. Subliminals give you a choice, a way of flooding your mind with enough positive input to offset the negative. In short, subliminals can set you free.

About the Author

Susannah Lippman is President of Alphasonics International, the company that pioneered much of the new technology. Their audios were selected for use by the researchers who tested all brands. She founded Alphasonics in 1987, after discovering breakthroughs in subliminal research, to bring this new generation of powerful personal growth tools to the public. For over 19 years their audios have been used worldwide, by individuals and by practitioners who offer them to patients. Susannah holds a master's degree in communications, has been a teacher of speech and communications, a writer, a producer for educational television, and Director of the Association for Humanistic Psychology, Eastern Region. She is author of *The Truth about Subliminal Audios*, a comprehensive report (from which this chapter contains excerpts). The complete report is available at http://www.alphasonics.com.

97

Listen to the Teachers around You

William E. Hablitzel

The snow was still falling, but for the most part the storm was over. It would take many days, however, before life in our small community would return to normal. Blizzards weren't something that happened in Ohio, but there it was, a thick blanket of snow that had been whipped into incredible roof-high drifts that blocked roads and curved around homes like sand dunes on a beach. It was in the earliest days of my career, and the fire academy hadn't adequately prepared me for what I would encounter during those cold January days long ago. For three days I sat huddled with colleagues in the cold dampness of the firehouse, gasoline generators supplying electricity for only our most essential needs. Rescue runs once escorted by police cars were now led by snow plows. The brightness of the snow stood in stark contrast with the darkness of our mood.

Paramedic training hadn't adequately prepared me for what I held in my hands. The frantic man tried to get his wife to the hospital, but the car was hopelessly stuck in the snow despite hours of desperate digging. The petite woman was frightened. It wasn't supposed to be like this. Her doctor had told her that she had another month. Instead of a warm hospital bed, their dining room floor had to make do. It was my first delivery.

Their infant daughter couldn't have weighed more than five pounds. The smallest hand that I had ever seen closed around my little finger as her squint opened to reveal brilliant blue eyes, eyes that seemed to focus on mine. With a sharp gasp her mouth opened, her chest rose, and I witnessed the miracle of the first breaths of life. The cold that had followed me for days melted away, and I was left with a sense of incredible awe and wonder. While only minutes into this life, those eyes seemed to speak of ageless wisdom. It was a contradiction that I did not understand at the time, but I had a long way yet to travel on my journey.

A decade would pass before I would see eyes like those again. The fire service had been just a stop on the path that I was to take, a path that would lead to medical school and an invitation into the lives of incredible people. Roger Harrold was one such person. I met him during my residency at the VA hospital. The VA was a great place to learn medicine. It was a world of fathers and grandfathers, of heart-touching stories and of lives in need. Inevitably, patients would become family. Such was the case with Roger.

Early one morning found me sitting on the side of Roger's bed. I had been up all night and still had many tasks to complete before I could go home, but at that moment Roger's bedside was the place where I most wanted to be. I had only known him for a month, but it was an intense month. Much of each day was spent with Roger. There had been physical exams to conduct, procedures to perform, and medication to administer. But there had been much more. We shared our thoughts, our dreams, and life itself. By the time I knew that Roger was dying, we were already family.

As I held Roger's hand, thickened and weathered from age and hard work, I was struck by his piercing blue eyes. They were eyes of infinite youth, of peace, and of great wisdom. With the most gentle of smiles and a soft gasp I witnessed the last breaths of life. It, too, was a miracle. While I had seen death before, I had never participated so completely. I was often touched by the brevity and fragility of life—one moment you are alive, and next moment you are not. But what came next? What would become of the experiences, memories, and knowledge that took a lifetime to collect? They were questions without answers, but in those eyes I had seen understanding of great depth. Indeed, there would be much more to come for Roger. His journey would not end that day.

Medical school, conferences, and journals all contributed to my knowledge of medicine, but they could not teach healing. An ancient Asian proverb tells us, "When the student is ready, the teacher will appear." My patients became my teachers, and those breaths of life from long ago helped me to get ready for the special lessons that they would bring to my life. The ability to wonder and to be open to all possibilities are not easy traits for physicians trained in tradition, but without them I might never have recognized my greatest teachers.

Alex was one of those teachers. A well-known figure in our community, he was the definition of success and accomplishment. While he had been a patient for many years, he was a difficult person to get to know well. Despite his success, he never seemed to smile, and I often wondered if he was happy. One afternoon, Alex stood waiting for me in an examination room. Two weeks earlier, Alex had died. He had been experiencing unusual sensations in his chest and collapsed, and died, in the waiting room of the emergency room. Had he not been at that place, at that time, he never would have been resuscitated and left the hospital alive. This day, Alex wore a broad smile when I entered the exam room. It was the smile of a happy man. "Dying was the best thing that ever happened to me," he said. In that moment I knew Roger had been right. There was much more to come after the last breaths of life.

There are moments in life powerful enough to change us instantly and forever. Far too often, though, these special moments come when we are not present to notice, lost in dramas of yesterday or our plans for tomorrow. Perhaps wisdom is living the richness that each day offers, being present to recognize those moments with the power to transform us, and seizing them before they can slip away into the currents of time.

Physicians are entrusted within the lives of their patients, lives woven from the threads of spirituality, touched by the mysteries of the universe, and filled with stories to tell. These stories can teach of a miraculous place and shine light on the path that will take us there. You do not have to be a physician, though, to learn of such things. These secrets of meaning and happiness are ours for the taking. They are hidden in the stories told by the old man down at the barber shop, displayed in the gardens of the lady next door, visible in the gaze of the stranger at the bus stop, and felt in the handshake of an old friend. They are everywhere.

We are surrounded by ways to improve our lives. Many of us won't, not for lack of desire, but because we have not learned to listen to the teachers around us and to wonder.

ABOUT THE AUTHOR

William E. Hablitzel, MD, author of the captivating book, *Dying Was the Best Thing That Ever Happened to Me: Stories of Healing and Wisdom along Life's Journey*, is a practicing internist in southern Ohio and an Associate Professor of Clinical Medicine at the University of Cincinnati College of Medicine. He has been recognized by the University of Cincinnati for excellence in teaching, and his work in rural health care was honored by resolutions passed by the Ohio State Senate and the Ohio House of Representatives. Visit his Web site at http://www.Sunshine-Ridge.com.

98

THANKFULNESS

Power of Thanks

Stuart Rosen

Gracias. Danke. Merci. Thanks.

Simple words with the power to bind, to build, and to behold. If you've ever gotten thanked or given thanks, then you know its power. Just the fact that you say it can be enough to make a difference, just as not saying it can make a difference in a negative way.

"Thank you" isn't just something that comes with "have a nice day" as you grab your paper or plastic. It's a sincere sign that something nice has occurred. It's not just an acknowledgement that you've been positively affected by something but a chance to return positive emotions back to the giver.

How can we tap into this powerful force?

- Be timely. Timing is perhaps the most crucial element of thanking someone. Waiting too long or forgetting altogether makes people wonder if you got that gift, if they did a good job, or if you really care. No hard and fast rule for what is a reasonable time in which to thank someone can be given, so "the sooner, the better" is always a good rule of thumb.
- Be appropriate. Sometimes, just a simple "thank you" will suffice. Most times, though, a more formal card (handwritten) will mean more than any gift. Of course, there are times when physical tokens of appreciation fit the bill, but be careful about going overboard as that makes one look like he's either trying to be impressive or is buttering 'em up for next time. Also, that sets up expectations of bigger and better for the next time, which is hard to keep up and really not what thanks are all about.

- Be receptive. Some people crave public attention. An announcement during an award ceremony or a toast during a special event might be just the thing to feed the ego as well as the spirit. For the shy crowd, that card and token are better. Giving thanks in the way that a person enjoys means that we care even more about him.
- Be personal. A thank you is even more powerful if some thought went into it. A book on a hobby he loves, a picture of his favorite place, or anything that is uniquely him says a lot.
- Be sincere. All the other elements are a part of our sincerity, but only a part. There's a knowingness that comes with a heartfelt thank you. Sometimes, it's obvious; other times, it's just a gut feeling, but something just rings true to the receiver. That's when thanks really hit home.
- Expect nothing in return. For a thank you to go deep into the soul of another it must be cast out without expectations, without conditions, without any strings attached whatsoever. Some people have gotten out of sorts because their thank you wasn't thanked. They're missing the point: it's all about the giving.

What If I Forgot?

What if, after reading this, you think, "Oops, I forgot to thank so-and-so." Now what? The fix is fairly simple: start with "I am really sorry," then go to step one above.

Guru-cize It!

The following is an exercise for you to try at home, at work, or anywhere!

> *Who should you thank?*
> Someone who did something nice for you.
> Someone you rely on.
> Someone you love.
> Someone who needs to feel appreciated.
> Everyone else.
>
> *What to do when someone thanks you:*
> Open up and let it in.
> Say, "You're welcome."

About the Author

A near-death experience at the tender age of five led Stuart Rosen on a lifelong pursuit of understanding and love. He became a motivational speaker by 11 and continues on some 30 years later. He became known as "Gurustu" during his radio days in Los Angeles and is the author of *Gurustu's Lil Words O' Wisdom* as well as numerous syndicated articles. Enlighten up with over 100 articles, "Dear Guru" letters, and cartoons at http://Gurustu.com.

99

The Cause of Unhappiness

Chuck Gallozzi

Is something disturbing, bothering, irritating, or annoying you? If so, what is troubling you? Is it a boss that is too demanding, a coworker that is too careless, or your children that are too noisy? Does the lack of civility, the increase in crime, or the apathy of young people upset you? Perhaps it is poor health, little money, or no respect that is making you depressed. With so many problems swirling around us, is the prospect of happiness a mere dream, an unattainable goal?

Did you ever learn that unhappiness is not caused by what happens to us but by how we interpret what happens to us? After all, in the last 50 years, brilliant thinkers have been hammering home this important point. Over and over again, Dr. Albert Ellis (Founder of Rational Emotive Behavioral Therapy), Dr. Aaron Beck (Founder of Cognitive Behavioral Therapy), and their followers have been proselytizing this truth.

It wasn't until recently that so much attention has been focused on the fact that unhappiness is caused by our attitude, not outside events. Yet, this teaching is hardly new, for Epictetus (55 ~ 135) taught that "Men are disturbed not by things but by the views which they take of them." Similarly, Marcus Aurelius (121 ~ 180) taught, "If you are pained by external things, it is not they that disturb you, but your own judgment of them. And it is in your power to wipe out that judgment now."

What is Marcus Aurelius telling us? Simply this: the true cause of our unhappiness is the decision we have made to blame others for it. This tactic of avoiding responsibility is self-defeating because it leads to a dead end; that is, we remain stuck, with no solution in sight. It is only after accepting responsibility that we can begin to analyze the causes of our behavior and look for ways to improve it.

If we already know that it is not the world but our opinions of it that cause our constant complaints, why do we continue to rob ourselves of happiness? One reason is that we fail to apply what we learn. Another reason for remaining mired in misery is force of habit. The good news is that we can break bad habits and return to the path of happiness.

1. Grapple with Epictetus' and Marcus Aurelius' teachings until you clearly understand them. Say to yourself, "People and events *do not* make me upset. Rather, I choose to make myself upset."

2. Become aware of your attempts to blame others for your discontent. Carry a small notebook with you. During the day, jot down examples of how you have falsely blamed circumstances and others for getting upset. Try to record at least three examples each day.

3. Set aside some time during the day to review your notes and correct your faulty thinking by assigning responsibility to yourself, uncovering the reasons you feel as you do, and reviewing your choices.

Example 1

"When I boarded the crowded bus on my way to work, I looked for an empty seat. I came to a spot where one man took two seats. He sat on one seat and placed his bag on another. Even though I was standing right by him, he did not remove his bag from the seat. He made me very angry."

The first step is to rephrase the sentence to make it truthful. Instead of thinking, "He made me angry," change it to, "I made myself angry (or I chose to become angry)." Now that you have shifted the responsibility to yourself, you can continue by analyzing your thoughts to uncover the cause of your anger.

For example, you may have thought, "That man *should* have been considerate. It upsets me when people are inconsiderate." However, if you choose to become upset whenever the world doesn't behave as you think it should, you are condemning yourself to unending misery as every day, you will meet situations that are contrary to the way you think they should be.

Instead of focusing on how things *should* be, why not focus on how things *could* be? Begin by understanding that everything happens for a reason. Every discomfort we experience is an opportunity to grow stronger and happier. Returning to the thoughtless bus passenger, what are some of the actions we *could* take?

1. We can practice being nonjudgmental. Perhaps the bus passenger was impolite because he was so engrossed in the book he was reading that he was unaware of your presence.

2. We can practice acceptance. When you learn how to accept things as they are by letting go of demands and expectations, you experience peace of mind.

3. We can practice patience. Perhaps the gentleman would have gotten up in a stop or two.

4. We can practice assertiveness. Without expressing anger, we can politely say, "Excuse me, I'd like to sit down."

Example 2

"Laura really hurt me when she ignored me at the party."

First, assign responsibility to yourself by changing the sentence to, "I chose to feel hurt when Laura ignored me." Next, try to uncover the cause of your feelings. For example, ask yourself, "Why do I have these feelings? Am I insecure? Do I feel worthless unless someone gives me attention?" Finally, what are some of your options?

1. You could attend an assertiveness course or study Nathaniel Branden's definitive book, *The Six Pillars of Self-Esteem.*

2. You could practice generosity of thought by giving Laura the benefit of the doubt; that is, you could say to yourself, "She's so busy, she probably didn't see me come in. You can't ignore someone you don't see!"

351

3. You could practice acting maturely by taking the lead and greeting her, instead of waiting for her to greet you.

4. You could practice courage by trying to meet new people at the party.

5. You could practice compassion by introducing yourself to lonely or shy people at the party.

By now, it should be clear that no one makes us upset. Rather, we choose to feel that way, but it is not in our interest to relinquish our happiness or to deny ourselves opportunities to grow stronger and happier. To turn things around, all we have to do is to become aware of how we blame others for our unhappiness, rephrasing our thoughts so that we assume responsibility. Then, we need to uncover the reasons why we feel the way we do and, finally, change for the better by acting on one or more of the positive options that are available to us. It may involve a little work to adopt this new habit, but don't you think your happiness is worth it?

ABOUT THE AUTHOR

Chuck Gallozzi, MA, is a Canadian writer, speaker, seminar leader, and coach. His articles are published in newsletters, magazines, and newspapers and are used by corporations, church groups, teachers, counselors, and caregivers. He is a catalyst for change who is dedicated to bringing out the best in others. To read more of his articles and subscribe to a free newsletter, visit http://www.personal-development.com.

100

VALUE IDENTIFICATION

Are You "Programmed" For Success . . . or Failure?

Larry Bilotta

Have you ever wondered why some people just have it all? They're well liked by everyone they meet, financially set, and attractive, but what stands out most is their beaming sense of self-confidence when they enter a room. It's almost as if they have a certain "presence" that gives off positive vibes.

Not everyone is this fortunate, however. Some people are faced with feelings of low self-worth; they struggle to maintain positive relationships and often feel resentful toward people who are better off than they are.

What's the difference? How can one person be so incredibly successful, while another person constantly struggles just to get by? The answer lies in what I call your "Invisible Lifestyle." Your Invisible Lifestyle is what made you into the person you are—you were literally "programmed" with the habits and beliefs that you follow (or refuse to follow) today.

Who were the programmers? Look no farther than your very own parents or guardians. Your parents unknowingly programmed you to become the person you are today. The reason I say "unknowingly" is because your parents raised you in the best way they could based on how *their* parents raised *them*. Because of the "brain wiring" of your original programmers (your parents), as an adult, you are duplicating the way they lived when you were young.

For example, let's say that you were raised in a household where both your parents were always there for you. They took an interest in you and encouraged you in everything you pursued. You grew up seeing your parents work hard every day and treat each other with respect. As a result, you grew up to have a successful career and a happy marriage because you work hard and treat your spouse with respect—just like your parents.

Now, let's look at another scenario. Imagine a life where you grew up in a neglectful household. Your parents never encouraged you or took an interest in anything you did—*ever*. Your father had a negative outlook on life because of *his* traumatic childhood, so all he knew how to do was to raise *you* the same way that his father raised *him*. As a result, you grew up with a negative outlook on life (just like your dad), and you have low self-esteem because nobody took the time to encourage you and take an interest in you as a child. Is this *your* fault? No, of course not! You did not ask to be "dropped" into your parents' household. It was the hand you were dealt in life, and now, as an adult, you're living out the consequences.

In these two scenarios you're living out what I call Invisible Lifestyle A—"A" stands for "always." What you didn't notice your parents doing as a child, you are faithfully reproducing today, and you don't have a clue that you're doing it.

However, there is one exception to this phenomenon. Let's say you grew up in a bad neighborhood with an alcoholic father. Everywhere you looked, you saw poverty, crime, and hopelessness. As a child, you couldn't wait to move out of the house. You saw your parents' lifestyle and were determined to not only be successful but to be nothing like your parents. While you were growing up, you took the necessary steps to put yourself through school, and as an adult, you have a positive self-image and do everything within your power to remain financially stable.

This is known as Invisible Lifestyle B—"B" stands for "bucking." What you couldn't stand your parents doing when you grew up, you won't stand for in your relationships today. Those who embrace the "B" Lifestyle do so in defiance of their family's values. The B Lifestyle can create the "black sheep of the family," and that goes for highly troubled families or for very successful ones. Invisible Lifestyle B has taken place when an inner city boy or girl goes on to pursue a successful career as a lawyer, while every one of their siblings end up in jail. On the other hand, a child from a wealthy family could go against his parents' values by recklessly spending and eventually filing for bankruptcy as an adult.

Now, I'm not telling you to place blame on your parents. Your parents raised you based on everything they knew at the time. It's all they knew. It's not their fault—it's nobody's fault. The key is to understand and accept the fact that the negative values you absorbed from your parents (such as your fear of failure, low self-worth, and jealousy) are programs literally wired into your brain.

If you have enough discontent with these, it is very possible to change that programming in your adult life, but simply knowing this is not enough. You must find these programs and learn how to "decommission" them. In other words, you need to know what to do and how to do it, especially if these programs seem to dictate your behavior. Do you do things over and over that other people might call "self-sabotage"? Are you attracted to a certain type of person you know you shouldn't be around, yet you can't help but feel attracted to him or her?

The source of this behavior is one or two negative programs from your childhood. These programs will prevent you (or your loved ones) from a better life. If your parents programmed you with some negative values that are causing you problems in your life today, it's *not* your fault, but it *is* your responsibility to do something about it.

You can start by thinking about how each situation in your life today is directly affected by your Invisible Lifestyle. The more you discuss your childhood memories of the way things were, the more you become consciously aware of them, and the easier they will be to decommission.

Over an entire lifetime, most people will not make the connection between their behavior as an adult and how their parents lived during their childhood. They will accept their parents' values without questioning anything, never knowing the real reason they continue to make the same mistakes over and over again.

But now you know better than that. Don't live your life under a blindfold. Create a better future by first identifying and then eliminating the values that are causing you trouble today.

ABOUT THE AUTHOR

Larry Bilotta is the leading authority on understanding people. He has been actively involved in helping people build their self-esteem, reduce their stress, and improve their marriages since 1993. If you'd like to learn how to "decommission" your undesirable programs, get your *free* copy of Larry's Special Report at http://www.selfesteemsecrets4women.com/report.html. Larry is also the author of a book, *Softhearted Woman, Hard World*, that helps women to make sense of the emotional pressure and guilt they experience in their everyday lives.

101

VOLUNTEERING

Success through Volunteering

Roger Carr

When we focus on improving our lives, our first thoughts tend to center around what we can do for ourselves. We create a vision, set goals, read books, and take classes. We take action by implementing what we have learned to fulfill our goals and make our vision a reality. These steps are important, and I perform these steps in my own life, but our attention should not be exclusively on ourselves. Rather, we should think about how we can make the world a better place, while at the same time advancing our own goals.

You know that volunteering a portion of your time is something that you should do, but are you aware that helping others can significantly enrich your own life and move you toward completing some of your goals more quickly? Have you thought about the benefits you could receive from volunteering?

- Build personal and professional contacts. Your ability to do significant things during your lifetime will grow by building a significant network. The other volunteers with whom you work will have unique abilities, experiences, and networks of their own that could aid you now and in the future. Get to know them, and support them in your unique way. They may find ways to return the favor.
- Develop skills. You can use volunteering as a way to enhance your skills. Volunteer opportunities are available for almost any skill you can name. If you have a goal to develop a new skill, volunteering can be one of the best ways to make that happen. Prior knowledge is not usually required. Voluntary experience is also an added bonus on your résumé. Not only can it show additional skills that you have obtained, but it also demonstrates your

willingness to give back to others. This is important to companies that support their communities and adopt charities.

- Share your skills with others. Mentoring is a terrific way to hone your own skills while feeling good helping others. You can help someone else add a skill to his résumé and be more successful as a result.

- Increase your personal satisfaction. Knowing that you are doing something to make a difference in the world will increase your personal satisfaction. Being needed and appreciated for contributing your time and energy to a cause will also build your self-esteem and self-confidence.

- Earn academic credit. Many colleges and universities are now giving academic credit for volunteer support to charities. If you are working on a formal education, academic credit for your time is a possibility.

- Make new friends. True friends can be a great source of encouragement when needed. Volunteering provides a tremendous opportunity to build friendships with other generous people. Find occasions to learn more about them. Find opportunities to encourage them; your encouragement can be as simple as a positive word or a handwritten note. Don't be surprised if the kindness is returned at a time when you need it most.

- Have fun. You have fun when you work with other caring people toward a common cause!

You will get more out of your volunteer experience than you put into it. If you are looking for a life change, consider giving to others as a part of your personal growth plan. Don't wait until you are successful to volunteer your time as volunteering can help you to become successful more quickly.

Identify a worthy cause, and donate some of your time to it. You will be glad you did.

ABOUT THE AUTHOR

To learn more ways to give, sign up for the *free* Everyday Giving e-zine at http://www.everydaygiving.com. Roger Carr is the founder of Everyday Giving. His life purpose is to help people help others. He lives with his wife and son in historic Fredericksburg, Virginia.

About SelfGrowth.com

SelfGrowth.com is an Internet super-site for self-improvement and personal growth. It is part of a network of Web sites owned and operated by Self Improvement Online, Inc., a privately held New Jersey–based Internet company.

Our company's mission is to provide our Web site guests with high-quality self improvement and natural health information, with the one simple goal in mind: making their lives better. We provide information on topics ranging from goal setting and stress management to natural health and alternative medicine.

If you want to get a sense for our Web site's visibility on the Internet, you can start by going to Google, Yahoo, America Online, Lycos, or just about any search engine on the World Wide Web and typing the words "self-improvement." SelfGrowth.com consistently comes up as the top or one of the top Web sites for self-improvement.

Other Facts About The Site

SelfGrowth.com offers a wealth of information on self-improvement. Our site:

- Publishes nine informative newsletters on self-improvement, personal growth, and natural health.
- Offers over 4,000 unique articles from more than 1,100 experts.
- Links to over 5,000 Web sites in an organized directory.
- Features an updated self-improvement store and event calendar.
- Gets visitors from over 100 countries.

Contact Information

ADDRESS: Self Improvement Online, Inc.
             20 Arie Drive
             Marlboro, New Jersey 07746
PHONE: (732) 761–9930
E-MAIL: webmaster@selfgrowth.com
WEB SITE: www.selfgrowth.com

Author Index

A

Allen, Jim M., 34–36
Angier, Michael, 114–115

B

Bacak, Matt, 140–142
Bailey, Mary Ann, 198–201
Baldasare, John, 12–15
Barnhill, Frank, 330-333
Bench, Doug, 47–50
Beneteau, Rick, 9–11
Bilotta, Larry, 353–356
Breitenbach, Marcia, 216–219
Brescia, Mike, 37–40
Brown-Volkman, Deborah, 62–64
Burg, Bob, 223–226

C

Carr, Roger, 357–358
Cole, Evelyn, 334–336

D

Dane, Douglas, 220–222
Davis, Steve, 202–205
Di Lemme, John, 165–166
Dietzel, Glenn, 227–230
Dwoskin, Hale, 91–94

E

Eikenberry, Kevin, 116–118
Emmett, Rita, 267–270

F

Frazer, Paul, 119–122

G

Gallozzi, Chuck, 349–352
Gates, Kathy, 99–102
Gordon, Molly, 69–71
Gorham, Richard, 238–241
Grado, Rebecca, 123–126
Gregory, Eva, 246–248
Grenier, Laurent, 277–280
Griswold, Bob, 302–305
Griswold, Jeff, 302–305

H

Hablitzel, William E., 342–345
Hajee, Karim, 259–262
Hale, Jacquie, 330–333
Harricharan, John, 253–255
Harris, Bill, 298–301
Hoss, Bob, 87–90
Hoss, Lynne McKenna, 107–110

I

Iris, Kristy, 162–164

J

Johnson, Darren L., 127–129
Johnson, Vic, 41–43

363

ABOUT DAVID RIKLAN

David Riklan is the president and founder of Self Improvement Online, Inc., the leading provider of self-improvement and personal growth information on the Internet.

His company was founded in 1998 and now maintains four websites on self-improvement and natural health, including:

1. www.SelfGrowth.com
2. www.SelfImprovementNewsletters.com
3. www.NaturalHealthNewsletters.com
4. www.NaturalHealthWeb.com

His company also publishes nine e-mail newsletters going out to over 850,000 weekly subscribers on the topics of self improvement, natural health, personal growth, relationships, home business, sales skills, and brain improvement.

David's first book—*Self Improvement: The Top 101 Experts Who Help Us Improve Our Lives*—has been praised by leading industry experts as the "Encyclopedia of Self Improvement." That book's success motivated him to continue publishing books which, like the one you're reading now, seek to improve the lives of others.

He has a degree in chemical engineering from the State University of New York at Buffalo and has 20 years of experience in sales, marketing, management, and training for companies such as Hewlett-Packard and The Memory Training Institute.

His interest in self-improvement and personal growth began over 20 years ago and was best defined through his work as an instructor for Dale Carnegie Training, a performance-based training company.

David is a self-professed self-improvement junkie – and proud of it. His house is full of self-improvement books and tapes. He took his first self-improvement class, an Evelyn Wood speed-reading course, when he was 16 years old, and his interest hasn't ceased yet.

He lives and works in New Jersey with his wife and business partner, Michelle Riklan. Together, they run Self Improvement Online, Inc. and are raising three wonderful children: Joshua, Jonathan, and Rachel.